"I Won't Stay Indian, I'll Keep Studying"

"I Won't Stay Indian, I'll Keep Studying"
Race, Place, and Discrimination in a Costa Rican High School

WITHDRAWI

KAREN STOCKER

University Press of Colorado

© 2005 by the University Press of Colorado

Published by the University Press of Colorado
5589 Arapahoe Avenue, Suite 206C
Boulder, Colorado 80303

 The University Press of Colorado is a proud member of
the Association of American University Presses.

The University Press of Colorado is a cooperative publishing enterprise supported, in part, by Adams
State College, Colorado State University, Fort Lewis College, Mesa State College, Metropolitan State
College of Denver, University of Colorado, University of Northern Colorado, and Western State
College of Colorado.

∞ The paper used in this publication meets the minimum requirements of the American National
Standard for Information Sciences—Permanence of Paper for Printed Library Materials. ANSI Z39.48-
1992

Library of Congress Cataloging-in-Publication Data

Stocker, Karen.
 "I won't stay Indian, I'll keep studying" : race, place, and discrimination in a Costa Rican high school
/ Karen Stocker.
     p. cm.
  Includes bibliographical references and index.
  ISBN 0-87081-816-3 (hardcover : alk. paper) 1. Indians of Central America—Costa Rica—
Education. 2. Indians of Central America—Costa Rica—Ethnic identity. 3. Indians of Central
America—Costa Rica—Social conditions. 4. Indian reservations—Costa Rica. I. Title.
  F1545.3.E84S76 2005
  305.897'07286—dc22

                                                                                    2005023311

Design by Daniel Pratt

14   13   12   11   10   09   08   07   06   05   10   9   8   7   6   5   4   3   2   1

To all the students at Santa Rita High School, in particular to Carmen, who suffered the consequences of my being *metiche,* Jacobo, Ileana, Rebeca, Juan Pablo, Joaquín, Sara, Carlos, Samuel, David, Adrián, Federico, Amelia, Yeison, Irene, Amanda, Martín, Elena, Nelson, Paula, Chico, Sofía, Alberto, Lisandro, Marco, and all the other underdogs.

Contents

Acknowledgments

ABOVE ALL, I EXTEND MY GRATITUDE TO THE COMMUNITIES OF NAMBUÉ AND SANTA Rita, to Santa Rita High School, and to all the individuals who contributed to this research. Although I cannot list them all, as I would like to retain their anonymity, I owe these individuals a tremendous debt. The Department of Indigenous Education of the Costa Rican Ministry of Education also provided considerable help in finding solutions to the issues described in this book. Those individuals who supported me while I was in Costa Rica are too many to mention by name, but thanks to several teachers, in particular *los de la soda,* for their friendship and insight. *Mil gracias a todos los alumnos, profesores, administradores, y miembros de las comunidades de Nambué y Santa Rita por sus contribuciones a este libro.*

I also acknowledge the Fulbright Foundation for funding the research that led to this project and the Latin American and Iberian Institute at the University of New Mexico and Title VI funding for providing the means by which I conducted the fieldwork described in this book. The University of New Mexico's Department of Anthropology and California State University, Bakersfield, provided the environments in which to write this book. To them, and to my colleagues and friends at each of these institutions, I am grateful. Thanks also to Cecilia Arguedas of the *Revista de Ciencias Sociales* at the University of Costa Rica.

I thank my academic committee at the University of New Mexico—which first read drafts of this book in dissertation form—composed of Karl Schwerin, Sylvia Rodríguez, and Les Field from the Department of Anthropology and Ann Nihlen from the Department of Language, Literacy, and Sociocultural Studies. Various professors from other departments were also extremely helpful along the way. Thanks to Kimberle López, Miguel López, Enrique Lamadrid, and Tey Diana Rebolledo from the Department of Spanish and Portuguese and Julia Scherba de Valenzuela from the Department of Education for their professional advice and interdisciplinary influence. Thank you, also, to Eva Encinias-Sandoval and Pablo Rodarte.

I owe gratitude to the late Ilse Leitinger for helping me formulate my initial anthropological investigations in Costa Rica and for subsequent mentorship throughout the years and to Julianne Williams for teaching me that advocacy and academics need not be mutually exclusive endeavors.

Many thanks to Bill, Marilyn, Andy and Corinne Stocker, and Esther Anderson for supporting me in innumerable ways at each stage of this process. Thank you to Paul Arbetan, Veronica Arias, Linda Banks, Debbie Boehm, Wesley Chenault, Kathy Freise, Michael Gaud, Marta Henriksen, Rebecca Hernandez, Joe Janes, Catherine Kleiner, Susanna Schaller, Kari Schleher, Mariann Skahan, Charlotte Walters, and Melinda Zepeda for their support in Albuquerque. In particular, I thank Mariela Nuñez-Janes for proofreading my translation of this work into Spanish. I also thank Kaylee Allen, Cristian Bogantes, Jocsan Brenes, Yaurins Castrillo Obregón, Sundey Christensen, Gowri Grewal, Walter López Portillo, Graciela Montiel, Kate Mulligan, Cindy Murillo, Mónica Sosa, and Jessica Wodatch for their encouragement from afar.

Various individuals provided scholarly feedback on this manuscript and advice on the publication process. The Interdisciplinary Research Group at California State University at Bakersfield—including Tanya Boone, Anne Duran, and Norm Hutcherson—as well as Liora Gubkin, Rich Malicdem, and Michael Ault offered invaluable aid. Finally, I thank the anonymous reviewers for their meticulous feedback and my editors, Sandy Crooms, Kerry Callahan, and Laura Furney, for their assistance throughout the process.

"I Won't Stay Indian, I'll Keep Studying"

Introduction: *"Mi delito es ser de aquí"*:[1]

RACISM AND PLACISM IN COSTA RICAN EDUCATION

IN 1977 A LEGAL PROCESS BEGAN THAT RESULTED IN THE TOWN OF NAMBUÉ[2] being arbitrarily named an indigenous reservation in 1979. This was done despite the fact that Costa Rican history claims the country's indigenous populations had become extinct in the colonial era, four centuries earlier. Nambué was one of twenty-three demarcated reservations where peoples self-identified as indigenous or where indigenous peoples were known to have lived at the time of colonization. Nambué fit the latter criterion. Although all of Guanacaste—the northernmost province of Costa Rica—is considered Chorotega territory, just one small area was selected to become the Chorotega reservation. This labeling did not make Nambué's inhabitants suddenly Indian—a stigmatized identity in a country that projects an image of whiteness. Instead, it effectively absolved all those people outside the reservation of this stigmatized label in spite of their similar cultural heritage. With the exception of a small white settler population, the people living in the towns surrounding the reservation shared the same cultural heritage of those inside its borders.

There were no significant differences in language, religion, or worldview between people inside and outside the reservation. Thus, the defining factor for Indian identity—at least ascribed Indian identity—became place of residence. If two siblings lived on either side of the reservation's boundary, only one might be recognized as Indian. A sixteen-year-old commented on this when he noted, "It's not because of the race but more because of the name [of the reservation]. I'm from the indigenous reservation, and for that reason they discriminate against me." When one student not from the reservation heard that I lived in Nambué, she asked jokingly, "*¿Qué, chola, profe?*" (What, Teacher, are you Indian?), thus pointing out the connection between place of residence and perceived race.

In 1999 students from Nambué attended high school outside the reservation in Santa Rita de Cascia (hereafter Santa Rita), a town dominated by a small settler population whose most prominent members identify as white and Spanish. In Santa Rita High School (SRHS), also dominated by this white, economically better-off settler population, students from the reservation met with daily discrimination. That discrimination, however, was based more on place than on race. According to the school's criteria, 80 percent of the student body shared the same ethnic heritage as students from Nambué, but for the most part only students from the reservation were perceived as Indian. It is significant that in this society the label *Indian* had connotations of backwardness and even inferior intellect. Thus, place largely determined ethnicity (which was discussed as race), and ethnicity determined one's academic potential in the eyes of a handful of racist, powerful, predominantly white teachers. Therefore, according to the dominant stereotypes at work, being Indian automatically set students up for being treated as inferior.

Not surprisingly, then, on the flip side of this racist—or placist—situation is the fact that many teachers viewed individuals from the economically better-off white settler families that constituted 20 percent of the student body (according to the school's statistics) as the best students. Students who were not from white settler families but who lived in the white-dominated town and were also of a relatively more privileged social class were also considered white, regardless of their skin color. During a discussion with Isabel, an eighth grader from Santa Rita, about her perceptions of students from Nambué, she pulled up her pants legs and showed me that she was white and not the same color as students from the reservation, as I had mistakenly perceived her to be. Thus, for students from the dominant town, place was also connected to race. A student who was not white by skin color but who was relatively well-off and resided in Santa Rita could sometimes pass as white by association. In some cases, however, social class was also an issue, as I saw students who had dark skin and who were from poorer Riteño[3] families chided for being Indian.

This intermingling of race, place, and class played out in the high school setting. In many cases, students from the dominant town who were too poor to be considered white were encouraged by select teachers to drop out. This was also the case for many students from the reservation. Samuel, a boy from Nambué just starting high school the year I did my fieldwork, had been the best student in his elementary school class inside the reservation. In contrast, in high school in Santa Rita he was immediately labeled (erroneously) as learning disabled and was asked by the school counselor to drop out—which he finally did at the end of the year. While explaining to his grandmother why he was always under the watchful eye of the school counselor responsible for disciplinary action, he stated, "*Mi delito es ser de aquí*" (My crime is being from here).

Because he was from the reservation, his actions were watched more closely by those who expected him to do poorly in school. He was called into the counselor's office on more than one occasion and falsely accused of crimes. Among the accusations were vandalism and theft, both of which were untrue, but they were expected of an Indian student according to the dominant stereotypes at work in the high school. In one instance Samuel's grandmother was called in and told her grandson was stealing money. The counselor based this claim on the fact that she had seen the student with a large quantity of money. Evidently, she assumed a student from the reservation would have to steal to have that amount of cash. In reality, the student was the treasurer of his class, and to carry out his job he had to collect money from classmates. In effect, he was being judged and punished for participating in school activities. Indeed, most student government members were from Santa Rita.

For students from Nambué, there appeared to be two extremes with regard to identity and school success. Some students from the reservation maintained indigenous identities but did poorly in school or, in many cases, dropped out. At the other extreme, some students attained school success but rejected Indian[4] identity and all that had to do with the reservation. Although numerous reactions existed between these two poles, for most students from the reservation, projecting an Indian identity seemed incompatible with school success. As we will see, in this setting an intricate intertwining of place, race, and class all but dictated possible school success for students from the Nambué reservation.

It is not unusual that a place and the people who reside therein come to be mutually defined.[5] It is the process by which places become emblematic of peoples, and vice versa, that was at work for the inhabitants of the Nambué reservation. In this community, place of residence and class status mingled to determine how one's race was perceived by outsiders and, for all practical purposes, determined the level of success a child from Nambué could attain in a predominantly racist high school outside the reservation.

Given that students from the reservation confronted discrimination frequently in school, they had come up with a variety of strategies to deal with this situation. Some took on an identity other than Indian (such as athlete, class clown, or bad kid). Some dropped out. Some accepted their assigned place and participated only minimally so as to pass unnoticed. Some students, however, relied on place-based strategies to confront the placism that affected them.

These place-based strategies included pretending to be from elsewhere when asked. (Getting on the bus to Nambué at the end of the day undermined this strategy to some degree, however.) Another strategy was tied to the rejection of Indian identity. Some students and other inhabitants of the reservation had sought federal unrecognition of their land as a reservation to remove their stigmatized, ascribed, and place-based identity. To combat the stigma of being from a town designated as a reservation, which, in turn, determined their ascribed identities, some students were involved in a small-scale movement to remove Nambué's reservation status and thus remove their stigmatized label. Given that inhabitants of the reservation had carried that label for over twenty-five years, however, this strategy was unlikely to be effective. Dropping out was one of the more popular strategies in 1999 for resisting the school's categorization of and discrimination against students from the reservation (although it may not seem beneficial in the long run).

For these students, place of residence became a limiting factor and a constricting badge. In the case of Jacobo—a poor student from the dominant town—race, class status, and being the son of a single mother may have led to his being considered Indian even though he did not live on the reservation. The limits this discrimination placed on his possible school success were evident when he dropped out. Jacobo explained to me that some teachers and one counselor had been successful in forcing him to drop out but that he wouldn't let them stop his education altogether. At the end of the school year he moved to another province, another place, where his ascribed identity was not in direct conflict with school success and educational opportunities. He also emphasized the connotations of Indianness and its opposition to school success when he told me his plans to continue studying elsewhere. He concluded with the phrase "*No me voy a quedar indio. Yo voy a seguir estudiando*" (I won't stay Indian. I'll keep studying).

The research described in this book, from its inception, has aimed to affect schooling practice and policy. Developed in conjunction with the community of Nambué throughout a six-year period prior to conducting this school-based study, in part as a result of my personal ties to the community, the project that forms the basis of this book has sought to be useful to the community of Nambué, to SRHS, and to the Ministry of Education. Thus, I contextualize this work within the parameters of applied anthropology, as well as within the bounds of critical education theory. Whereas much of the latter literature has addressed schools in the United States, mine seeks to provide a comparative perspective by providing a Latin American example.[6] Thus, I contribute to a growing body of literature surrounding schooling in Latin America.[7] In particular, Costa Rica's spin on nationalism and ethnic diversity proves rather different from the mix in other parts of Latin America.[8] Although my work focuses on students, I also address as many aspects of school life as possible through attention to teachers, parents, and communities. I acknowledge the influence of each of these groups in the high school's crucial role in shaping identity.[9] In this manner, I place my work within the context of that of more recent scholars, as I will discuss in greater detail later, who recognize the role of human agency and resistance within social reproduction theory.[10] I also situate this book within the realm of critical race theory while paying particular attention to the role of place in the social constructions of race and ethnicity. Finally, I see gender not as a separate topic but as one that merits attention throughout my discussion of race, ethnicity, identity, and schooling.

I begin my analysis of schooling and identity in a Costa Rican high school by outlining the development of this research project, the methods used, and my stake in the work described here. As an applied anthropologist linked to the reservation community through years of interaction, personal ties, and marriage yet seemingly tied to Santa Rita on the basis of my race, I confronted numerous dilemmas with regard to accountability and representation. This unique position also affected the way individuals in the high school viewed, judged, and responded to me. The theoretical works from which I draw in Chapter 1 address reflexivity in ethnographic writing,[11] the role of women anthropologists in the field and a women's ethnographic tradition,[12] and the tensions that can exist between female anthropologists' professional and personal, marriage-related, or gender roles.[13] The project that forms the backbone of this book stems from 1,125 hours of participant observation in 1999, from interviews of students of various communities, teachers, administrators, family members of students, prominent community members, and Nambueseño youth who either never attended high school or who dropped out.

Following the consideration that schools often reflect and perpetuate the beliefs and attitudes found in the surrounding community,[14] in Chapter 2 I provide a historical and ethnographic portrait of Santa Rita. After innumerable years of settlement by the Chorotega and their descendants, a group of white settlers—led by the local priest, Father Sánchez—"founded" the town as it is now known. These founding families continue to hold considerable power and prestige in this community that identifies itself as Catholic and Spaniard (albeit several generations removed from Spain) within what one teacher described as "an oasis" of whiteness in a province otherwise characterized by Chorotega heritage. In Chapter 2 I present early examples of ethnic conflict that underlie the rift that exists today. The chapter also addresses the founding of SRHS by the same priest to whom the community attributes its development. Here I provide examples of racist attitudes expressed by students in school that mirror those present in the surrounding community.

In Chapter 3 I portray Nambué from historical, insider, outsider, and scholarly perspectives from the social sciences. I contrast the historical account of Costa Rica as devoid of indigenous inhabitants with the legal discourse that labeled Nambueseños as such in the 1970s and with subsequent social science research that has frequently categorized the country's twenty-three reservations along a hierarchy of perceived ethnic legitimacy. The chapter addresses the tangible effects and those on personal identity of the contradictory definitions and expectations of indigenous Costa Ricans expressed by these various perspectives. I address the preconceived notions and stereotypes many outsiders hold of Nambueseños. The chapter includes excerpts of interviews with several teachers that demonstrate the stereotypes of the reservation that exist in the school. I outline the basis of the discrimination Nambué's residents faced in high school as revolving around place of residence, which in turn defines ethnicity. The chapter also draws from anthropological and other literature regarding place to elaborate upon how Nambueseños conceive of their community in light of outsiders' stereotypes.[15] I examine identity as a personal and shifting construction, as Nambueseños do not agree upon the appropriateness of their community's reservation status or on the Chorotega ethnic identity imposed upon them.

Also in this chapter I consider anthropological theory regarding the social constructions of race and ethnicity. Many traditional markers of ethnicity are inapplicable to this case in which those discriminated against and many of those who discriminate share an ethnic heritage and in which *mestizaje* (the process of racial mixing resulting in the mestizo population) has erased such clear boundaries. The mechanisms of boundary maintenance used in the absence of more traditional ethnic markers are also addressed here.[16] I follow García Canclini, Bonfil Batalla,[17] and others in seeing ethnic identity as a dynamic process, not as a stagnant given. I relate Bonfil Batalla's notion of *"desindianización"* (de-Indianization) to the process by which social science in Costa Rica has all but erased the Chorotega from modern existence. In sum, ethnicity is socially constructed, and the maintenance of boundaries between one ethnic group and another is key to that construction. Of particular importance in this chapter is the role of place of residence as a significant aspect of racial and ethnic constructions of self and other.

In Chapter 4 I examine the numerous ways ethnic categorization took place in the absence of many traditional ethnic markers. This chapter discusses the ways teachers and students drew lines between "us" and "them" in the high school to divide students into various social groups. These methods included racial and ethnic divisions, as well as gendered ones and those related to place of residence and social class. I describe how students' place of residence and, in turn, their status, as well as other factors such as religion and social class, affected their access to school, to particular classes in the vocational track, to extracurricular activities, and more. Furthermore, I examine the way social class affected participation in school activities and basic coursework. This chapter also examines the techniques individuals in the high school used to maintain those divisions. Such strategies included tracking, favoritism by particular teachers, gossip, stereotypes, and ridicule. Some of these tactics were overt and individualized, whereas others were built into the school system. Certain teachers explained many of them as choices Nambueseños made that kept them low on the social ladder. Through various mechanisms, students learned where within the social hierarchy they were assumed to belong.

In Chapter 5 I investigate overt curriculum and teaching methods, the ways students' economic limitations affected their perceived standing as "good" or "bad" students, and who benefited most from the high school experience in Santa Rita. At SRHS, students were taught about their own national and local identity through a direct curriculum. I argue that lessons of identity were among the most lasting lessons the high school imparted. Most frequently, however, these lessons were not taught in such a direct manner. More often they were inculcated through subtle and enduring means. In this chapter I discuss the ways an official curriculum was taught to students at SRHS in accordance with guidelines set forth by the Ministry of Education.

In Chapter 6 I examine the numerous vehicles through which the relative values placed on different identities were communicated within the high school. This chapter focuses on the ways students were taught identity—both racial and gendered—

in the classroom. Whereas an earlier chapter investigated tactics such as tracking for students deemed inferior, this one focuses on lessons taught implicitly or tacitly, in most cases with regard to what is often termed *hidden curriculum*.[18] I tie this to Bourdieu's concept of habitus by examining how the classroom was both constitutive of and constituted by the social categories through which students were taught their imposed identities. I discuss some of the effects of this labeling in accordance with various theories on the topic.[19]

With regard to the teaching of gender roles, girls were at once taught to suppress and to develop femininity. They were likewise taught to discredit ideas surrounding gendered work roles while they were placed in classes that reinforced those ideas. This sexism was both built into the school system and imposed by students.[20] Along with teachings of ethnic and racial identity, I address the value placed on whiteness as taught in various classes—both directly, through curriculum, and indirectly, in extracurricular activities. Finally, in this chapter I examine teachers' policing of interracial student couples, which underscored the school's agenda of promoting, prizing, and protecting whiteness. Through hidden curriculum and direct teachings, students were taught their social location within a hierarchy marked by place, race, class, ethnicity, and gender, as well as being taught which intersections of these categories were acceptable and which were not. Habitus and the naturalization of these teachings obfuscated the way they differentially opened doors or shut them to various students' futures.

Finally, in this chapter I examine what futures were available to students from Santa Rita, to those from the twenty-seven other communities served by the school (including Nambué), and for those who graduated versus those who did not. In particular, I question whether the high school experience was of value at all to students from the reservation. To discuss these issues, various theories from anthropology and education are helpful in illuminating the relationship between schooling and the workplace.

Chapter 7 centers upon the question of student resistance and human agency in the high school. After questioning what constitutes resistance and reviewing anthropological theory on the matter, I provide numerous examples of student resistance and examine tendencies within each strategy with regard to gender, ethnicity, and other variables. I pay attention to power and resistance as phenomena that go hand in hand. I include within my conceptualization of resistance smaller, less visible acts of resistance that some may dismiss as insignificant.[21] Each aspect of schooling I address in this book—the ascription of stigmatized identities, preferential treatment in teaching, teaching style, the teaching of gendered and racial identities and the relative values of these identities, uniforms, and tracking—met with student resistance in one form or another. In this penultimate chapter, I pay special attention to dropping out as a tactic of resistance.[22] I also address the frames for explaining what I consider discriminatory acts, as different students, parents, and teachers saw them.

In Chapter 8 I address possible ways to intercede and affect policy at the levels of the reservation, the school, and the Ministry of Education. I consider the contributions of this project in terms of theory and practice, examine how it has been received by the communities involved and its potential applications to Costa Rican educational policy, and address the ethical dilemmas I faced in carrying out the project.

In short, this book explores the boundaries of race and place within and between two communities in Costa Rica and examines how race, class, place, and gender inform relationships of power dynamics both between and among students and teachers. The book addresses the dynamics at play in a high school geared toward a powerful, privileged numerical minority in which xenophobia and racism abound. What is discussed in the high school in terms of "race," however, encompasses much more than color and includes social class, place of residence, and ethnicity. Although I pay special attention to racism in school as it affects students from the reservation in particular, the book includes discussions of various school-related phenomena as they affect students of different social groups. I focus on the mutual effects of schooling and ethnicity, the institutionalized barriers to academic success for students from the reservation and others, and how ethnic, racial, and gendered identities are taught in the school to the extent that school success and professed indigenous identity seemed to be at odds at SRHS.

NOTES

1. "My crime is being from here."

2. This, like all other names of places, students, and teachers in this book, is a pseudonym.

3. Those from Santa Rita are known as Riteños. I will refer to those from Nambué as Nambueseños.

4. Some residents of Nambué prefer this term to *indigenous*. Although I use both terms and I recognize that some readers might take issue with the term *Indian*, I often use the term to draw attention to the fact that this categorization or label has had significant effects on those who bear it. I do not in any way wish to convey the pejorative connotations of the term. Many of those in favor of the label have reclaimed it, and some of those against it are not in favor of it precisely because of the constraints circumscribed upon them as a result of the labeling process. That process is of central interest to this book.

5. For other works that address this phenomenon, see Blu 1996; Casey 1993; Frake 1996; Relph 1976.

6. In this I respond to Levinson and Holland's (1996: 3–4, 15) call for increased attention to the comparative perspective.

7. See Levinson 2001 and Rival 1996 on Mexico; Luykx 1996 and 1999 regarding Bolivia; López, Assáel, and Neumann 1984 with regard to Chile; and Arnove 1986 for a focus on Nicaragua.

8. Although many Latin American countries revere an indigenous past (although they may not recognize the complex contributions and cultural borrowing of present-day indigenous peoples), Costa Rican history largely denies its indigenous past. In this manner, Costa Rica provides an interesting example through which to examine the construction of nationalist belonging as it relates to race and ethnicity.

9. Here I place my work in the same context as others who view schools as key sites of "cultural production," as Levinson, Foley, and Holland (1996) call it. Others who acknowledge this aspect of schooling include Yon 2000 and Luykx 1999.

10. Authors in this category include Apple 1993; Bourdieu and Passeron 1977; Ferguson 2000; Levinson 2001; Levinson, Foley, and Holland 1996; Luykx 1999; MacLeod 1987; McLaren 1982; McRobbie 1978; Willis 1977; Yon 2000.

11. In this I follow Rosaldo 1993 and M. Wolf 1996.

12. I draw from the work of Abu-Lughod 1991; di Leonardo 1991; and Enslin 1994 for this analysis.

13. In this discussion I refer to the work of Tedlock 1995.

14. In this consideration I follow Aronowitz and Giroux 1993; Bonfil Batalla 1990; Foley 1990; McLaren 1982; Ogbu 1978.

15. Blu 1996; Casey 1993; Kahn 1996; Relph 1976; Tuan 1992.

16. Following Barth 1969.

17. 1990 and 1989, respectively.

18. Gearing and Epstein 1982; Spindler 1982; Wexler 1989; Wilcox 1982.

19. Such as those proposed by Oboler 1995; Rist 1970; Romo and Falbo 1996.

20. This is in accordance with what Holland and Eisenhart 1990 propose.

21. Following Comaroff and Comaroff 1991; Kondo 1990; McLaren 1986; and others.

22. See Thomas and Wahrhaftig 1971.

The Husband's Anthropologist

Positionality of an Unwitting and Unwilling Double Agent

> The feminine narrative is . . . often marked by conflicts between the personal
> and the professional. There may be a tension between the conventional role
> that includes ambition or a vocation.
>
> —Barbara Tedlock[1]

> Introducing myself into this account requires a certain hesitation both
> because of the discipline's taboo and because of its increasingly frequent
> violation by essays laced with trendy amalgams of continental philosophy and
> autobiographical snippets. If classic ethnography's vice was the slippage from
> the ideal of detachment to actual indifference, that of present-day reflexivity
> is the tendency for the self-absorbed Self to lose sight altogether of the
> culturally different Other. Despite the risks involved, as the ethnographer I
> must enter the discussion at this point to elucidate certain issues of method.
>
> —Renato Rosaldo[2]

Although my research focus was on the ascribed and projected identities of Nambueseño students, my own identity—both the aspects of it that I projected and those imposed upon me—soon became an equally salient issue. My fieldwork experience was wrought with the tension between roles described by Barbara Tedlock in the quotation that begins this chapter. I straddled several seemingly opposed communities of belonging. I crossed, invaded, and transgressed gendered, racial, professional, and personal realms, which in my experience were far less clearly delineated than their concise labeling suggests. Although it has become customary to position oneself within anthropological narrative, this suggests that it is, in fact, possible to situate oneself concisely while maintaining a sense of belonging to conflicting realms. Another—although seemingly separate—trend in anthropology is to recognize the shifting nature of respondents' affiliations.[3] As with the identities of my respondents, I must represent my own as equally multifaceted.

As a woman married at that time (prior to and throughout my fieldwork in 1999) to a man from Nambué (who was a student at Santa Rosa High School [SRHS] years ago) and as an active participant in the community of Nambué off and on for several years, my affiliations with and loyalties to the reservation should have been clear. Indeed, I professed these loyalties from the start to teachers, administrators, and students; and my residence within the reservation and in the house of my in-laws—who were noted members of the reservation community—supported my affiliation with the community of Nambué. My status as a white, North American–educated woman, however, led some white teachers and residents of Santa Rita to expect that I ought to move out of the reservation and into their community. It appeared to me that whiteness gave me an assumed belonging in the white settler community of Santa Rita. Furthermore, in conversations with some white teachers, my marriage to an Indian man was constantly questioned as traitorous to my race. Perhaps because of my whiteness, the few overtly racist teachers (although they knew the focus of my research) spoke freely about students from the reservation using derogatory terms and manifesting their stereotypical assumptions. Although this conflicting positionality between my professed identity and others' perceptions of it was the most visible one in the school setting, it was but one axis of the entangled web of positionality in which I lived throughout that year of fieldwork.

Although I made it clear to students that I was neither a disciplinarian nor a teacher (a necessary assurance to gain rapport with them), the last-minute resignation of an English teacher at the beginning of the year obligated me to fill that void until another could be hired. This led to intense ambiguity surrounding my status with regard to students. At some points of my research I was viewed as a peer of students, and at others I was seen more as a teacher. The conflict between these two roles was especially manifest when students had confided in me about cheating techniques and resistance strategies used in the classrooms of select, prejudiced teachers, and I was subsequently asked by the administration to substitute for an absent teacher slated to proctor an exam. This sort of ambiguity required a careful negotiation of my positionality both by me and by the students.[4]

A final area in which positionality was problematic was the way my role as an anthropologist (invited to give lectures to the local branch of the university) clashed with my role as wife and daughter-in-law (which prescribed that I stay at home when not at the school). One result was that once, my policeman brother-in-law paid me a surprise visit as I lectured in a male professor's classroom, and frequently my actions were carefully monitored by my extended family. Although my very presence on the reservation in 1999 was as a result of my role as a doctoral candidate conducting fieldwork, gender roles in rural Costa Rica mandated that my role as wife take precedence. My position was not unlike that of numerous anthropologists' wives whose research (often unacknowledged and either used or usurped by their anthropologist husbands) was secondary to their husbands' professional efforts.[5]

Thus, my positionality—with regard to both the roles I presented (as wife, daughter-in-law, anthropologist, student, and longtime friend of reservation inhabitants and students) and those imposed upon me (traitor to my race, teacher, and *gringa*—white, North American woman) deeply affected the realms open to me, the data available to me, and the degree to which I was accepted in any given circle. Discussions of positionality often assume that ethnographers fit within some clear-cut category from which their biases can be understood. Even anthropologists who do not identify as ethnically, racially, or nationally mixed or as "native anthropologists," however, may surpass the categories placed upon them or to which they assume belonging.[6]

Even a researcher dedicated to making his or her loyalties and biases clear in the field may be held accountable by opposing factions. One's affiliations and roles may cross and clash in ways that have a profound effect on the research being carried out. This issue of multifaceted positionality and seemingly contradictory loyalties is important to education researchers who utilize qualitative methods, especially those involving participant observation and other ethnographic methodologies. It sheds light upon the practical application of these methods to educational research while unpacking common ethnographic views of researcher positionality.

GENDER IN FIELDWORK

The concept of women's roles in fieldwork being secondary to and defined by their husbands' roles is not new to anthropology. These women are often referred to as "anthropologists' wives"—women who conducted fieldwork but whose work is discussed in conjunction with or as part of their husbands' work rather than being legitimated as proper anthropology because the women did not follow the usual academic channels. Although some of these women later became recognized anthropologists, I will focus here on those whose wifely status took precedence over other aspects of their reputations. Sometimes, too, their work was not acknowledged at all but rather was usurped by the male half of the research "team" into his published work. Other anthropologists' wives published their own, nonacademic accounts of their travels but steered clear of the academic realm.[7] Thus, women's ethnography has existed for some time, although it may not have received the same credit as men's more "professional" accounts.

In many cases, this female tradition in ethnographic writing follows a different format than works deemed ethnographic. Women's anthropological writings may be more family focused, more attentive to life history, or more self-reflexive.[8] Other female ethnographic works have attained sufficient respect from academe to be used widely in anthropology classes (such as Marjorie Shostak's *Nisa*), but their authors are still referred to as anthropologists' wives (even Shostak, whose work is more well-known and widely used in anthropology than her husband's). Although these women rarely receive acknowledgment as researchers, they may get recognition as legitimizers of their male partners' social roles—as married men, their husbands could be viewed as fitting into a more normal role in the society under study by virtue of having a wife.[9]

It is at this point that my own experience in balancing the roles of wife and anthropologist converges to some degree with those discussed here. In spite of my having jumped through the academically prescribed hoops to become a legitimate anthropologist-in-training conducting fieldwork, many people in my field site still viewed me as a wife. It was through this lens that all my other actions were judged.

Like Elizabeth Enslin, I was married to "the Other" and was intensely involved in his kin's family life.[10] Although I had enjoyed a sort of honorary male status as a single female fieldworker in previous years, that was no longer the case when I conducted fieldwork as a married woman.

Prior to my marriage, I could move more freely in areas generally limited to men (such as the pool hall, the general store during the afternoon social hour, and on hikes with friends—all realms closed to most rural Costa Rican women). For a married woman, such activities were frowned upon. My interviews with families and individuals I had known for six years and with whom my conversations had never been suspect were suddenly a source of worry for my overprotective in-laws. Interviewees questioned my being in my field site alone, unaccompanied by my spouse. In the high school, teachers who had met me unaccompanied by my husband turned the conversation to him repeatedly. My role as wife shadowed the role I had traveled there to fulfill—that of a researcher and doctoral candidate. In spite of having begun my fieldwork in Nambué two years before my marriage, at this point in my career it was my husband who gave me entrance into the field (like so many other feminist scholars who gain access through male privilege or introduction).[11]

Given this precarious position in which I am not the anthropologist's wife but the husband's anthropologist, I must write within the "women's tradition" of ethnographic writing, including perhaps more of my personal life than I would like.[12] Yet I must also follow the conventions of "traditional" (read "male") ethnographies, which display the rigmarole of academia coursed prior to fieldwork and utilize a language and writing style demonstrative of that academic background. I seek recognition as an anthropologist who carried out her work professionally but who was working in a context in which the professional was extremely personal. My personal life (and others' perceptions and opinions of it) colored my anthropological persona at every turn. Thus, I participate in both the women's ethnographic/wifely tradition and that of my male counterparts—the "legitimate" anthropologists. Still, I must be careful not to overemphasize my insider status as a woman married into the community.[13] Rather, as a result of significant differences between most Nambueseña wives and me, my position was wrought with privileges and freedoms not available to most Nambueseña wives but that are accorded (albeit in an unearned manner) to whiteness and U.S. nationality in the so-called Third World.

ETHNOGRAPHIC ACCOUNTABILITY AND
VIEWS OF THE RESEARCHER

It is not only on both sides of this gendered frontier that I stand, however. To complicate matters further, I must write in such a way that my informants will be willing to read this account, which I promised to (and did) return to them, in translated form. Yet at the same time, I must write in a language appropriate to the academy, which will be taken seriously by the Ministry of Education in Costa Rica (which requested a copy of my written analysis). Enslin battled with this same issue in questioning to which audience—one in the United States or the community of study—she was ultimately accountable and to which she ought to direct her writings.[14]

Kirin Narayan, in her article on insider anthropologists, challenges the insider/ outsider binary and questions the ascribed outsider status of "non-'native' anthropologists" who are committed to long-term study in one area.[15] She suggests that some of these anthropologists have gained a certain entrée into insider status. Indeed, members of the community have told me that Nambué is my *pueblo*. My belonging and loyalty to it are unquestioned by those who reside there. Thus, like many insider or native anthropologists, I, too, have always been accountable to the community in which I studied. As a result, I am quick to censor what I write in the name of privileging personal relationships over academic conventions. When I began to straddle the line of two rival communities of study (rather than just Nambué), however, this position of loyalty became increasingly precarious.

I consider myself extremely biased toward the side of Nambué in the Nambué/ Santa Rita rivalry, and I made this bias clear at every opportunity. By virtue of my race, however, some white teachers in Santa Rita seemingly considered me part of their community, frequently asking me how long I "had" to live in Nambué before moving to Santa Rita. These individuals made derogatory comments about people of color in front of me, perhaps thinking I would agree. They considered me a traitor to my race for having married someone from the reservation. Thus, if I was seen, at least in part, as an insider in both communities, although I both considered and presented myself as partial to the Nambueseño cause, to which must I be accountable? The anthropological ideal that one must not jeopardize his or her respondents in any way seems to imply that all informants are on the same side. For an anthropologist studying a subordinate community within a dominant one, that line is less easily drawn. Thus, I find myself an unwitting and unwilling double agent.[16] I declared my loyalty to Nambué from the start, yet I was given a certain degree of membership within the dominant Riteño community. To support one is to betray the other. Certainly, when I presented my findings of racist teaching practices by several teachers in the high school, many teachers felt betrayed.

I found myself accountable to conflicting parties, placed in the role of wife even though my primary identification was that of anthropologist. Additionally, my professional duties were constrained by those of my role as daughter-in-law. At once insider and outsider, servant and traitor to various communities and subgroups (gendered, racial, and professional), I found myself in a position my anthropological forefathers[17] perhaps found less precarious. Thus, I write this account of my fieldwork and my research with a personal slant. It cannot be otherwise, as my professional and personal identities—both ascribed and projected (like those of the Nambueseños who contributed to this research)—at different times converged, overlapped, or seemed to be isolated worlds. I can write neither from the perspective of the anthropologist's wife nor from that of the seemingly detached observer, as my work was always carried out betwixt and between the sometimes contradictory worlds of wife and anthropologist, academician and activist, honorary Nambueseña by marriage and residence yet accepted Riteña by race and class.

To those with whom I worked, at various times I fulfilled all the roles of the feminine archetypes found in Latin American literature. Different groups and cliques saw me as embodying various roles: as *puta,* by gossips who imposed stereotypes of promiscuous *gringas* on my professionally dictated requirement of interviewing men as well as women; as *la sacerdotisa* or perhaps *monja,* as many interviewees compared my job to that of a confessor; as *madre* in the minds of those who viewed all adult women—especially married ones—as potential mothers (my lack of offspring in spite of my marital state merely slated me as a bad, unfulfilled mother); and as *Malinche*—traitor to my race (as evidenced in my marriage to a Nambueseño and my residence in Nambué instead of Santa Rita). I was *la esposa devota,* yet strangely *solterona* (doting wife, yet unaccompanied and unsupervised by my husband); *guerrillera* in my fight against discrimination toward Nambueseño students; and finally, *la bruja.* Many Nambueseños defined witches as women who had nothing better to do than transform themselves into beasts and bewitch people. Similarly, in their view I had no recognizable occupation for which I deserved pay. Just as I was *la bruja,* I was also *la embrujada*—my marriage was widely considered a result of witchcraft, in part because of the racist idea that no *gringa* would marry an *indio* for any other reason. In another situation, it was unclear whether witchcraft was at work, whether a humorous situation was the result of divine intervention, or if I could chalk it up to karma. At any rate, here is an anecdote related to my position of power as outsider anthropologist and the events subsequent to overstepping my bounds as a visitor by perhaps accepting too much power.

POWER DYNAMICS IN THE FIELD

Toward the end of my year of fieldwork, many teachers at the school in which I conducted my research requested that I give a presentation about my findings. On the one hand, I am dedicated to the practice of making one's research available to the community that made it possible and to returning significant data to the population involved in the study for that information to be used to good ends. On the other hand, much of what I had observed was extremely disturbing to me and implicated many of the same teachers who requested the report. I meticulously drafted a presentation in which I elaborated several examples of discriminatory behavior I had observed while being careful to omit examples whose perpetrators could be easily identified. The result was a rather lengthy and disquieting exposition that left half of my audience (made up of teachers and other school personnel) disappointed in my not having been more direct and the other half furious at my insolence. As Profesor Sergio, a teacher who supported both my work and my findings, explained to me later, I had come off as an arrogant outsider telling insiders what to do and meddling in situations that did not pertain to me. This was a role I never meant to embody, and I did so only in response to the solicitation of teachers from both factions.

Neither in that meeting nor in this document was my intent to vilify teachers. Indeed, the majority of teachers at SRHS were dedicated. They all had to work within bureaucratic constraints and an unpleasant work environment created by the gossip and criticism of approximately eight powerful, racist teachers who spurred the rapid turnover of other teachers. Other researchers, too, have struggled with how to present convincing critiques of schooling and teachers' roles in oppression without being overly critical of overworked, underpaid, and insufficiently appreciated professionals.[18] In this book, I hope it will be clear that no particular group of teachers was always stellar or consistently detrimental to students.[19] At the meeting in question, however, in the words of Profesor Sergio I had come across as *"la prepotente dama del norte"*—the supreme (or supremely arrogant, perhaps) Lady of the North.

With mixed feelings, not satisfied by the fury of those angered by my speech or by the disappointment of those who expected more finger-pointing yet, oddly, feeling that I must have reached the middle ground, given these reactions, I looked forward to the walk home. It had been raining nearly every day for approximately six months but, since the last two days had been dry, I decided to chance taking the muddier but otherwise more pleasant route. I assumed that the hour's walk under a green canopy filled with the calming sounds of howler monkeys and birdcalls would help clear my head of the conflicting emotions that revolved therein.

I walked cautiously at first, assuring myself that only surface mud remained. When convinced that I was correct I stopped stepping so carefully—and I immediately sunk knee-deep into an enormous quicksand-like pool of thick mud. Standing up to my knees in mud, I realized that to get out I would have to stick other limbs into the mud. When I finally emerged from the pit, I was caked in mud up to my elbows. Any other day my reaction would likely have been tears of frustration. This particular day, however, I laughed unstoppably. It was as if, after having played the role of the Ugly American and the Bad Anthropologist Who Imposes Her Views on Others all afternoon, I needed to be taken down a few notches. And step by muddy step, I was. Ironically, in the variety of Spanish used in this region, pointing out people's faults or criticizing them excessively (as many thought I had done in my presentation) is expressed by the verb *embarrar*, or its more distinctly campesino version, *embarrealar*—to muddy. After having engaged in mudslinging, *embarrealando a los profesores,* for the better part of the afternoon, I had now quite literally muddied myself. Had I been Nambueseña, I might have suspected witchcraft. Had I been Riteña, I would perhaps explain this as stemming from the hand of God. Being neither, however, I decided on poetic justice as a more adequate explanation.

Regardless of the cause of my mishap, I still needed to get home. Often, on days I walked home, nobody passed or offered me a ride. Although I hoped for that situation on this particular day to avoid embarrassment, I was not so fortunate. I passed ten students on bicycles, five cars (mostly filled with teachers, some offering rides and others questioning my odd appearance), and the teachers' carpool bus (chock-full, of course).

The following day I returned to school dreading the coldness of teachers insulted by my presentation. Although I did confront some of that, most of the comments had more to do with my appearance the previous afternoon. One rumor suggested that I had gotten into a brawl over my research results—a rumor I did little to dispel, preferring that explanation to "I fell in a mud pit." The sticky situation, however, served to balance the power dynamic once again—to the extent possible—between the teachers and me. The teachers implicated in my discussion of inappropriate and racist practices in school and I returned to school the next day significantly humbled and thus able to coexist in the high school's uncomfortably cramped surroundings. The mud pit experience terminated my role as *la prepotente dama del norte* and returned me to my usual status as clumsy *gringa*/anthropologist/wife (although not necessarily in that order).

In the anthropological world, I am like the anthropologists' wives (because of my positioning in the field), yet I have gone through the ritual process of coursework, proposal writing, and exams that made me a bona fide anthropologist. I was neither teacher nor student yet oddly both. Those who knew me well in the field realized that I did not fit the existing stereotypes of *gringas,* yet I was not quite *tica* either.[20] I did not fit neatly into either the male or the female role—I had more freedom than most women in town, yet my placement in some male realms was questioned and curbed. In short, I was the husband's anthropologist, and I can write from no other perspective.[21]

A relatively recent trend in anthropology urges ethnographers to include themselves in their texts.[22] For me, it cannot be otherwise. At the risk of falling into the self-absorption of which Rosaldo warns, I present this reflexive account of the ways in which I positioned myself and was positioned in spite of myself during my fieldwork. Following theorists who suggest that experience and theory are not mutually exclusive camps,[23] I incorporate the multivocality of my own perspective, as I utilize polyphony in the accounts of those with whom I worked in the field to reconcile the seemingly contradictory positions from which I conducted this research.

METHODOLOGY

Although the project began, albeit in another form, during my first visit to Nambué in 1993, I carried out the research described in this book in 1999. I chose to conduct research both within and outside of the reservation—in the high school—to see the differences in behavior among Nambueseño students in both places. I suspected that students might behave and be treated differently in diverse contexts within the high school. Therefore, I observed assorted homeroom classes in their interactions with all of their teachers to better capture the various facets of student life.

In all, I conducted 1,125 hours of participant observation in the high school, following fourteen (of a total of seventeen) homeroom classes for one week each to all their classes, assemblies, and other activities.[24] In this manner, I observed students of every grade level and from all places of residence served by the school in their daily interactions with one another and with school personnel. I conducted participant observation in the high school four days each week for the duration of the school year (from February to December). In addition to classroom observations, I interviewed all twenty-eight Nambueseño students as well as twenty-four former students from Nambué (including both graduates and dropouts), eight Nambueseños of high school age but who never attended, and several Nambueseño parents of students. I tape-recorded interviews with teachers and administrators and followed a loosely structured interview protocol.[25] Although the ordering and phrasing of questions often varied in accordance with individual conversation styles, I addressed the same topics with all the teaching and administrative staff. The interviews ranged in length from approximately twenty minutes to two hours (most lasted about an hour), depending on each conversant's prolixity and willingness. I attended staff meetings and outings and conversed with teachers informally on a regular basis. I did not tape-record interviews with students but, rather, took careful notes either during or following interviews. When students asked to see the notes, I showed them (and translated) notes that related only to them. As with the teacher interviews, I tried to address the same issues with each student or group of students through open-ended questions.

In addition to interviewing Nambueseño students, I interviewed three to four non-Nambueseño students from each homeroom class I observed, and I participated in frequent informal conversations with innumerable students of various grades and places of residence. It is impossible to quantify my informal interviews on campus and in the reservation; my friendships with individuals in both contexts rendered it difficult to determine where a conversation stopped and an interview began, and vice versa. Whereas some might argue that such a lack of "detached observer" status might diminish the validity of my research, I consider that detachedness is not necessarily an asset to socially engaged research. In addition to carrying out participant observation in the high school four days a week, I taught English once a week to sixth graders in Nambué's elementary school at the request of community members. There I became familiar with the attitudes and opinions of those on the verge of entering high school.

I obtained formal, written permission to carry out this study from the director of the school prior to my arrival at the field site. I also solicited permission from Carmen, my sister-in-law, who was a student at the high school during my fieldwork year. I sought permission from teachers and staff at the first staff meeting of the year, when I explained my study, and each time I entered their classrooms or sought to interview them. When I interviewed students, I began with a brief explanation of my interest in studying school culture, but I did not request written permission from them. Likewise, in Nambué I sought and received verbal permission to carry out this study from families within the community and from parents of Nambueseño students when I went to their homes to interview them directly. I made a conscious decision to avoid seeking written consent from these families based on previous experience in Nambué in which my attempts to get written permission caused suspicion and evoked a negatively remembered era in Nambueseño history in which the written word overpowered the spoken word, resulting in people losing land through written agreements while verbal ones, in the minds of many Nambueseños, had outlined other stipulations than those written and recognized legally.[26]

As I explained earlier, I conducted my research from both within and outside. I enjoyed a closeness to the Nambueseño students and parents that developed through-out several years, as this project changed shape to better conform to the community's needs and requests. As a result, the project took on greater significance in accordance with my increasing familiarity with Nambué and its most salient issues. This study, which evolved from one focusing on gender identity and machismo to a study of ethnic identity, led me to the high school site, where Nambueseño youths had made it clear that their ethnic identity (ascribed and projected) was drawn into its sharpest focus. From 1993 to 1999, I conducted fieldwork through intensive periods, varying in length from ten days to two years, during which I carried out well over 200 interviews and innumerable hours of participant observation. During those periods I came to focus on inhabitants' opinions of the reservation and of their ethnic identity. That research, too, informs the present manuscript.

In this book I have mixed ethnographic portraits of both Nambué and Santa Rita, six years of fieldwork that culminated in the 1999 school-based study, and theory from the fields of anthropology and education with regard to the social construction of race, ethnicity, and identity in order to elaborate on the nature of the discrimination against Nambueseño students and others at Santa Rita High School. I begin with ethnographic portraits of the two communities.

NOTES

1. Tedlock 1995: 277.

2. Rosaldo 1993: 7.

3. I have chosen to use the term *respondent* instead of *informant* or *collaborator.* The word *informant* suggests a very unequal power relation in which the "informant" is hired or otherwise obligated to inform one's work. Still, I do not wish to downplay the power dynamic inherent in most anthropological research by renaming those who have made this study possible as "collaborators," as that implies a more equal footing and benefit for all. Although I have engaged in a good deal of collaborative work, I feel the use of the term *collaborator* may be misleading.

4. Others who straddled a similar line between student and adult status (often as adults conducting graduate research with adolescents in schools or as adults conducting research in schools where they found themselves more involved with youth than with other adults) include Dolby 2001; Ferguson 2000; Levinson 2001; Luykx 1999.

5. See, for example, Enslin 1994.

6. See, for example, Jackson 2004; Limón 1989; Narayan 1993; Zavella 1993.

7. For additional insight into "anthropologists' wives," see di Leonardo 1991: 6; Tedlock 1995: 267; Tsing 1993: 223; M. Wolf 1996: 215.

8. See Abu-Lughod 1991: 152 for a more extensive analysis of women's ethnographic works.

9. See Tedlock 1995: 272.

10. See Enslin 1994: 549.

11. See Abu-Lughod 1993; D. Wolf 1996: 9 for other examples.

12. Various male readers of previous drafts have questioned why I elaborate on positionality at such length. One suggested that I relegate the effects of my gender on fieldwork to a footnote. Had my gender been the equivalent of a footnote to the whole research experience, that might be appropriate. It affected my fieldwork constantly, however. Interestingly, female readers have applauded my inclusion of this topic in the manuscript. It seems to me that the type of fieldwork experience that is taken as standard, or as the default experience in anthropology, is one that is free of gender issues. I find this ironic, given the high proportion of women to men currently in the field of anthropology. In my view, this makes it even more important to analyze gendered experiences in written accounts of fieldwork.

13. See also Enslin 1994: 550–551.

14. Ibid.: 553.

15. Narayan 1993: 677.

16. Although the language of agents and spies and its connotations may be unbecoming to anthropologists and I do not wish to fulfill such a role (indeed, I have taken pains to be up front about my study all along), it is appropriate to the way anthropologists are often perceived. Some students—until I cleared up their doubts—did think I was a spy for the administration. Aurolyn Luykx (1999: xxiii) also experienced this feeling of anthropologist as spy.

17. Here I use this gendered term on purpose.

18. See Levinson and Holland 1996: 19; López, Assáel, and Neumann 1984: 5, 282; Luykx 1999: xxviii, 242; McClaren 1986: 209.

19. See also Yon 2000: 127 on the difficulty of labeling a particular individual as good or bad given that "individuals come from contradictory locations and occupy contradictory positions." Just as this is so for teachers, it is also true for students. Although I portray students as exemplifying particular attitudes or beliefs, no student is emblematic of his or her entire community's beliefs, nor is any one person entirely without compassion or altogether bad. I do not wish to pick and choose examples that portray any individual in a particularly negative light, but I also do not want to downplay the severity of some individuals' negative influences.

20. The term *tico* and its feminine counterpart, *tica,* are nationalist labels used by Costa Ricans to describe themselves.

21. For another careful consideration of the effects of researchers' feminine gender on research, see Luykx 1999: xxiv–xxv.

22. See, for example, Geertz 1995: 65; Rosaldo 1993.

23. See Kondo 1990: 300; Tsing 1993: 32.

24. Although I thought students might be uncomfortable being followed in this way, often students asked when I would follow their class again. Students from the few homeroom sections I did not observe so thoroughly (because of time constraints) sometimes expressed regret at having been left out.

25. See Appendix I for interview protocols.

26. See Luykx 1999: xxi for additional comments on the ethical dilemmas regarding consent, whereby explicit consent is requested of adults while students, who form the backbone of the study, have less power over what a researcher can do.

2

The Founding Father

AN ETHNOGRAPHIC PORTRAIT OF SANTA RITA

PROFESOR ANTONIO, A HANDSOME (BY RITEÑO STANDARDS) MALE TEACHER, WAS the protagonist of numerous rumors. If he spoke to the teenage girls who swooned over him, gossip had it that he was taking advantage of female students. When he purposely avoided conversations with the girls, however, the gossip network in this exceedingly homophobic Catholic community declared him gay. The teachers' lounge—dominated by a group of mostly white teachers, primarily from Santa Rita—was almost constantly abuzz with rumors of pregnant students, community scandals involving students' parents, and judgmental chatter displaying a simultaneous fascination with and fear of homosexuality. One afternoon, hoping for a ride to the entrance of Nambué, I asked Profesor Sergio, a male teacher who owned a car and whose route home went right past Nambué, what time he was going home. Profesora Rosa María, a teacher with a penchant for gossip, overheard my question. Her jaw dropped as if I had just openly arranged a tryst. Students soon filled me in on the teachers' rumors, according to which Profesor Sergio and I went to the coffee shop across the street from the school and did "who knows what." Potentially scandalous uncertainty was perhaps more captivating than crossing the street to find out what actually happened.

Although this hearsay is not directly connected to the Founding Father of Santa Rita and although he is critical of such rumors, he is not above them. In fact, this priest often finds himself the protagonist, if a reported actor in defamatory rumors can be termed such. Nonetheless, the gossip is one defining characteristic of the town that owes its development (and its high school) to his particular brand of Catholicism and leadership. His history and that of Santa Rita—almost always recounted as one and the same—are vital to a study of the high school located in the town.

Several theorists dedicated to anthropology and education assert that schools not only reflect but also perpetuate the attitudes and practices of the communities in which they are located.[1] They acknowledge that although schools do instill the dominant values of the communities in which they are housed, we must not underestimate the role of human agency.[2] I agree that the view of school as a mere reflection of dominant society neglects resistance (a phenomenon I will discuss shortly), but we should not underestimate the role of the school in socialization or the influence of dominant society on what is considered worthy of teaching. Schools do perpetuate social hierarchies, but they do not dictate how students respond to such structuring. In later chapters I will address how students react to the school environment. In this chapter I focus on the culture of that environment, as embodied in (or reflective of) the dominant values, attitudes, behaviors, and customs of Santa Rita. To begin to address these, however, a history of the town is necessary.

RITEÑO HISTORY

Santa Rita, a town in the province of Guanacaste in northwestern Costa Rica, is located 314 kilometers from the capital city of San José. As a township (as opposed to the small town and governmental seat by the same name, often referred to as central Santa Rita), Santa Rita comprises 215,000 square kilometers. According to an article published in Costa Rica and focusing on this town and the township that shares its name, "Santa Rita is a township conformed by two cultures which have integrated."[3] The article goes on to explain that in the pre-Columbian era, Santa Rita belonged to the territory occupied by the Chorotega. Around 1910 it was populated by people from Nambué and from various townships located in the Central Plateau of Costa Rica, such as San Ramón, Atenas, and Palmares.

The handful of families named among its founders include no common surnames from Nambué, however. At the present time, the inhabitants of Nambué and the remaining Chorotega are considered synonymous, as will be discussed in Chapter 3. Thus, the early "founders" of Santa Rita are those of Chorotega descent who already resided in the region prior to 1910, plus the immigrant families mentioned as "founders" earlier. These founding families, like the majority of those in their townships of provenance, are of Spanish descent, fair-skinned and fair-haired, and Catholic. Their history in Santa Rita parallels, to a large extent, the "foundational fictions"[4] of Costa Rican national history.

According to national historiography, the Spaniards who came to this country in search of riches were sorely disappointed upon realizing that the name they had given to Costa Rica was a misnomer. Riches were not to be found, nor were there abundant Indian slaves to be exploited—or so goes the myth.[5] The purported idyllic result of these conditions, as Costa Rican historians explain, was a classless nation of laborers on equal footing with one another. It is widely considered that would-be conquerors, finding neither riches nor exploitable labor forces, set about cultivating the land for themselves.

Similarly, although the first immigrants to the township of Santa Rita "came in search of famous buried treasure and riches, many stayed to work the land."[6] By a Riteño author's account, the general makeup of the population parallels that of the country as a whole (at least as the foundational fictions would have it). Guido Durán notes that most contemporary inhabitants of the township of Santa Rita were born there, of parents from the Central Plateau, although "a small portion are of Guanacasteco descent" (meaning they are originally from the province of Guanacaste, in which Santa Rita is located, and implying that they are of a different ethnic and racial heritage than the white Riteños).[7] The descendants of the original immigrants to Santa Rita expressed the goal to "work hard," much like their forefathers.

THE FOUNDING FAMILIES OF SANTA RITA

Although the aforementioned families from the Central Plateau of Costa Rica are known to have been among the first non-Guanacasteco residents of Santa Rita, Riteños invariably give credit for the town's founding to Father Abel Sánchez, a Spanish missionary priest who came to Santa Rita in 1961. He was sent there by Father Arrieta, now the Bishop of Costa Rica. In Durán's words, "We can say without fear of being mistaken that in [Santa Rita] there is no work of progress and development that does not carry the mark and the direct intervention of Father [Sánchez]."[8] Among these works of progress are the building of passable roads (still a relative term), the town's first nutrition center for expectant mothers and small children, regular medical attention, the obtaining of land titles, leadership seminars, the formation of the Association of Integral Development (Asociación de Desarrollo Integral, the local governing body), construction of the Catholic church, an agricultural center, the creation of Santa Rita as a district (in 1965), the designation of Santa Rita as a township (in 1971, at which point it ceased to pertain to the township of Majapiñao), and the establishment of the Colegio Técnico Profesional Agropecuario de Santa Rita—the local vocational high school, which is the focus of this book—in 1972.[9] As Profesora Rosaura, a teacher from Santa Rita, explained, "The Father's vision, as creator of this high school, was a marvel."

The priest, in my interview with him, described his contributions to Santa Rita more humbly. According to Father Sánchez, the first settlers came to Santa Rita in 1931. They came from the Central Plateau of Costa Rica seeking escape from the economic depression that reigned there. At the time, "This was a no-man's land, public land," said the priest. Other founding families note that land was inexpensive in Santa Rita at the time, and a family unable to afford to continue living in the

Central Plateau could sell land there and buy a more substantial farm in Santa Rita. According to the priest, the settlers came from San Ramón, Puriscal, Palmares, and Atenas and began to work the land. They planted rice, beans, corn, and coffee and began raising cattle. They lived without running water, doctors, or electricity. In other words, according to Father Sánchez, "they lived by the hand of God." These founding families (recognizable by their prestigious surnames) form "part of the mythology of Santa Rita," as reflected in the words of Jaime, a young student from one of these "important" families who discussed them with the same awe and placed them upon a similar pedestal as a resident of the United States might do regarding the Kennedys.

According to members of founding families, Santa Rita in the early days was in dire need of a priest who could attend to the community's spiritual needs more frequently than the less than monthly basis that was common before Father Sánchez's arrival. Father Arrieta responded to the community's request by promising to send a priest if Riteños would aid in the construction of a seminary in the Central Plateau. Both parties kept their end of the bargain, and Father Sánchez was sent to Santa Rita, where he began his community development efforts. In 1961, Father Sánchez arrived in Santa Rita with what he called "a development plan" and immediately "went about developing." He saw to the construction of buildings, roads, aqueducts, electric lights, and other basic comforts. Giving credit to the settlers as well as to his own designs, the priest explained that these were the things "we founded." Later, he also started a cooperative, the high school, the clinic, the coffee processing plant, and the agricultural center.

At the time, the government started schools of various types—some with an agricultural focus, others with a mechanical bent, and still others with an industrial specialization. Father Sánchez requested an agricultural school with the idea of having landowners' children study agricultural techniques to utilize in Santa Rita. Originally, Father Sánchez was the director of the high school, and he ran it with the goal of teaching students to improve farming techniques and establish businesses that would allow them to stay in the countryside rather than having to migrate to urban centers to seek employment. The priest notes that, as with many of his other plans, this one eventually "deviated from its objectives."

Don German, a respected member of the community and son of a founder, remembers how Father Sánchez saw to it that Santa Rita became an official district of its township, Majapiñao. District status accords greater autonomy and local governing power to a town with sufficient population to merit it. According to Don German, the community had already requested that the local government of Majapiñao make Santa Rita a district, and Majapiñao had refused. Father Sánchez communicated with the Costa Rican president, who told him to petition for district status again, and if it was not granted, the president would see to it that Santa Rita was made a district by executive decree. Riteño oral history has it that Majapiñao rejected the community's subsequent petition, and a community member warned officials, "You'll see—Santa Rita will be a district within the year." Soon afterward,

Majapiñao received word that by executive decree, Santa Rita had been made a district. Following up on this bit of history, I asked various community members about Majapiñao's resistance to making Santa Rita a district. One community member suggested, "They didn't like us white people." Another suggested, laughing, "They felt strange that we occupied the place."

CARTAGOS AND GUANACASTECOS

The reference to occupation reflects the racial rivalry that still exists between white Riteño settlers, referred to as Cartagos (in reference to a town from the Central Plateau), and mestizo or indigenous Guanacastecos (named for their province of origin) in the region. Costa Rican folklorist, author, and political figure Miguel Salguero alludes to this rivalry in his description of the township. He notes that whereas Santa Rita was originally populated by the Chorotega, the tribe, which was

> the object of persecution on the part of the Spaniards, has survived, nevertheless, and currently there is an important nucleus [of the Chorotega] village with the name of [Nambué]. The rest of the territory was populated by emigrants, mainly of Cartago origin, or from the towns from the country's interior, such as San Ramón, Heredia, Atenas, Puriscal, and others.[10]

Just as the history (both oral and written) of the foundation of Santa Rita mirrors the nation's colonial history, the relationship of Nambué, as a "nucleus" of Chorotega survival, to predominantly Spanish, white Santa Rita parallels that of the province of Guanacaste to the whole nation. Although the nation projects an image of whiteness and Europeanism, it relies on the province of Guanacaste's customs for its national folklore.

In spite of this, Costa Ricans from Guanacaste generally experience a great deal of discrimination in predominantly white areas of Costa Rica (such as the Central Plateau). They are often referred to by the derogatory label "*Nicas regalados*" (pronounced *regalaos,* in mimicry of the stereotypical and stigmatized speech of Guanacaste)—roughly, "leftover Nicaraguans." This phrase refers to the history of Guanacaste, which belonged to Nicaragua prior to its annexation to Costa Rica in 1825. In a country where xenophobia dominates and a strong prejudice exists against Nicaraguans, the term is deployed derogatorily as a formidable insult.

Santa Rita, in a way, annexed Nambué as well to have sufficient population to merit its own township status (rather than continuing to belong to Majapiñao). Without Nambué's sizable population included within its borders, the nascent township would not have received its change in status. Many members of the larger Riteño community, however, look down upon the current inhabitants of Nambué. What several Riteños referred to as a "rivalry" was called "prejudice," "underestimation," "disrespect," and "racism" by Nambueseños who felt the exclusion from the township of Santa Rita alluded to by Salguero in separating Nambué as a "nucleus" of difference.

The township as a whole, in 1998, had a population of 6,027 individuals spread out among the twenty-eight communities the township comprises.[11] The largest community, with a population of 1,526, shared the name of the overall township. The clinic estimated Nambué's population as 696 individuals—a statistic considered too low (by approximately 300 people) by elementary schoolteachers in Nambué who conducted a systematic survey of the reservation. According to Santa Rita's annual report to the bishop, the high school had nearly 500 students (of which 80 percent were from towns other than Santa Rita and 20 percent were from Santa Rita, according to school officials).

In spite of constituting a numerical minority in the school, students from Santa Rita were the powerful few against whom all others were measured. Profesora Delia, one of the school counselors, compared the "*viajantes*" (travelers)—the 80 percent of the school body that travels to school from somewhere other than the town of Santa Rita—to "the rest" of the student body. It is significant that "the rest"—the standard—referred to a numerical minority. It was widely considered (and Profesora Delia's comments reflect this view) that it was the traveling students' responsibility to mingle and work their way into predominantly Riteño peer groups rather than it being the Riteño students' responsibility to include them.

The comments from some traveler students also reflected the priority given to students from "central Santa Rita." In commenting on the difficulty of a recent exam, two traveler students told me that "even the most intelligent ones" did not have time to finish. Having been under the impression that the girls with whom I spoke were among the most intelligent in their class, I asked who these smart kids were. They told me they were the girls the teachers thought were bright—but that in reality "they're intelligent at copying." These traveler students referred to a clique of Riteña girls upon whom I frequently observed teachers doting.

Guanacasteco Displacement and Exclusion From Santa Rita

The lesser status of those not from Santa Rita was even more evident in the case of Nambué. Indeed, it appeared that outside of the school context, the other communities included in the township, although perhaps not on equal footing with central Santa Rita, more nearly approximated its status than Nambué did. This was evident in interviews with the founding families of central Santa Rita. In one case I asked the child of a founding family if anyone was here when the "first settlers" arrived. The individual responded, "There were many people, but [only] Guanacastecos"—a fundamental difference in the categorization of people. The person added, "They went about leaving." Others, too, characterized the displacement of Guanacastecos by Riteños under the rubric of personal choice.

The "free decision" of Guanacastecos[12] to leave their land was expressed by other founding families as well. One founder's son (one of the respected elders of the community in 1999) recalled how cheaply his father had bought land and added that the Guanacasteco people left for other areas. His wife added, "They didn't like us,

the white people." Several grown children of founding families remembered frequent mortal fights (often with machetes) between Cartagos and Guanacastecos.
These situations were described with different tones of severity and disapproval.
One sympathetic Riteña remembers that as a young girl she hung from her father's
legs begging him to stop a fight so neither party would be hurt or killed. A founder's
daughter spoke of violent ethnic conflicts and then concluded, laughing, "We had to
tame them." Profesora Alodia, an adult daughter of another founding family—and a
teacher at the local high school—commented, amid laughter, that many Guanacastecos
call Cartagos or Riteños "intruders" and say "that we arrived to usurp lands where we
had no reason to be and that we took everything away from the Guanacastecos." She
added that such commentary has died down. Others agreed that violent clashes were,
indeed, commonplace but specified that they mainly took place among Guanacastecos.

What was once settled through individual brawls seems to have moved into the
governmental realm. In 1999, Nambué still sought equal representation—in the form
of requesting district status from Santa Rita, much as Santa Rita had from Majapiñao
years ago. Some officials explained that Nambué's population was insufficient to merit
that status. That same year, however, two communities smaller than Nambué—even
by the Riteño statistics many Nambueseños alleged to be deliberately skewed—were
made districts. District status gave these communities greater power of representation in local government as well as direct control over federal resources.

Communities without district status were subject to the municipal government
of Santa Rita, which disbursed funds as it saw fit. In practical terms, this meant
(according to the mayor and many Nambueseños) that the towns dedicated to tourism or coffee production, which brought income to the township of Santa Rita,
received priority over requests from Nambué for such projects as covering the dirt
road with gravel so it might be passable in the rainy season, thus allowing students to
attend school consistently and permitting those employed outside the reservation to
get to work.

The exclusion of Guanacastecos from greater Riteño belonging has been a
fundamental part of the township's history and a sore point for Guanacastecos in
general and for Nambueseños in particular. Similarly, other characteristics of Santa
Rita have also remained fairly constant over time. The priest separated himself from
Santa Rita's political and social exclusion of Nambué when he chided Riteños, in
sermons and radio addresses, for not supporting activities held in Nambué. Father
Sánchez, however, seemed to embody many of the other defining characteristics of
Santa Rita. Elements of Riteño identity hinged upon such issues as Spanish national
and cultural origin, whiteness and the higher social class that correlated with it, and
religiosity in the form of Catholicism.

FATHER SÁNCHEZ

Father Sánchez—originally from Spain—is a white-haired, white-skinned man
of short, stocky build, with a thick Castilian accent and good intentions. While in the

seminary in Spain, he had dreamed of going to the Congo. He explained, "Africa enchanted me." Physical weaknesses, however, prevented him from being sent there. Instead, his superiors decided he would go to the Americas. He was to be sent to Cuba in 1954, "but then the war exploded," explained Father Sánchez. Instead, he was sent to Costa Rica for five years. After those five years, however, he did not want to leave his development projects half finished, so he stayed. Catholic leaders, in response to the priest's problems (which he did not specify to me), tried to send him to Panama and Puerto Rico on different occasions. He did not want to go, however, and asserted that they could not send him against his will. Thus, his missionary work, as he categorized it still, continued in Santa Rita in 1999.

As both religious leader and founder of the town, he had strong influence in Santa Rita. As with any prominent community figure, Father Sánchez both enjoyed immense support from many and had to deal with negative accusations from a few. Some of these accusations were made in the context of gossip and others in the form of political criticism. Gossip and hearsay focused on the priest's alleged offspring throughout the region. Political criticism, often relying on gossip to further discredit the priest and curtail his leadership from the political to the merely spiritual, suggested that he used his role as religious leader in the township's communities to tell people for whom to vote. Assorted teachers accused him of pressuring them to pass the children of prominent citizens of Santa Rita when they had failed academically. In the priest's opinion, those who disagreed with his ideas regarding education and the direction the high school had taken accused him of being a "dictator" if he intervened in school affairs once he was no longer the director of the high school. Others still referred to the priest (perhaps ironically, in an environment in which Indianness was looked down upon) as the cacique of the township supported by a council of elders—children of founding families now grown and influential in the community in their own right.

SANTA RITA'S PRESENT CULTURE

The spirituality, whiteness, and Spanish origin Father Sánchez seemed to embody were perhaps taken to extremes by some of his more powerful parishioners, thus creating an environment that not only reflected but espoused a preference for these qualities or characteristics. The result was a widespread, odd mix of Catholic dogma and extreme racist and religious intolerance for those not fitting this image. The best example of the deep-set nature of these preferences is seen in a thirteen-year-old boy, whom I will call Jaime, from a prominent, well-off family in Santa Rita.

I spoke with Jaime early in the school year, during his first year of high school. My conversations with him began one day when I went to observe his class and we were waiting for the teacher to arrive. Jaime asked me if I lived in Santa Rita. When I replied that I lived in Nambué, he responded in apparent disbelief, "But on the way out of Nambué, right, not in the very heart?" I informed him that, in fact, I lived in the social center of Nambué, smack dab in the middle of the town. Shortly after this introduction, I asked Jaime if he had ever been to Nambué and how he liked it. He responded with a diatribe that left me speechless.[13]

Jaime began, "I'm going to be honest with you. I'm not going to lie to you. I have racist tendencies." I asked what he meant by that, and he responded with these thoughts on Nambué. "There, I feel like I'm in a different environment. Among another race." I asked how this was so, and Jaime said "since they're black." I told him I thought those who were usually referred to as black in Costa Rica lived in Limón (an area populated largely by Afro-Caribbean peoples), as I had not heard the Spanish word *negros* used in conjunction with any other area of Costa Rica. Jaime altered his terminology, "Well, not black [negros] but dark [*morenos*]." I asked, point-blank, "So you don't like Nambué because of racism?" Jaime corrected me, "No, I said 'racist *tendencies,*' not racism." I asked where he got these ideas. He tapped his temple and said, "I invent them."

Tongue-tied, I did not continue this topic, and I began to speak to other students nearby. Jaime, however, proceeded to volunteer information about his "tendencies": "The only race [different from his own, he implied] with which I sympathize is the Asian one." He explained that he did not know why, but all that was Asian enchanted him. Interestingly, there were no Asian students in the high school and no Asian inhabitants in Santa Rita. Other individuals explained at different times that once a Chinese Costa Rican family had moved to Santa Rita and begun a business, but nobody would patronize the store, so the family moved.

Jaime turned the topic to what relatives who had visited Alabama had told him of the Ku Klux Klan. I asked if he approved of that. He said, "No, it's one thing for me not to sympathize with [black people] and another to kill them." He elaborated on this distinction between not liking a racial group and discriminating against its members: "If you were black, I wouldn't not talk to you. Although I wouldn't like you, I would talk to you."

I learned from fieldwork lore in methods classes that the good anthropologist is not supposed to judge or to let on what his or her true opinions may be when in conflict with those of respondents. In this case, however, given my race and what many Riteños assumed would be my agreement with dominant Riteño culture and values (as discussed earlier), I feared my silence on the matter might be taken for tacit approval. Thus, I crossed the anthropological line and let Jaime know that I disapproved of his racism. Jaime defended his position as resulting from how he was brought up.

"I was raised to be a Spaniard," he explained. I asked what that entailed. He provided several examples. "I don't play with dirt. I never played with dirt. I don't eat with my mouth open." I informed him that I also do not eat with my mouth open or play with dirt, but that does not make me a Spaniard. Jaime agreed, "No, because they raised you as a North American." Stumped, I asked what else is Spanish. Jaime said that to be Spanish is "to be cultured." I asked what he meant by that, and he replied, "To be educated; to know. They [Nambueseños] don't know." Jaime also noted that being Spanish is about getting good grades and not enjoying physical labor. When I again asked what else is Spanish, Jaime replied that he did not know and suggested I ask him more questions.

Taking him up on his offer, I asked what they did differently in Nambué from the Spaniards in Santa Rita. He and a Riteño cousin said, in unison, "Everything." I asked for examples. Jaime suggested, "Because of their culture, they're dirty. They smell bad." Then he added, "Some [of them], not all." He also said those in Nambué hold and attend dances. I asked if my going to dances made me Nambueseña. Jaime, seemingly exasperated with my ignorance, said, "No. You don't understand me. They go to dances but also hold dances just for them—like to call the rain." I asked if he really believed that. He said yes and repeated that in Nambué they held rain dances (a belief likely gleaned from stereotypical representations of Native North Americans in old westerns or other television shows broadcast in Costa Rica, as this has never been a custom in Nambué, according to both collective memory and written history).

Arelys, another Riteña of a prominent family, backed me up and told him that was not the case. I agreed, noting that in my six years of visiting Nambué I had never seen a rain dance. Jaime explained, "I am referring to the culture they have that is of indigenous heritage." Stymied by his use of remarkably anthropological language, I was unable to come up with a clever response. Instead, I asked what other examples he could give. His cousin said, "They aren't impeccable. It's not that they're dirty, but they're not impeccable."

Jaime added, "They don't speak." He said they have cultural and grammatical differences. I asked, "Do they speak differently?" He said yes but was unable to give any examples. His cousin suggested that Nambueseños have accents. She added that she knows a Nambueseña who does not add the phrase "with your permission" to her speech, as polite Riteños and others do. She said a woman from Nambué went to her mother's house (presumably to work as a domestic servant) and did not say "with your permission—she just grabbed things."

At this point I was reduced from spoken responses to just shaking my head in disbelief that there was such an enormous perceived difference between the inhabitants of Santa Rita and those of Nambué—a mere seven kilometers away.[14] Jaime, perhaps responding to my head shaking, added, "But you think I disrespect them." I agreed that, indeed, it seemed so. He explained once again, "But no—disrespecting them isn't the same as just not liking them." Later in the year, Jaime questioned my interest in Latin America and explained that he was not a fan of the region himself. He asserted that of the Latin American nations, only Costa Rica and Argentina appealed to him. He explained, "As you know, I am racist [no longer clinging to mere 'tendencies'], and other than Argentina, Costa Rica has the largest European population."

This is perhaps the most extreme, explicit, and lengthy example of openly racist commentary I heard in Santa Rita. As such, it should not be taken as representative of the whole community's sentiment toward Nambué. Indeed, Arelys listened to this conversation with Jaime and often interjected comments that indicated she did not believe him, did not agree, and was perhaps as disgusted as I was by his comments. The ideas I heard first from Jaime, however, I did hear later from other Riteños (one by one, not in such a long, direct commentary as Jaime presented). Thus, although the severity of Jaime's opinions may have exceeded that of most community members, the underlying ideas regarding the difference and inferiority of Nambueseños to Riteños were, I found, pervasive and dominant in the community of Santa Rita and perceived as such by outsiders.

Outsider Views of Santa Rita

Several non-Riteño teachers characterized Santa Rita as racist. Some then clarified that they only referred to white Riteños—perhaps, not coincidentally, when nonwhite Riteños were within earshot. Outsiders also characterized Santa Rita as 100 percent Catholic. In fact, there were several Jehovah's Witnesses and Evangelical families as well, but both Riteños and outsiders viewed the community as overwhelmingly Catholic. I got the impression that it was not so much that the town of Santa Rita contained no non-Catholics but that non-Catholics did not quite count as Riteños. Class mixed with race to function in a similar fashion—either to exclude poorer and darker families from Riteño belonging or to give wealthy nonwhite members of the community honorary white, Riteño status. In the Introduction I described Isabel, one such girl who was *morena* (in my perception) from a wealthy family that resided in Santa Rita and who took pains to convince me of her whiteness.

Racial categorization was by no means always related to color. Assimilation to cultural ways common to a "white" population or attainment of an economic status comparable to a dominant white community could result in conferral of a different racial status, along a continuum that conflated whiteness with wealth at one extreme and placed darkness and poverty at the other.[15] Race and class intermingled in ways such that it may not be useful to consider which was primary but rather to explore how they mixed in different situations and with what outcomes.

I examine this conflation of class and race more thoroughly in Chapter 3. At this point, however, the concept is of import to the view of Santa Rita as a community of white, economically powerful families whose whiteness and economic power may have influenced one another significantly. For the time being, it will suffice to present one more example of the assumption that Riteños were wealthy. In a presentation to seventh graders about drug use and its effects, Profesora Delia addressed the issue of "distortion of reality" as an effect of drugs. She gave two examples of distorted realities: "I can't think I am [Mexican pop singer] Thalía when I am Profesora Delia. I can't say I'm from Santa Rita when I am from a family of limited resources."

La Rectitud Andante and Riteño Discourses on Sexuality

Another characteristic of residents of Santa Rita, according to outsiders I interviewed, was that "they play at being very puritanical," in the words of Profesor

Miguel. Profesor Sergio, a non-Riteño teacher (often the subject of gossip by Riteños), referred to Santa Rita as a community characterized by the "maintenance of almost Victorian morals," demonstrated through "almost inquisition-like observations." As the subject of numerous Riteño rumors with no basis in reality, I am inclined to subscribe to this perspective as well. This was so much the case that it was reminiscent of Foucault's descriptions of Victorian culture.

Foucault asserts, "For a long time, the story goes, we supported a Victorian regime, and we continue to be dominated by it even today. Thus the image of the imperial prude is emblazoned on our restrained, mute, and hypocritical sexuality."[16] This statement could have been written about the powerful core of Riteño teachers in charge of both the local gossip mill and, not coincidentally, the teachers' lounge and referred to sarcastically by Profesora Belisa (a non-Riteño teacher) as *la rectitud andante* (a walking monument to righteousness). In this repressive setting, sex and inappropriate relationships were taboos to be policed, but in many cases they were made existent by the gossip itself. Although some illicit relationships may have existed in the high school, rumors suggested that they happened with much greater frequency than was the case. Thus, gossip created a perceived reality. Sex was seen everywhere (including where it did not exist) and extensively decried. Rumor, in Santa Rita, worked to police sex.

This is perhaps why Profesora Rosa María interpreted my asking a male colleague for a ride to the entrance of Nambué as a come-on. Likewise, it may explain why my eating lunch or drinking coffee with a male teacher was rumored to be a cover-up for illicit sexual goings-on. Indeed, my speaking to male teachers at all (required by an anthropologist intending to interview 100 percent of the teaching staff) took on a different, scandalous meaning in local gossip that embellished it. Profesora Genofeva, a non-Riteña teacher, described Santa Rita (and the Riteño teachers' clique in particular) as "a snakes' nest; everyone speaks badly of everyone."

More in keeping with Foucault's discussion, sex in Santa Rita was a topic of constant speculation and conversation, revealing perhaps more about the minds of the gossips than about the reality they purported to observe and report.[17] Whereas the Riteño gossip mill held that sex must not be in any way (directly or indirectly) present in the school where it might negatively influence students, thus leading them astray, it was the gossip itself that made sex ever-present and passed rumors on to students.

The careful policing of sex (in terms of both squelching illicit relationships and demanding that sex occur only for procreation in socially approved pairings) was made painfully clear during the Mother's Day celebration put on by the male teachers for all female teachers and high school staff (not limited to those with offspring). At the Mother's Day luncheon I had the misfortune of choosing a seat (in a prime observer's position) at the corner where two long tables with teachers on both sides joined. Across from me sat three Riteña teachers integral to the gossip mill and *la rectitud andante*. Because it was Mother's Day, the conversation logically turned to questions of why, as a twenty-eight-year-old married woman, I had no children.

This was a question I had been asked frequently, and I responded with my standard answer that this was not the best moment in my career for motherhood. Usually, that was sufficient. Unfortunately, this was not the case on Mother's Day. Subsequently, I was lectured on how it was unacceptable for a married couple not to have children, on how such couples marry only for sex, on rumors of couples in the United States who refer to their pets as children, and on the selfishness of childless couples. Profesora Natalia then asked me point-blank, "Are you or are you not in favor of someday having a child?" The teachers at both tables looked at me as I stood trial. On this occasion, the policing of my sexuality was not limited to unfounded rumors, but rather I was directly criticized for shirking my reproductive responsibility.

Although I felt it personally when it was directed toward me at that luncheon, such vigilance regarding what was deemed moral responsibility was not limited to me. Two male teachers, not from Santa Rita but who resided there during the week, complained of not being able to go out for a beer after work for fear of the gossip network reporting such immoral activity. Another refrained from attending a school dance (attendance at which was mandatory for teachers) because, should he dance with anyone, rumors would fly. An administrator noted that such civilian policing was not limited to social activities. This individual used the word *vigilance* to refer to Riteño community members' penchant for watching at what time school employees arrived and left the school and where else their travels took them. Students also complained of being watched off campus by community members during lunch breaks (and reported for infractions embellished from daily, nondisruptive activities).

Riteño Values as the Standard for SRHS

Surveillance was not the only way students were affected by the dominant attitudes of Santa Rita, including those manifested through gossip given to hyperbole. Teachers' estimations of other teachers, based on rumor and the elements deemed central to belonging in Santa Rita (whiteness and wealth, residence in Santa Rita, and following "Spanish" culture) eventually made their way to student conversations. These criteria were also used to evaluate students in many cases (as I will discuss in detail in Chapters 5 and 6). In short, without a doubt the dominant culture of Santa Rita that privileged whiteness, wealth, Spanish descent, Catholicism, and residence in Santa Rita was also reflected and perpetuated in the school.

Teachers often related readings or subject matter to how "we" live—and "we" almost invariably reflected Riteño ways.[18] Profesora Rosaura, a Riteña literature teacher, compared a penitent's self-inflicted beatings to how "we [Catholics], when we pray, we strike our chests softly." "We" students of traveler Profesor Arnoldo went to Mass when a Riteño community member died or when a Mass was dedicated to the school—and those who were not Catholic had to bring written permission not to attend. Those who did not attend (even in one case I witnessed in which going to Mass was a last-minute plan a student could not possibly have foreseen) were graded down for absence.

"We" had telephones in our homes, to include our number as an answer on Riteña profesora Eugenia's English test or to phone our parents (although at the time central Santa Rita was the only community in which many families had telephones in their houses). "We" had money for extracurricular activities or out-of-the-ordinary school supplies. "We" students of Riteña profesora Marta Iris's class were described as dependent upon modern conveniences such as refrigerators, washing machines, coffeemakers, electric rice cookers, and "the indispensable video recorder" (although several students at the school who did not live in Santa Rita did not even have electricity, much less expensive appliances that depend upon it). "We" students, according to the principal, would travel to other countries someday. In other words, it was assumed that the standard student fit this mold—in spite of the recognized fact that only 20 percent of the student body was from central Santa Rita.

Indeed, social differences such as those noted between the dominant town and others outside of school were also apparent within the school. In Santa Rita the priest's model as a white, upstanding, pious Spaniard-turned-Riteño perhaps got exaggerated and pulled in directions the priest himself would have been unlikely to view as upholding the tenets of Catholicism. Father Sánchez was among the first to criticize the gossips and the excessive privilege of some Riteño families that allowed them to be above suspicion in even the most serious cases. Still, he was inextricably tied to the dominant attitudes and prejudices in Santa Rita, as exemplified by Jaime's diatribe.

I present one final example to demonstrate the link between the priest's presence in Santa Rita and its inhabitants' projected piousness. The high school began planning a Halloween dance as a fund-raiser. The local government of Santa Rita, however, declined to lend the school the community meeting hall for such an event, with the argument that Halloween was a diabolical import from the United States capable of corrupting youth, and the municipality preferred to support activities that "rescued" Costa Rican values. The month before the thwarted dance would have taken place, however, and—not coincidentally—when the priest was vacationing in Spain, the municipality lent the community meeting hall to an organization to hold a bikini-modeling pageant.

I learned of this happening while writing notes in the teachers' lounge, adjacent to the principal's office (whose walls did not reach the ceiling, making it less than soundproof). Profesora Aracely—a teacher from Santa Rita who was unusually quick to play devil's advocate, stand up for the underdog, and fight against unwritten Riteño privilege in the school—was placing a complaint. She expressed the opinion that "the devil is more present" in a hall full of women parading in bikinis under the lustful gaze of the community's men (and, I might add, the descendants of the illustrious founding families) than he is at a high school Halloween dance. Her interlocutor explained the contest's occurrence as a result of the priest's absence—not directly citing hypocrisy on the part of the community or its selective use of Catholic dogma. Santa Rita is no more guilty of hypocrisy or nonuniformity in its residents' points of view than any other community. When a heterogeneous community presents itself as homogeneous in its projected whiteness, wealth, Spanish heritage, and Catholicism (and such an image was seemingly upheld and legitimated in the mythologized figure of the priest), however, that hypocrisy is all the more evident. It is these assumptions and contradictions regarding who constitutes Riteño society that were reflected and perpetuated in the high school attended by members of twenty-eight distinct communities, including Nambué—to which I now turn.

NOTES

1. For such analyses, see Aronowitz and Giroux 1993: 9; Bonfil Batalla 1990: 199; Foley 1990: 138; López, Asséel, and Neumann 1984: 8; Luykx 1999: 295; McLaren 1982: 21; Ogbu 1978: 352; Yon 2000: 126.

2. See Alonso 1992: 418; Giroux 1989: 141; Luykx 1999: 295–296.

3. N.a. 1990: 4; translation mine.

4. Sommer 1990.

5. Edelman and Kenen 1989: 2 decry this myth, whereas others, such as Monge Alfaro 1959: 128 and Rodríguez Vega 1953: 16–19, 21, promote it.

6. Durán 1990: 17; translation mine.

7. Ibid.: 7; translation mine.

8. Ibid.: 6; translation mine.

9. Ibid.; translation mine.

10. Salguero 1991: 170; translation mine.

11. This information is drawn from the 1998 statistics from the local clinic, which conducts a survey each year.

12. Guanacastecos were, in some cases, referred to as "*cholos*," a word indicating, in Costa Rica, a step down in authenticity from Indian to a more mestizo, assimilated version still not considered part of any other community or ethnicity.

13. I was not recording the discussion or taking notes as it occurred, but I wrote field notes on it immediately afterward. Thus, what I present here should not be taken as a verbatim record of the conversation but rather as my perhaps flawed recollection of it, although it includes phrases I took care to memorize.

14. The high school, located in the center of Santa Rita, is nine kilometers from the center of Nambué.

15. See Field 1999: 191 for a discussion of the link between whiteness and wealth, and Wade 1997: 99 for insight into the complex intermingling of race and social class.

16. Foucault 1978: 3.

17. Ibid.: 17–49.

18. See López, Asséel, and Neumann 1984: 282, 361 for a similar analysis of how Chilean school curriculum imparts dominant culture. See also Pinar 1993: 60 for an account of how a curriculum demonstrates whose knowledge is most valued. See Luykx 1999: 203–204 for the curricular content of cultural capital in a Bolivian normal school geared toward teaching dominant ways of being. Dolby 2001: 48 writes of a South African high school with a predominantly black student population that nevertheless promoted a white image for the entire school. Yon 2000: 37 writes of "us," implying

"white Canadians," in the Toronto high school where he worked. Similarly, Levinson 2001: 311 notes that by promoting a homogeneous image of the nation, the Mexican secondary school where he worked all but erased ethnic difference. Furthermore, not only do all of these works address the teaching of a particular ethnic or racial identity as the standard, but Levinson 2001: 311 and Luykx 1999: 158 also note that maleness was the standard within the dominant ethnic group.

3

Ni chicha ni limonada[1]

IDENTITY POLITICS IN AND ABOUT THE RESERVATION

IN MY INTERVIEWS WITH THEM OVER THE YEARS, SOME INHABITANTS OF THE CHOROTEGA Indigenous Reservation expressed the opinion that they were labeled *indigenous* only as a result of their residence within the boundaries of a reservation. Others considered that Nambueseños' practice of "traditional" culture—the preparation of certain foods, narrative tradition, living in thatched-roof houses (*ranchos*)—was symbolic proof of their Indianness. Several enthusiastic participants in the building of a *rancho* in 1998 considered such symbols emblematic of belonging in the national culture (and in contradiction to indigenous culture), which has adopted these symbols and adapted them for its own use. As is evident in the case of the Chorotega of Costa Rica, the expression of ethnic distinctiveness is only one facet of the negotiation of identity, which involves self-identification as much as external categorization, the influence of dominant discourses on the definitions of ethnic groups, and the malleability of cultural symbols used by different parties to prove and disprove ethnic and racial affiliations.

Fredrik Barth asserts that it is the maintenance of the boundaries between ethnic groups that truly defines the groups rather than the cultural features that lie within those boundaries.[2] Nevertheless, many cultural markers people interpret as the defining properties of ethnicity are in fact related more to cultural elements or manifestations. In some cases these practices might be indicative of ethnic distinctiveness, but at times they fall short of other groups' means of definition. Other scholars contend it is the labeling process that takes place at borders that is of foremost importance in the construction of ethnicity and that is integral to distinguishing one ethnic group from another.[3] In this chapter I discuss various forms of creating and maintaining ethnic distinctiveness and how identity was construed both by and for the inhabitants of Nambué. The purpose of this chapter is to place my work within a theoretical context regarding ethnicity, race, and identity. I present both insider and outsider opinions of the reservation and of the label residence within it conferred upon its inhabitants. In particular, I emphasize how place of residence has become one of the most significant defining factors of ethnicity for Nambueseños.

Many anthropologists discuss a variety of ethnic markers as indicative of a group's distinctiveness. By emphasizing these markers, members of ethnic groups can assert their ethnic difference.[4] Although there exists much debate over what constitutes an ethnic group, definitions commonly take such everyday items or practices—like kinship, religion, language, appearance, and nationality—as definitive. The unique history and circumstances surrounding the reservation, however, make the traditional markers of ethnic identity less appropriate to the Nambueseño case.

HISTORY OF THE RESERVATION

In 1977 the Costa Rican government started establishing reservations in areas where people claiming indigenous identity continued to live in traditional ways and in areas where indigenous populations were known to have lived at the time of conquest. In all, twenty-two reservations were established (and one has been added since) for the members of eight ethnic groups[5] seen as corresponding to one of those two categories. Nambué fit the second of the two. In the colonial era, the Chorotega inhabited the Nicoya Peninsula in what is now Costa Rica. Although the Nicarao also inhabited this region at the time of conquest, there was no discussion of establishing a Nicarao reservation. I have argued elsewhere that this may reflect a nationalist project and the xenophobia that exists toward Nicaraguans in general.[6] This alludes to the existence of underlying, unspoken motivations for the creation of reservations in Costa Rica and the criteria used to do so. Indeed, some of the details surrounding the establishment of reservations are murky, even for those intimately involved in this process. One social scientist consulted on the matter spoke of its motivations in vague terms and asked that I not identify him or her. Given the lack of clarity surrounding the official reasons behind the reservations, various opinions exist surrounding the purpose of the reservation system.

Although one of the Nambueseños who originally supported gaining reservation status for Nambué argued that the primary motivation for the establishment of reservations was the recovery of land for indigenous peoples, other sources suggest otherwise. One author reports that CONAI (Comisión Nacional de Asuntos

Indígenas—the National Commission on Indigenous Affairs) was set up "to provide technical help and legal protection to the Indian groups. According to one study, however, a focus has been to convert the Native Americans into more standard peasants, and to ignore the problem of helping them to find ways to retain their lifestyle."[7] According to CONAI, the reservations were established with the express goal of assimilating the indigenous populations. In the words of the law that created the reservations, the goal was to "promote social, economic, and *cultural* improvement of the indigenous population with the aim of elevating its conditions of life and to integrate the aboriginal communities to the development process."[8]

A non-Indian teacher in Nambué at the time encouraged Nambueseños to promote Nambué as the site for the Chorotega reservation in order to receive land from the government (part of the reservation program included the government buying land from white settlers within the reservation areas to redistribute to Indians at no cost). Six Nambueseños followed his suggestion. With the teacher's assistance, these individuals drafted criteria that supported Nambué as an appropriate site for the Chorotega reservation. Topping the list of proof of Indianness, according to one representative of that small group of pro-reservation activists, was the inhabitants' physical appearance. The list also included housing practices (the presence and construction of *ranchos*), the fiesta that accompanies the construction of such a house and pays laborers with traditional foods and drink, and another festival in the region for which Nambueseños almost always served as *mayordomos*. The source explained that "the *mayordomo* was the most Indian [person] who ran the [festival]" and that "the most Indian" person was always found in Nambué. The criteria also included the fabrication of pottery then practiced by one community member, the production of traditional foods, the abundance of pre-Columbian artifacts found in Nambué, and a reputation for witchcraft (tied to Chorotega practices) within the community.

The man did not list the name of the community, but it is in fact one of the few surviving Chorotega words from the Mangue language. This source also did not include the collective memory, passed through generations, of forced labor for Spaniards in the construction of a colonial church that still stands in a nearby town. This representative of pro-reservation activists from 1977 told me many people were willing to claim indigenous identity to get free land. He added, "Now people have their land, and they don't want to be indigenous because of the discrimination."

Many people both within and outside of Nambué have accused the Nambueseño reservation promoters of opportunism. The same is said of those who projected Chorotega ethnicity to obtain free land but who later denied that identity. Other reservations in the country consider that Nambué and one other reservation were given reservation status under the condition that they would vote for certain (nonindigenous) CONAI representatives. The representative of the 1977 pro-reservation group with whom I spoke acknowledged that Nambué was used in this way by CONAI but said it was a situation of mutual benefit. CONAI used Nambué's representative to support its non-Indian leaders' decisions, and Nambué promoted an Indian identity not held by all its inhabitants in order to procure land.

Nambué's first representative to CONAI was successful in obtaining land for those inhabitants willing to claim indigenous identity. He was so successful, in fact, that shortly after becoming Nambué's official representative, CONAI transferred the man to a reservation at the country's other extreme where a language other than Spanish was spoken and the customs were nothing like those of Nambué. The consequence of his transfer was that he was placed in an area where his activism and advocacy were rendered ineffective.

BENEFITS AND DISADVANTAGES OF RESERVATION STATUS

Nambueseños in favor of the reservation in the 1990s pointed to the protection of land (by means of the prohibition against the sale of land to outsiders) as a main benefit of the reservation. Prior to Nambué's establishment as a reservation, white settlers had been buying land rapidly and cheaply. Several Nambueseños reported people being cheated out of their land by settlers who essentially traded homemade liquor for signatures in a system that privileged signed titles over the spoken word as proof of landownership. Protection of land was also listed by those opposed to reservation status, however, as one of the reasons such status was detrimental to their economic situation. They noted that if they could sell land to non-Indians, they could move elsewhere. As it was, however, no Indians in Nambué could afford to buy their land, so they were forced to stay. Among Nambueseños, there was an overwhelming sense of people feeling trapped in their community. Although reservation status protected individuals from opportunistic outsiders, it also prevented insiders from leaving at will.

Those who were pro-reservation in recent times pointed to the fact that Nambué could theoretically get funds, access to health care, and housing assistance through CONAI rather than through the usual labyrinthine bureaucratic process. Reservation opponents noted that these benefits were purely theoretical and that their supposed existence prevented Nambueseños from obtaining the services or goods through the regular bureaucratic processes. Non-Indian municipal governmental offices considered that Nambué was not entirely their responsibility and often used the theoretical, CONAI-provided benefits as an excuse not to provide actual ones. Unfortunately, CONAI did not take sufficient responsibility for Nambué either.

Although the reservation itself encompasses three small communities, I focus on that which shares the name of the entire reservation and is also the largest of the three. Many Nambueseños and numerous outsiders did not realize that any communities other than Nambué formed part of the reservation. The fact that two other communities exist within the reservation bounds, however, is significant. Of these three communities, only one—Nambué—corresponds to the township of Santa Rita. The other two continue to belong to the township of Majapiñao, as Nambué used to. The mayor of Santa Rita explained that this condition of being split between two municipal governments was the source of Nambué's problems. It requires an inordinate amount of bureaucratic coordination to accomplish anything at the level of the entire reservation—such as fixing the road. The two municipal governments (of Santa Rita and Majapiñao), in such situations, can point fingers at each other to indicate under whose responsibility Nambué as a reservation falls. Working with two municipal governments in this way only increases the phenomenon known locally and colloquially as *tortuguismo* (turtleism), whereby bureaucratic channels seem unending and any project takes a frustratingly long time to see completion—if it ever does.

Some inhabitants of the reservation explained differently the municipal government's relative inactivity on projects requested by Nambué. One respected community member considered that from the point of view of local government (at the municipal level, in Santa Rita), "Nambué is a parasite." Economically speaking, it contributed nothing to the township (such as revenue from tourism or the coffee industry, which other towns had to offer) yet drained resources from the same. Thus, the reservation's incongruence with other local, political boundaries did not aid Nambué's situation. Its division into parishes paralleled the reservation's split membership in two municipalities. This division, by which Catholics from Nambué proper attended church functions in Santa Rita and those from the other two communities corresponded to the parish of Majapiñao, further inhibited reservation-wide organization. This, however, was not the priest's main criticism of the beginning of the Chorotega reservation.

According to Father Sánchez, who administered Mass in Nambué, "The reservation was imposed, and it was imposed too late. They would have had to impose it 100 years earlier to continue the [cultural ethnic] line." In contrast, by the time Nambué was made a reservation, there was no longer an indigenous structure of leadership, a pre-Columbian system of land tenure, or a Chorotega (Mangue) language. Many Nambueseños shared this view.

CONAI AND NAMBUÉ

Whereas Nambué's first representative gained some tangible benefits for the reservation's inhabitants, the situation changed in subsequent years. Later representatives of the reservation reported that after the advantages of having reservation status were no longer visible, Nambueseño representatives were merely coerced into approving CONAI officials' actions. Such coercion took the form of physical threats and underhanded manipulation.[9]

CONAI's manipulation of Nambué has had serious consequences, but the results of this coercion have had as much negative effect on CONAI as on Nambué. In 1997 CONAI came under increased scrutiny of the various reservations. The Costa Rican Legislative Assembly began revising the law that governed both CONAI and the reservations, and state delegates consulted all the reservations with regard to how this legislation might better serve their needs. This project was known as the Legal Project for the Autonomous Development of Indigenous Communities (Proyecto de Ley Para el Desarrollo Autónomo de los Pueblos Indígenas). Representatives of the Legislative Assembly visited each of the twenty-three reservations to pass out copies of a proposed revision of the law.

Although the effort was relatively successful overall, it had some drawbacks. In the Teribe, Bribrí, and Cabécar reservations in Térraba, Ujarrás, and Cabagra, respectively, it became evident that the director of CONAI had hired men to incite the "white" colonists within reservation lands to protest the assemblies to protect their interests.[10] Thus, intimidation inhibited full participation by reservation inhabitants. Once these communities were able to meet in a nonthreatening environment, however, members did voice their opinions.

In Nambué there were no direct efforts to sabotage the consultation, but not all inhabitants were notified in sufficient time to be able to attend. In their defense, the state delegates asserted that they announced the meeting in several ways: through a newspaper ad (a paper not readily accessible to Nambueseños), a telephone call to the attendant of Nambué's only telephone[11] (who was locally notorious for never passing on messages), and dissemination of pamphlets by mail to be read and discussed at the meeting (which never reached many community members, given the slow mail service in the country).[12] Not having prepared for the meeting by reading pamphlets outlining the suggested new law, the inhabitants of Nambué were unable to give sufficient input on the issue.

One community member suggested that the meeting never would have worked because the officials tried to divide the community into groups to discuss parts of the law. This person viewed such a strategy as a way to prevent anyone from becoming familiar with the entire law. Even if sufficient time had been allowed to prepare, however, there were additional obstacles to the meeting's success. As the proponent of the preceding theory explained, "CONAI has always come here with lies." Given that Nambué was rarely included in Costa Rican pan-Indian activities, Nambueseños were already suspicious of their inclusion in this event.

Mistrust of state government officials and of CONAI also impeded the success of this process. CONAI had a history in Nambué (and elsewhere) of manipulating indigenous presence and words. Nambueseños, as I found out in interviews after the consultations took place, thought this was just one more instance of CONAI pretending to serve their interests that would result in a twisting of their words to their detriment. Prior to the consultations, CONAI called together representatives of each reservation to voice their opinions about the way CONAI was run. According to the CONAI representative who called for Nambueseño participation, this was an invitation for indigenous peoples to demand Indian control over the organization. Representatives from Nambué and other reservations traveled to the capital city to insist on assuming indigenous control of CONAI. Meanwhile, CONAI representatives undermined their presence by passing out leaflets to observers explaining that presence as indigenous support of CONAI as it was being run.[13] An inhabitant of Nambué recalled this incident, noting that she was encouraged to go to the meeting when the person who called to invite her (presumably from CONAI) told her father that he would help get her a job with a delegate of the Legislative Assembly working for the defense of indigenous peoples in Costa Rica. Under this assumption she went to the meeting, where she was used as one more "example" of indigenous support of CONAI.

More recently, CONAI was suspect in a fraudulent situation whereby monies supposedly directed toward high school students from Nambué never arrived. During the year of my most recent fieldwork in Nambué (1999), a member of the community obtained employment with CONAI. He found that two students in Nambué were listed as receiving scholarship money for school. I asked the students if they were aware of receiving scholarships, and they were not. They contacted the Nambueseño official working with CONAI to investigate the situation, and when I left the field in December 1999 they still had not received the funds.

NAMBUESEÑO CAUTION TOWARD OUTSIDERS

This mistrust of officials resulting from interactions with CONAI was not limited to that organization. The same wariness existed with regard to social scientists and education officials. I learned of the apprehension toward social scientists early in my interactions with the community of Nambué. In 1993 some community members explained to me that too many researchers had gone to Nambué with the intent of learning all they could, thus furthering their own careers without doing anything in return for the community. From that time on I made a point of contributing to Nambueseño society in ways asked of me and, in some cases, in ways I suggested but that received community approval, permission, and support. These ranged from making tamales for community events, taking advantage of my height to cut the best leaves on banana trees from which to wrap tamales, providing child care, giving English classes, tutoring, writing recommendation letters for Nambueseño students and job seekers, and collecting a volume of oral narratives (published, with the narrators credited for their contributions).[14] These actions, among others, qualified me as "sufficiently humble" (the greatest compliment a gringa could receive in Nambué, where stereotypes of North Americans included stinginess, selfishness, and an exploitative character). Various Nambueseños explained, in retrospect, that it was my humility that led people to continue to talk to me, entertain my questions, and willingly and knowingly further my career.

Other social scientists have been less fortunate than I, in my own view, and less deserving, in the eyes of many Nambueseños. In 1994 I witnessed three social science students from the local branch of the University of Costa Rica leave frustrated. Some individuals who have been (and continue to be) helpful to me in my research turned these students away, claiming to know nothing. One person in the community suggested that they look to me for information, which they did. In 1999 students from local universities again sought me out for information on Nambué.

Some of these students tried to conduct interviews in Nambué, and others did not. Those who did experienced the rage of individuals tired of being classified by people of their same ethnic heritage as somehow different and more Indian. In one case a pair of researchers—one from nearby Majapiñao and the other from neighboring Santa Rita—arrived unannounced to interview Nambueseños on "their process of transculturation." The general store owner resented their assumption that anyone in Nambué could know more about the topic than a man from Majapiñao and a Riteña who had lived all their lives with the same customs as Nambueseños. A local schoolteacher was furious at their presumptions. This teacher initially told her interlocutor that she was no different from any Riteño, with the possible exception that she was more educated because she had worked for five years in San José, she was a professional, and she did not ask ridiculous questions. The teacher let the local student of social sciences know she was unable to talk about the days when loincloths were en vogue in Nambué because she was not alive in that era.

This Nambueseña teacher continued to express her resentment of the local student. She asked exactly what "transculturation" he wanted her to tell him about, since she had always lived just as she did then. The student explained that by transculturation he meant influences from other countries, and he gave the example that as part of his own transculturation he sometimes ate hamburgers. The teacher exclaimed "so do I!" and stressed that she was no different from him. A local university professor explained to me that students who aspired to teach social studies (often of the same ethnic heritage as those they interviewed) were frequently sent either to Nambué or to Guaitil (a town in Guanacaste that produced ceramics like those unearthed by archaeologists in the region) to ask questions about culture. The Nambueseña teacher agreed that this was the case and that when they arrived in Nambué, such students wondered where all the Indians were because the individuals they encountered were just like them.

It is this repeated exploitation and manipulation of Nambueseños by organizations, scholars, and institutions that have led to their understandably heightened use of caution in dealing with officials and outsiders. At the meeting with delegates from the Legislative Assembly whom many Nambueseños assumed to be CONAI officials in disguise or individuals manipulated by CONAI, one respected member of the community, Pedro Pablo Pérez, explained why members of the community were unwilling to make hasty decisions regarding laws that would rule the reservation. First, they had no time to think the proposed laws over and discuss them with those unable to attend the meeting. Second, the last time a decision was made by the few for the many, Nambué ended up with reservation status—a decision with which many disagreed. He addressed his fellow Nambueseños when he stated, "I understand the worry, on your part, of settling issues like this, in one blow, but it is as the *campesino* saying goes: he [sic] that burns himself on milk even blows on cheese curd [*El que se queme con leche hasta la cuajada sopla*]."[15] Such caution may come from a long history of imposed definition from outside the reservation.

CONTRADICTORY DISCOURSES ON
CHOROTEGA PERSISTENCE IN COSTA RICA

Discourse has the capacity to create, rather than simply reflect, local identities. By purporting to objectively describe reality, various texts turn into authoritative voices that determine the ways readers perceive that reality.[16] In the case of the Chorotega of Costa Rica, three dominant indigenist discourses—historical, legal, and anthropological—have formed a trinity of contradictory yet definitive authoritative voices regarding the description and definition of Costa Rican indigenous peoples.

These three discourses simultaneously create both an absence and an ambiguous presence of indigenous peoples in Costa Rica generally and of the Chorotega in particular. History, legal discourse, and anthropology have each, in their own way, constructed a vision of the nation that ostensibly aims to assimilate and define indigenous peoples but that in practice results in excluding them from the nation as a whole. Furthermore, these discourses render invisible or insignificant the social class differences among citizens, thus creating a vision of a homogeneous nation. To some extent, the citizens of this nation and the Nambueseños have internalized the various perspectives promoted by these discourses.[17]

Along the fissures of these discourses, however, seeps a marginal discourse that contradicts the way the dominant voices have erased the Chorotega from the present-day Costa Rican nation. Within Nambué, this voice emerges through oral history and collective "memory." This "memory" recalls events the homogenizing discourses attempt to erase: indigenous peoples' history of relegation to the fringes of society, social stratification, and even forced labor. The three dominant discourses regarding attitudes and practices toward Costa Rican indigenous citizens are history, which has erased them from the modern nation; legal discourse, which officially declared their existence and enclosed them in reservations with the goal of acculturation; and anthropology, which has evaluated each reservation according to a constructed hierarchy of perceived "authenticity" or legitimacy in each community's merit of reservation status. Each of these discourses has turned into a "reality" for Costa Ricans generally, as well as for those labeled as Chorotega Indians.

Costa Rican historiography has excluded indigenous people from the modern nation. It is widely believed (although erroneously so) that there were scant indigenous populations in Costa Rica at the time of Spanish colonization. Of the eight ethnic groups now recognized as having once existed within the country's boundaries, early-twentieth-century Costa Rican historian Carlos Gagini considered the Chorotega the tribe of greatest importance.[18] This importance, however, was apparently already relegated to the past by Gagini's time, as manifested by the fact that he never writes of the Chorotega in the present tense.[19] Another turn-of-the-century historian describes the "complete disappearance" of the Chorotega.[20]

According to these perspectives and others like them that abound in Costa Rican historiography, it appears that the theory of ethnicity or of "Indianness" that dominates Costa Rican history is based on essentialist purisms. This type of purist perspective falsely suggests that indigenous peoples have lived unchanged throughout time, never mixing with other ethnic groups or adopting outside customs.[21] That a national myth should be taken as fact is not uncommon.[22] Costa Rica's official historical discourse treats indigenous peoples as if they can exist under this label only if they have remained frozen in time, in complete cultural stasis.[23]

In 1977 Costa Rican law contradicted this historical discourse when it first created twenty-two reservations, thus acknowledging the existence of eight indigenous ethnicities. The creation of indigenous reservations in Costa Rica was one aspect of the effort to create a homogeneous nation by targeting particular ethnic groups for assimilationist projects. Through this process of "cultural improvement," which, according to CONAI, motivated the creation of reservations, it was evident that in Costa Rican indigenist politics, Indianness was something to be contained and eventually eradicated.[24] In this manner, legal discourse recognized the existence of indigenous peoples within the Costa Rican nation, but only with the contradictory goal of ultimately eliminating them by means of forced acculturation.[25] Ironically, although reservations were created to promote assimilation, their being set apart promoted instead (among some members) an increased sense of ethnic difference. Thus, in some cases the imposition of a given identity, through the establishment of the reservation system, could lead to a reaffirmation of ethnic distinctiveness.[26]

In the case of Nambué, the Chorotega reservation, and what Costa Rican folklorist and politician Miguel Salguero refers to as a "nucleus" of Chorotega survival,[27] the designation of a parcel of land as an indigenous reservation did not suddenly cause its inhabitants to be described as Indians in the 1970s but rather had the curious side effect of absolving those outside the reservation's borders from that stigmatized label. The result was a sort of placism, if you will—a form of discrimination based on a specific place of residence perceived as an indicator of racial difference and inferiority.[28] During my various stints of fieldwork between 1993 and 1999, I observed that inhabitants of the reservation had come to be systematically discriminated against by people (often of the same ethnic heritage) living immediately outside the reservation's borders, as those borders, in the quarter century since their demarcation, had come to have the effect of labeling those within as Indian—a stigmatized label in a country that projects a view of homogeneous whiteness with pride and holds an estimation of Indianness as synonymous with backwardness.

Like legal discourse, Costa Rican anthropological discourse has also supported its arguments with primordialist views of ethnicity. Although the state, through law, paradoxically created indigenous reservations to diminish Indianness and to promote assimilation, Costa Rican anthropologists have declared the inhabitants of Nambué insufficiently Indian to merit reservation status, thus becoming complicitous in the negation of Nambueseños' Indian heritage as proclaimed by historiographic discourse.

In large part, Costa Rican anthropologists have traditionally defined Chorotega customs (in the Boasian tradition of quantifiable inventories of "purely" Indian traits or ceremonies) as lost traditions once they came to be considered national patrimony. Above all, anthropologists point to the lack of an indigenous language within the Chorotega reservation, where community members speak only Spanish, as proof of the Nambueseños' acculturation.

Although Costa Rican anthropologists recognize that other Costa Rican tribes find themselves in a process of transculturation—characterized by the appropriation of outside customs or cultural elements—they consider that the Chorotega have already acculturated. Costa Rican anthropologist María Eugenia Bozzoli de Wille describes the Chorotega as individuals who are no longer indigenous, given their lack of customs distinct from those of people living immediately outside the reservation.[29] Instead, she considers Nambueseños to be campesinos or mestizos. According to this view, indigenous culture can only be considered indigenous when it is opposed to mestizo culture. When Nambueseño culture approximates mestizo culture, it is considered less that the mestizos have appropriated elements of indigenous tradition than that the Indian has acculturated.

Although her experience within Nambué was brief—she passed through approximately fifteen years ago[30]—Bozzoli de Wille's assertion that the inhabitants of Nambué are more campesino or mestizo than indigenous has had a great impact. Anthropologists who have published subsequent to her writings have ignored Nambué in their considerations of Costa Rica's indigenous populations.[31] The classification of Nambué as no longer indigenous and the adoption of this perspective by other anthropologists and by the inhabitants of reservations considered "more legitimate" in Costa Rica have resulted in Nambué's current position on the lowest rungs of the legitimacy ladder, which to some extent determines the distribution of federal funds to the various reservations as well as the respect accorded to each by the pan-indigenous community.

What the Costa Rican anthropological perspective fails to recognize is that stripping a community of its purported ethnic identity (or ethnic label in this case, where identity may differ from the label for many individuals) removes a potential rallying force, thus increasing the possibility of exploitation.[32] In the Costa Rican context, anthropology pretends to protect "legitimate" indigenous groups by distinguishing them from the more "acculturated" ones to preserve indigenous tradition. By designating Nambueseños as acculturated, however, social scientists deprive many Nambueseños of their identity and do not take into account that their influence is responsible for leaving Nambué, as a reservation, "*sin el santo ni la limosna*"—literally "with neither saint nor alms"—and figuratively falling through the cracks.[33] Caught in a bureaucratic double bind, in the 1990s the community of Nambué no longer received sufficient federal funds (distributed to other, so-called more legitimate reservations) because of what was viewed as its insufficient Indianness. Yet it also received scarce funds from its local municipality, which claimed that CONAI was responsible for providing economic aid to Nambué. Furthermore, as a result of living within the borders of a reservation, Nambueseños still had to confront discrimination and prejudice that existed on a local level—in schools, clinics, and businesses that surrounded and supposedly served the reservation.

INSIDER VIEWS OF DEFINITIONS BY OUTSIDERS

When discourses construct social realities, they can influence the very people they purport to describe. Within Nambué, all the perspectives previously mentioned (the historical, legal, and anthropological) regarding the identity of the reservation's inhabitants coexisted simultaneously during my fieldwork and articulated with anthropological theory from the United States and elsewhere regarding the social construction of ethnicity. Some reservation inhabitants I interviewed agreed with dominant versions of national history that insist the Chorotega became extinct centuries ago, be it as a result of European pathogens that preceded the Spaniards (already colonizing nearby regions) in the 1500s or directly as a result of the conquerors' violence. Other Nambueseños agreed with legal discourse that recognizes the existence of indigenous peoples in Costa Rica, and some of those believed the reservation system protected them. Still others promoted the leading anthropological perspective that claims that although the Chorotega did at one time live in and around Nambué and were ancestors of the current inhabitants of Nambué, the present-day inhabitants are no longer indigenous but mestizos—both racially and culturally. The opinions of other inhabitants of Nambué did not follow closely any of these three discourses, although the contradictions among the three have had their effect on identity as well.

As one Nambueseño explained, referring to the ethnic limbo in which inhabitants of Nambué find themselves, "*No somos ni chicha ni limonada. No somos nada*" (a phrase that translates figuratively as "We're neither one thing nor another. We are nothing"). It seems the authors of the dominant discourses did not take into account that now, more than ever, the people they mean to describe can and do read, negotiate, reject, and internalize these definitions.[34] In Nambué, the debate surrounding whether community members were Indians or mestizos was both common and constant. Within and among families and generations there was no agreement regarding ethnic identity or the appropriateness of Nambué's designation as a reservation.

Viviano Aguirre, a former community leader (whose point of view does not reflect the opinion of all Nambueseños), spoke about the objectification of the community as a result of its being designated a reservation. Speaking with government officials in a community meeting, he explained:

> The government entities, the institutions, see the people of Nambué as if we were a clay vessel, as if we were a [museum] piece, they don't value us and they hold us like a relic: [Nambué], the Chorotega Indigenous Reservation. . . . They see us like an object . . . those that don't know us, or they think that we wear a feather on our head[s] or a loincloth, and it's different, we're different, and maybe we're the community that's most different from the others, and although we feel proud to be Chorotega indigenous people, we want progress, our own intellectual progress, that of our children, and that of the children of our children.[35]

This quote refers to the Costa Rican Chorotega Indians' relegation to the past (as presented by historiographic discourse) and to the perception that the Nambueseños are different from other indigenous communities in the country (as Costa Rican social scientists suggest). Furthermore, it implies that in spite of this transculturation, they continue to be indigenous. Another community member, in favor of neither the community's reservation status nor its corresponding imposed indigenous identity, explained the reason behind his resentment of Nambué's indigenous label. He noted that other reservations in the country were different. As examples, he proposed images of people in Talamanca—a Bribrí and Cabécar reservation in the southeastern part of the country—bathing in water they later drank, lacking toilets, and making beverages using unhygienic processes (images that do not entirely resonate with my observations gleaned from fieldwork there in 1994 and that, ironically, are similar to the stereotypes outsiders might hold of Nambué itself). At the meeting in which Aguirre presented his opinion, a delegate from the Legislative Assembly congratulated Nambué on its "progress" beyond that of other reservations and lauded Nambué as "the best indigenous reservation of the country, because it has better services, it has water, lights, a school, a church, and everything."[36]

In the excerpt of Aguirre's speech quoted earlier, Nambué's former community leader comments indirectly on the contradictory definitions of the present-day Chorotega, which create for them an externally imposed identity crisis. None of these discourses adequately defines the Costa Rican Chorotega Indian—perhaps because none of their developers consulted the Chorotega when forming their definitions. Nevertheless, not all Nambueseños questioned these dominant discourses. The variety of identities projected by different residents of Nambué became evident to me through fieldwork carried out from 1993 to 1999. Two important foci of the interviews I conducted during those years were the question of identity and Nambueseños' opinions of the reservation. I found that approximately 50 percent of residents identified themselves as indigenous and 50 percent did not, with no clear lines of division along family, generational, or other identifiable lines.[37] I stumbled onto the topic of identity while familiarizing myself with the village during my first few days there in 1993. Having just spoken to Gerardo, a prominent community member who happened to mention his pride in his indigenous identity (not at all related to the research I was conducting at the time, which included Nambué as one of four rural communities under study), I was walking past what I later found out was the house of Gerardo's sister, Socorro. Without having met me, Socorro waved enthusiastically and shouted, "Hello! You know there's nothing indigenous here!"

This intriguing salutation—juxtaposed with Socorro's brother's positive evaluation of his own identity as indigenous—was my first clue to the identity crisis that divided the community. I soon became aware that within Nambué there was no agreement regarding whether the inhabitants were Indian. Some Nambueseños I interviewed drew upon conventional anthropological categories as proof of their Indianness. According to others, the preparation of traditional foods, knowledge of medicinal plants, particular narrative practices, and the presence of pre-Columbian artifacts in the reservation were not unique to Nambué but were common throughout the region—thus illustrating that Nambueseños were no more Indian than anyone else in the province of Guanacaste and should not be singled out as such. These same Nambueseños, who opposed both the designation of Indian identity and the reservation status of their land, asserted that the *ranchos* did not prove a connection to the ancient past but, rather, indicated a connection to the inhabitants' current, poor economic condition. To explain the variety of identities professed in Nambué, it is useful to examine some theoretical considerations of what constitutes an ethnic group.

ANTHROPOLOGICAL DEFINITIONS OF ETHNIC GROUPS

Some anthropologists consider that some consciousness of membership must exist for a group to be distinctive.[38] Although anthropologists and policy makers in Costa Rica have defined groups on the basis of their outwardly visible ethnic markers, several scholars advocate the use of emic identification as the preferred method of definition.[39] Others view self-definition as only one important component of ethnic identity. For some anthropologists, like Bozzoli de Wille and those who follow her lead, the lack of overt differences between a designated ethnic group and those around them might overshadow their self-identification and become proof of their nondistinctiveness. Perhaps self-identification is only one definitive element of ethnicity. An external categorization of people is also necessary to validate their difference.[40]

This brings up two important issues. The first is the nature of ethnic markers as dynamic rather than static, as they are often assumed to be and as many commonly accepted markers of ethnic difference suggest. The other is the nature of identity as self-defined or as externally ascribed. Quite simply, the assertion of ethnic difference is not easily defined by following a less than exhaustive list of essentialist markers. Nor is it so simple as viewing the determination of ethnicity as a two-sided issue between self-definition and ascription, for the two are intimately intertwined. As is evident in the case of Nambué, a people might fall back on anthropological lists of traits or customs to prove their ethnic difference to outsiders in particular situations.[41]

Along with physical and cultural markers, many scholars and other individuals take place, birthplace, or homeland to be an important element of ethnic difference.[42] Some members of the Chorotega populations of Sutiava and Monimbó (Nicaragua) also assert their Indianness on the basis of having been native to particular communities for multiple generations.[43] Even so, the Chorotega of Nicaragua are rarely recognized as an indigenous group at the national level. The category of common descent, in both cases, is very much tied to place. For some Nambueseños interviewed between 1993 and 1998, their tie (through birthplace in the general region) to the people who lived there in colonial times (and were at that time recognized as Indian) was integral to their identity. In spite of the artifice and arbitrary nature of the borders, some ethnic groups have internalized imposed political borders as legitimate ethnic markers.[44] In spite of this self-identification of some Nambueseños as Indian, the Chorotega are not always included in lists of ethnic groups residing within the country.[45]

In contrast, according to Jeffrey Gould, membership in a specific Nicaraguan community (in a set place) was a crucial marker of Indianness in the early part of the twentieth century.[46] Thus, place is an important marker of identity for some people within the Chorotega communities of Costa Rica and Nicaragua, who base their identity on birthplace in the place where their ancestors once lived. Residence within these territorial boundaries may also ascribe indigenous identity to those who do not identify themselves as indigenous—as is the case for some members of both the Costa Rican and Nicaraguan Chorotega communities in which inhabitants do not all agree upon ethnic identity.[47] This lack of agreement makes sense, given that the Indian label affects individuals in different ways.

A PHENOMENOLOGICAL VIEW OF PLACE

A number of phenomenologists, geographers, and social scientists interested in the significance of place have noted that place takes on meaning in accordance with the experiences lived therein and the sentiments held toward it.[48] As it happens, in Nambué, sentiments toward this homeland varied dramatically from one person to the next. These sentiments varied in accordance with the range of experiences that contributed to the formation of sentiments surrounding this place, which were influenced by individual social identity. It is to these various identities and differently perceived meanings and designations of place that I now turn.

Nambué was many different places to those who lived within it and who faced the corresponding association of being inhabitants of the reservation. It was perceived differently by a lifelong resident who faced discrimination frequently than by a young person returning home for a weekend visit from the capital city. Likewise, it was experienced differently by a visiting anthropologist, able to take in the beauty and enjoy the scenery, sounds, and company—or even to study a phenomenon as frustrating as prejudice—without being subject to the discrimination faced by permanent residents.

Even for such a visitor, Nambué can be many different places, in spite of its small size. One is struck by the lush greenery covering the mountainous terrain crosscut by rivers where spirits are said to lurk at night (making the spots where a road or a path crosses the river a wholly different place at night). Also salient are the humid heat, already just barely bearable at 8:00 A.M., and the cacophony of sounds beginning much earlier—the most impressive of which I heard was sparked by an early morning pig slaughter in preparation for a fiesta.

The squeals began around 4:00 A.M., accompanied by the low murmurs and laughs of the men charged with killing the pig, butchering the meat, and cooking the fat-lined skin into *chicharrones* (fried pork rind). The squeals set off the howler monkeys earlier than usual, whose low, rumbling, guttural calls soon mixed with the high-pitched overlapping staccato chirping of wild parrots and a host of other avian tones—some wild, others domestic. Pet dogs joined in, contributing howls and barking until the volume was tremendous.

As the men dispersed to butcher the meat and the noises of the natural soundscape died down, those of the household began to crescendo, beginning with the rhythmic pounding of tortillas into near-perfect, uniform roundness on a wooden counter.

This was followed by parental admonishments for children to get out of bed, increasing in volume in accordance with the number of times they were ignored. By 7:00 A.M. the sounds of Nambué were usually at full volume. The only sound capable of drowning out conversations, orders, televised Mass, radios, the wooden wheels of sugarcane-laden oxcarts passing over a rocky dirt road, and cars passing by was an afternoon downpour on a tin roof, creating a roar so strong it could make all conversation impossible. For me, indeed, place is a container of memory.[49] But even for an anthropologist passing through or trying her hand at ethnography, Nambué was more than one place.

The lush greenery present in the rainy season turned golden in the dry season. In the golden hills I saw tangles of vines and appropriately named "monkeys' ladder" vines never noticed in the rainy season. The landscape was not all that changed throughout the year. In a given visit, the population changed as well. Young people returned from the banana plantations for rest or recovery or because some plantations fired all laborers for a minimum of two weeks every six months to avoid having to pay benefits. Others left town to work as domestic servants, and still others passed through between factory jobs. Relatively few young people stayed in Nambué year-round to farm family land or work as agricultural laborers. The elder population remained more constant, sometimes accompanied by toddler grandchildren whose parents were making a living in the city (a near impossibility in the region surrounding Nambué).

Individuals perceived Nambué differently according to how residence within it had affected them. Thus, it makes sense that in Nambué there was no agreement within or among generations of families regarding the reservation or the ethnic identity of those who resided within it. Approximately half of those I interviewed on the matter were opposed to Nambué's reservation status. Indeed, Nambué as a reservation was a very contested place.

ETHNICITY, RACE, AND THE FLUIDITY OF IDENTITY

To this point I have discussed indigenous identity with regard to ethnicity (or ethnic markers) as opposed to race. I do so to make the distinction—made, perhaps, more by scholars than by those living this situation—that ethnicity denotes difference but that race is a result of difference marked on the body.[50] Race is never only about skin color, however. Indeed, multiple phenomena combine to produce our conceptualizations of race in any given context. As is discussed in detail throughout this book, race in Nambué and its surrounding area had much to do with place of residence, social class, and other indicators of social status (such as whether a student had a single parent or lived with two parents).[51] In short, race is socially constructed, and each construal of it is integrally tied to historical circumstances and local social relations.[52] Even this conceptualization, however, can prove constricting. Not only is race cultural rather than biological, it is dynamic even as a social construct. It is a process, and, as such, it shifts and changes according to the context.[53]

In a similar fashion, I take the concept of identity to be both fluid and processual as well.[54] Identity is not to be taken as a given; people simultaneously craft an identity and have identities imposed upon them.[55] Identity is tied to external definitions, as well as to projections from within and to hierarchies of status and power.[56] Identity is not monolithic but is multifaceted and crosscut by issues such as race, ethnicity, age, gender, social class, and much more.[57] Identity, thus, is relational, and it is also situational, as individuals might foreground one aspect of identity in one situation and another in a different context.[58] Finally, identity is constantly in formation. As noted, people's experiences as labeled individuals affect their identities. The idea of identity as both ascribed and achieved, or imposed and self-defined, is particularly important to the case of Nambué.

The variation in identity within a group whose members bear the same label calls into question the necessity of a consciousness of membership as an ethnic marker, given that not all people deemed members of an ethnic group will consider themselves such or will consider that their group is distinctive. Individuals (and peoples) will represent themselves at times in one light and at other times in another light, as the situation dictates.[59] Although it is necessary to recognize some degree of plasticity in ethnic markers, two anthropologists warn of dangers in this. Peter Wade questions whether the overemphasis on "fluidity" may in fact be damaging to some communities whose recognition relies on existence acknowledged throughout history.[60] Richard Jenkins notes that although it is appropriate to acknowledge a certain amount of choice in matters of ethnicity, people cannot always decide for themselves how they will be categorized by those more powerful than they and what repercussions this might have.[61] Thus, such situational identity or shifts in ethnic ascriptions are not always possible.

STIGMATIZING LABELS AND THE IMPOSITION OF IDENTITY

It is not always the groups in question that proclaim or maintain their distinctiveness. In some situations, others maintain groups within boundaries through the ascription of stigmatized or otherwise imposed identities. Thomas Eriksen notes that in most cases the assertion of ethnic difference is a process by which two groups see themselves and are seen by one another as distinct.[62] He recognizes, however, that ethnic identities may also be imposed by the powerful upon the less powerful.[63] In Mexico (as elsewhere in Latin America), indigenous identity has often been imposed from without and has carried some negative effects and considerable stigma.[64] Such imposition and negative definition are often enacted through the processes of othering and labeling.[65]

Although the concept of stigmatizing labels perhaps brings to mind (and certainly includes) local pejorative or derogatory name-calling based on stereotypes, a form of labeling that has had an effect at least as lasting, if not more so, is scholarly labeling. Certain ethnic groups have accepted many of the scholarly yet essentialist descriptions of themselves and incorporated some of the more primordialist ethnic markers into their self-definitions. There are also dangers in critiquing past academic, primordialist labels, however, if they have become part of a group's self-identification, given that this might delegitimize an ethnic group—with dire political consequences.[66] In addition to affecting those people it describes, social scientific discourse can affect political discourse or policy. Costa Rican anthropologists' estimations of the relative "legitimacy" of the country's reservations have influenced the amount of federal funding reservations receive. Thus, anthropological perceptions have affected legal and local definitions of Indianness.

Thus far I have focused on the potential negative effects of labeling on ethnic groups. The internalization of negative stereotypes is by no means the only way ethnic groups confront labeling. Ethnic groups may also appropriate positive stereotypes,[67] using such essentialist notions and definitions as a political rallying force for collective action.[68] Be it positively or negatively, ethnic groups are affected by external definitions that frequently become incorporated into the emic definition of the group described. Whether it results in stigmatization or mobilization of an ethnic group, ethnicity may be a result of internalized, imposed labeling from without. Therefore, the category of emic description or self-identification is not as pure and simple as it may at first appear. It more than likely includes impositions from outside.

Hybridity, *Desindianización*, and National Appropriation of Chorotega Culture

Just as ethnic groups may appropriate descriptions of themselves from the dominant group, they may appropriate other elements of dominant culture as well. For example, Judith Friedlander notes that much of what is defined as "Indian" in Mexico is of Spanish colonial origin.[69] Appropriations from the dominant culture by minority ethnic groups, however, tend to be seen by outsiders and urban Mexicans as departures from "pure" culture. From this point of view, any change over time in a given culture (or in the static stereotypes often held of it) can be interpreted as "culture loss."[70] Nevertheless, the lack of recognition that cultures do not exist in stasis has led to accusations of what Guillermo Bonfil Batalla calls *desindianización* (de-Indianization) against members of ethnic groups who do not remain within their ascribed status or their traditionally accepted ethnic markers. According to Bonfil Batalla, *desindianización* is the "loss of original collective identity as the result of the colonial domination process."[71] Recognized or not, approved of or not, such appropriation of dominant culture by ethnic groups is common. Downplayed, perhaps, is the equally frequent appropriation of ethnic groups' customs and symbols by dominant groups. Nation-states have often drawn upon and incorporated "ethnic" elements to promote "national" distinctiveness.[72] In this manner, the use of the Guatemalan *traje típico* (traditional regional form of dress) in the Miss Universe pageant is not interpreted as a *ladina* turning Indian[73] in the same way an indigenous woman adopting dominant styles of dress might be viewed as undergoing de-Indianization. Nevertheless, such mutual appropriation is less frequently acknowledged, and national appropriation of ethnic groups' customs is less commonly criticized.

This view of de-Indianization is common among anthropologists in Costa Rica with regard to Nambué, the Chorotega Indigenous Reservation, and Quitirrisí, the Huetar Indigenous Reservation. The inhabitants of these reservations are largely considered *mestizados,* acculturated or simply no longer Indian on the basis of their lack of customs that are distinguishable from those of the surrounding communities.[74] There is no standard legal definition of Indian in Costa Rica other than the understanding that the Indian population is coterminous with people residing within reservations. Given this lack of definition, for a custom to be uniquely Indian, then, it must be practiced only within a reservation. In the case of Nambué, to be viewed by Costa Rica's leading anthropologists as legitimately Chorotega, a custom would have to be limited to an area of 6.63 square miles—the area constituted by a politically defined, geographic boundary that denotes reservation land. Although ethnic boundaries are said to be permeable and unable to constrain the culture within,[75] beliefs of *desindianización* and the power of social science and political discourses to create reality suggest otherwise. This exaggerated construction is especially apparent when one looks closely at the situation in Nambué.

A further irony of the Nambueseño case is that Costa Rican social scientists, in claiming that Nambueseño customs are no different from regional or national customs, are failing to recognize the cultural appropriation of ethnic customs that has taken place within the dominant culture throughout centuries. What has come to be recognized as *lo típico costarricense*—typical Costa Rican culture—includes dance, food, and narrative practices considered by many to be of Chorotega origin.[76] Therefore, by practicing customs appropriated by the nation-state but perhaps originally their own, modern-day Chorotega are seen as "proving" their acculturation and are thus accused of *desindianización.*

Bozzoli de Wille might consider most of the ethnic markers the 1977 pro-reservation activists used to promote Nambué as the site for the Chorotega reservation (such as housing style and traditional food preparation) to be markers of regional or national identity rather than of ethnic distinctiveness (given the lack of acknowledgment of cultural appropriation by the nation-state). Ironically, the one practice from this list that she considers a true "remnant" of Chorotega culture—ceramic production—is a reinvented tradition.[77] It was reintroduced by a North American Peace Corps volunteer, as explained by Nambueseños who took the class she offered. To merit the ethnic label *indigenous,* the 1977 pro-reservation activists had to assert their ethnic distinctiveness along lines acceptable to anthropologists—once again reinforcing the way social science and other discourses create, rather than merely reflect, realities for ethnic groups. Ethnic labels, be they local, academic, or political, do not necessarily match an entire group's self-image (or the various self-images that might exist within one group) and may conflict with one another.[78] As seen in the example just cited, labels and their accompanying stigma[79] may also become incorporated into the group's image of itself.[80] Daniel Yon notes that categorizations can be both "claimed and resisted at the same time."[81]

The process of acculturation, effected through the imposition of dominant cultures through schools[82] or through stigma that leads to the undercommunication[83] or the masking of ethnic difference when possible,[84] needs to be seen as something other than a process resulting in *desindianización* or "culture loss." The shifting nature of ethnic markers and the appropriation of other cultural elements need to be recognized as legitimate dynamics common to ethnic groups, so that stasis is not a necessary requirement for recognition. Guillermo Bonfil Batalla and Alejandro Marroquín suggest a way of defining Indianness that is less dependent on misleading markers of ethnicity. In their views, Indianness ought to be understood as generated by historical conditions and recognized as an imposed, artificially homogenizing category.[85] These definitions do not depend on cultural content and therefore do not require that such cultural markers remain static. Likewise, Edward Spicer's view of ethnic persistence allows that a people can continue to exist as such despite significant cultural change.[86]

LOCAL RESPONSES TO CONTRADICTORY DISCOURSES ON THE CHOROTEGA

Although some Nambueseños saw themselves and their neighbors as modern Chorotega Indians—an oxymoron for some—others saw themselves as mestizos or *cruzados,* terms that indicate they considered themselves of mixed racial heritage and as acculturated, former Indians. What is clear from this mix of opinions is that Nambueseños, or the so-called modern-day Chorotega, were familiar with all the discourses that have tried to define them. They knew these discourses, negotiated them, and applied them in different contexts according to various agendas. Those who wanted to remove their community's reservation status (as I discuss later in the chapter) employed the anthropological discourse that said Nambueseños were no longer indigenous peoples but rather were acculturated campesinos or mestizos. Those in favor of maintaining the reservation or those who projected an indigenous identity (although these two groups did not comprise the same individuals) followed historiography's primordialist arguments. Instead of agreeing with the historians that the Chorotega no longer existed, however, they utilized the ethnic essentialisms to demonstrate their continued existence.

Noted scholar Homi Bhabha notes that national historiography, which generally serves to homogenize the nation, many times erases the less becoming moments of national history and makes citizens "obliged to forget" them.[87] The Costa Rican myth presented by historians—which conflates race and class while postulating that no social stratification existed in colonial Costa Rica because of the relative lack of indigenous peoples in the country—has come to represent national reality for many Costa Ricans. In spite of the myth of a Costa Rican egalitarian society of homogeneous Spanish descent, a marginal discourse exists inside the reservation that challenges the idea of national history. In reference to the western world in the postcolonial age, Bhabha notes that it is through memory that opposing (unofficial) histories manifest themselves.[88] Betwixt and between the dominant discourses that define Nambueseños in one way or another without consulting them, a "collective memory" and corresponding oral narratives have emerged that contradict the dominant discourse and remember what national history tries to forget.

Oral histories of colonization may be indicative of ethnic belonging, according to some scholars.[89] This is the case in Nambué, where an elderly woman recalls that her grandmother told her about a time when Nambueseños were required to take firewood and egg whites (to be used in adobe) to the site where they were building what is now known as "the colonial church." This church, built by indigenous *encomienda*[90] labor, still stands in the nearby town of Majapiñao as physical evidence of the "memory" that could not have come directly from her grandmother but that came from earlier ancestors, passed orally from one generation to another. Others told me how some ancient Nambueseños buried themselves alive along with their possessions when the Spaniards arrived, since they preferred to die by their own hand rather than by that of the conquistadors. These "memories" reveal the *encomienda* service that existed in the colonial era of this presumably egalitarian nation that Costa Rican historians would have us believe had no indigenous forced labor or violence against its native inhabitants or even existing indigenous peoples. Thus, this minority discourse reveals what the official "history" has suppressed. Such "memories," passed through generations, may constitute (for some) an element of ethnic belonging and a tie to indigenous people whose existence, unlike now, was acknowledged in colonial times.

SHARED HISTORY, CONTINUED OPPRESSION, AND CLASS-BASED STATUS

This idea of shared history, along with shared custom and culture, is important in setting one ethnic group apart from another.[91] Thus, a shared history that sets Nambueseños apart from accepted national history is significant. Some consider that a shared class history, or a history of oppression, is a binding force that might denote a group as enduring, or as a "persistent people."[92] The imposition of Nahuatl as a lingua franca in the colonial era and the subsequent imposition of Spanish could conceivably constitute "shared history" (an accepted ethnic marker) but instead serves as "proof" of acculturation for many social scientists in Costa Rica.[93] The phenomenon of shared history indeed serves as an ethnic marker for various Central American groups. In addition to having a language imposed upon them, the shared history within (and among) a variety of little-recognized Central American indigenous groups includes a memory of colonization and oppression and a class status often seen as indicative, if not constitutive, of their ethnic status, as I discuss shortly.

In addition to a shared history of oppression, continued oppression also figures into Indian identity for many people.[94] Indeed, Bonfil Batalla claims the only similarity among all people classified as Indian is their categorization as such (and their resulting lower social status) by those in greater positions of power.[95] This history of oppression is related to the class status that has come to identify indigenous peoples in Costa Rica and elsewhere in Central America. Many scholars debate the relation between class and ethnicity, however, although it is commonly cited as mutually defining.[96] Various scholars make a compelling case for the ways economic status has played into ethnic categorization.[97] Others note that although at times ethnicity and class converge, at times they do not.[98] For this reason and others, many scholars warn against the conflation of the two categories.[99]

In spite of such warnings, both inside and outside of Costa Rica, class has replaced ethnic identification in much scholarly writing and has become synonymous with ethnic identity for many members of ethnic groups.[100] In Costa Rica, Bozzoli de Wille and subsequent authors influenced by her consider the Chorotega and the Huetar more similar to nonindigenous campesino communities than to other indigenous communities of Costa Rica.[101] Marroquín protests this sort of replacement of ethnic classifications by class categories among academicians, stating that the term *campesino* lacks the nuanced (and stigmatized) connotations of the term *Indian*.[102] One author in particular cites language as an "obvious difference" between the two categories.[103] Although language is often taken as emblematic of ethnic identity, this is not necessarily the case for class-based identity.

Language and Ethnicity

The tie between language and ethnic distinctiveness is so strong that scholars often conflate the two.[104] In Nambué, language is frequently mentioned as a marker of ethnic difference on a local level but not on the national level. The tie between language and culture is so strong in Costa Rica that on the national level (both in the capital and in the larger Costa Rican pan-indigenous community) it is considered that the use of Spanish (rather than an indigenous language) disqualifies Nambué as a "legitimate" reservation. It is considered that an extinct autonomous language reflects an extinct culture. On the local level, however, this link between language and culture is also strong, but it worked to the opposite effect. Given Nambué's demarcation as a separate political/cultural entity, there existed a strong perception (among many outsiders) that inside the reservation Nambueseños spoke a different language. Individuals from outside the reservation have at times heard a Nambueseño speaking Spanish and sworn it was another language.[105] Thus, what constitutes a distinctive language is debatable. For some scholars (such as Bozzoli de Wille and her followers), policy makers, and laypersons, it appears that a language capable of setting an ethnic group apart must bear little resemblance to the dominant language spoken around that group. Other scholars' views, however, are less constraining. Language, according to Spicer, must include some distinct elements—such as a specialized lexicon, including terms differentiating the group from others—but it need not have an entirely distinct vocabulary.[106]

What constitutes an indigenous language is also an issue. Social scientists in Costa Rica have signaled the lack or loss of an indigenous language as the key to ethnic groups' illegitimacy, but their views of language are often as purist as their views of static ethnic markers. Although it may be true that these ethnic groups do not speak languages wholly distinct from Spanish—and they are among the first to admit that any indigenous languages once spoken in their area are long forgotten—the Spanish spoken in these areas may still retain influences from indigenous languages.[107] At any rate, it diverges from the national standard.

Many Nambueseños told me *historias*—and they stress that these are "histories" (thus implying that they are factual accounts) and not "legends" or "myths"—of spirits and witchcraft. These histories were narrated in so-called bad Spanish, which, incidentally, was peppered with Nahuatl words.[108] Nahuatl replaced the Mangue language spoken by the Chorotega in the colonial era and was used as a lingua franca by Spaniards throughout Mesoamerica. The Spaniards' efforts to promote Nahuatl were probably facilitated by the fact that, as a result of extensive precolonial trade routes throughout Central America, some level of bilingualism and comprehension of Nahuatl already existed. In spite of this linguistic history, however, the dialect spoken in these narratives is recognized not as an indigenous language but only as poorly spoken Spanish. Anthropologists have largely based claims of the supposed de-Indianization of Nambueseños, or their ceasing to fulfill definitions (or stereotypes) of Indianness, on language loss. The language used in these narrations, however, reminds us of the forced assimilation that occurred in the colonial era as the Spaniards promulgated the use of Nahuatl rather than Mangue and then of Spanish rather than Nahuatl.

A language presumed dead in Costa Rica[109] (which is manifest in a sprinkling of Nahuatl terms and Mangue place-names in an otherwise Spanish-language spoken text) emerges in the context of oral history when Nambueseños comment—through narrative—on how one should speak, on social structures, on ceremonies no longer practiced, and on traditions long ago declared to be witchcraft or diabolical.[110] This marginal discourse contradicts the Costa Rican anthropological discourse that states that no ancient indigenous traditions remain in Nambué while simultaneously utilizing traditional anthropological categories, such as the presence of oral history, as proof of Indianness.

The Limits of Academic Discourse

Anthropological discourse has at times legitimated and at other times delegitimated indigenous identity for Nambué. As Bonfil Batalla notes, "[D]e-Indianization is, socially, the result of violence, although individually it may come to be represented as a free decision."[111] Anthropological discourse in Costa Rica has failed to recognize the cause of Nambué's de-Indianization and language loss and has punished the reservation for this through delegitimization. As Latin Americanist Martín Lienhard asserts, "[T]o see 'the Indians' under the label of campesinos is to negate their exoticism."[112] Nevertheless, to see the indigenous person as necessarily possessing certain exotic traits is also to essentialize him or her. To prove their aboriginal heritage in a form credible to Costa Rican social scientists, Indian peoples now are virtually obligated to exoticize themselves, since otherwise they are "mestizo until proven Indian" and the burden of such proof is on them. Those who have been defined by national discourses, however, are capable not only of managing those discourses but also of proposing alternative ones. It is these marginal discourses that comment on those who do not take into account their own opinions, experiences, or identities when defining them—or judging their "legitimacy"—as a cultural entity.

The cultural fictions that predominate in Costa Rica—historical, legal, and anthropological discourses—are contradictory and incomplete. Marginal texts—coming from the community level in Nambué—contradict, manipulate, and add to them, thus salvaging "forgotten" historical aspects. In this manner, marginal discourses demonstrate the heterogeneity and hybridity of a nation presented as homogeneous by dominant discourses.

The Nambueseño case is unique in many regards. First, whereas throughout the Americas the trend toward a push for greater autonomy of Indian peoples appears to be gaining momentum, in Costa Rica the reverse seems to be the case. Be it as a result of de-Indianization, the assimilationist goals of the reservation system, or long-standing exclusionist policies, indigenous groups in Costa Rica have had to fight to be considered Costa Rican nationals. In this context, autonomy as a goal would be counterproductive to the effort to secure Costa Rican citizenship. Although citizenship was less elusive for inhabitants of the Chorotega reservation, a representative of the Bribrí reservation in southeastern Costa Rica commented on the irony of the difficulty in attaining citizenship for those who consider themselves Costa Rica's first citizens.[113] Thus, in Costa Rica a push for autonomy of indigenous peoples has been eschewed in favor of an insistence on recognition of their belonging to the nation. For Nambueseños, local belonging has also been difficult to attain as a result of living within a reservation that has set them apart.

PLACE-BASED RESISTANCE

The discrimination faced by Nambueseños is largely place-based—resulting from residence within the borders of a reservation, not from markedly different customs or ethnic background. Thus, Nambueseño efforts to overcome such discrimination and definition by outsiders have also been place-based. One of the most interesting of these efforts was a fight for federal derecognition as an ethnic group and withdrawal of reservation status. I have witnessed or heard of four examples of attempts (some formal, some informal) to remove Nambué's reservation status, all of which occurred during the 1990s. All were complicated by the community's lack of agreement on this issue.

The first case I heard of was Socorro's attempt to get a lawyer to help Nambueseños petition against reservation status. Because of Socorro's strained relations with the rest of the community, I was informed, her effort was unsuccessful. The second attempt to which I was privy occurred during an interview I conducted with

Nambué's youth group in 1997. One youth estimated that 90 percent of the young people were against reservation status. In light of this, he expressed the hope that in the future I (the visiting, aspiring anthropologist) would help them abolish the reservation. I will return to the third strategy shortly, in greater detail. The fourth strategy to remove Nambué's reservation status was through local elections in January 1998. Carlos, a young man from Nambué, ran unsuccessfully for local government under the slogan "youth and action." His platform included removing Nambué's reservation status.

The third attempt of which I am aware—and the one best documented here—occurred in a 1997 meeting (at which I was not present but of which I obtained a transcript) between the reservation of Nambué and delegates from a federal committee regarding indigenous issues. The delegates met with each of the twenty-three reservations in Costa Rica seeking input for revision of the law that created the reservations in the first place.[114] Community members were soon pleading with the delegates to abolish Nambué's reservation status. Even some of those who had held pro-reservation opinions for years provided reasons against maintaining the reservation.

The reasons presented in favor of removing reservation status were familiar. Some referred to the ways in which Nambué has never been like the other ("legitimate") reservations. Others alluded to Nambueseños having successfully achieved the original assimilationist goal of the first law, noting that they are more like mainstream Costa Rican society than the inhabitants of other reservations. The government delegates acknowledged that in contrast to the other reservations, Nambué was "up to date" and "at a higher level than the others."

Those who supported using the delegates' presence to plead their antireservation case urged, "We want to be free." A woman who insisted several times that "we want to be free" based her request for derecognition and the abolition of the reservation on the lack of difference between the inhabitants of Nambué and those of surrounding communities in the province of Guanacaste not labeled indigenous. She stated, "If the Indigenous Reservation has brought us problems, we don't want to say that we don't want to be Indians, let that be very well understood; the fact that we don't want the Indigenous Reservation is not that we don't want to be Indian, nor carry Indian blood. I feel proud to be Indian, because all of us *Guanacastecos* carry Indian blood."[115]

Symbolism for a Complex Communal Identity

Upon hearing about this attempt at derecognition, it appeared to me that the lack of agreement between pro- and antireservation Nambueseños had narrowed since my original interviews on the matter (conducted in 1993 and 1994). The number of people willing to openly declare their indigenous identity appeared to have increased, and it seemed the two factions on different ends of the identity debate (those proclaiming and those denying indigenous identity) had joined the effort to abolish the reservation in order to stop being singled out as Indians locally and thus avoid discrimination. This impression of increased unity, however, was deceiving.

Shortly after the 1997 meeting with the delegates, the community held an *empajo* (the fiesta that accompanies the thatching of a roof), a type of celebration that had not occurred on a large scale in Nambué for years. A new community meeting hall was built in the style of a *rancho*—the style of building reminiscent of pre-Columbian times. People of various opinions concerning Nambué's classification as a reservation turned up at the *empajo* to help with the *rancho's* construction and thatching. Yet this image of seemingly unified activity is also deceptive. I present it here to emphasize the variety of identities present among the "Chorotega" of Nambué.

Given many Nambueseños' past resentment at being represented by archaeological symbols and stereotypes of Indians, it is interesting that the community chose this traditional indigenous style for its new meeting hall. The hall would house potential future antireservation meetings with government delegates, events following multicommunity soccer tournaments, and dances that would bring people from a variety of places to Nambué. I found it surprising that the Nambueseños had chosen to represent themselves publicly in a manner that might reinforce outsider views of their Indianness. The community-wide effort to build the *rancho* culminated in perhaps the ideal physical representation of the identity debate in Nambué.[116]

Yet this irony—of a town trying to emerge from the stigma of imposed identity while seemingly promoting the very identity its citizens protest—is appropriate, given the malleability of this symbol. The *rancho,* to some, evokes the memory of an Indian past. To others it serves as a reminder of the Indian present and all that this entails, including a socioeconomic condition that dictates a certain lifestyle for many who cannot afford a more popular cement model of housing.

In 1997 I participated in a lengthy discussion with Nambué's youth group regarding identity and opinions of the reservation. Nambueseño youth reported that years ago a reporter had visited the reservation with the intent of sharing her perceptions of the town with the national public. The reporter published a photograph of a *rancho* in poor condition, accompanied by the caption "In Nambué, they only eat meat when lightning strikes a cow."[117] This is emblematic of the commonly accepted symbols of Indianness and their association with poverty.

At the same time, the *rancho* is a regional symbol for Guanacasteco culture, for those individuals who see themselves as allied more with a regional identity than with an ethnic one. Thus, the *rancho* symbolically encompasses the interpretations of various contradictory discourses. It can elicit the historical message of extinct Indianness, the legal image of persistent indigenous existence, and the anthropological view of an ethnic-turned-class identity. It is a symbol that both permits and presents the image of Nambueseños as at once all of these permutations of their imposed identity and thereby of the self-proclaimed identity of many Nambueseños as being nothing—"*ni chicha ni limonada. No somos nada.*"This most recent representation of Nambué still does not agree on one identity for all its inhabitants. It is at least and at last, however, a self-definition that does not speak for all but allows individuals to interpret their own identity and at the same time acknowledge the variety of ways outsider definitions have influenced those inside the reservation.

NONACADEMIC, OUTSIDER VIEWS OF NAMBUESEÑO IDENTITY

Local outsiders, too, realized that issues surrounding identity divided Nambué. One Riteña teacher summed up this observation—acknowledging the lack of agreement on ethnic identity, citing the discord surrounding the advantages or disadvantages of the reservation, and alluding to accusations of opportunism in "accepting" reservation status:

> Nambué is a problematic community, let's say, [because] among them they [the residents] haven't agreed on what they want to be, if it is favorable to them to be a reservation [or] if this has been harmful to them. Sometimes I think that first they need to accept their condition. They say, "We're not Indians." Well, their features are those of Indians. . . . But far from feeling ashamed, they should feel proud to be Indians. . . . Sometimes it is convenient for them to be Indians and sometimes it isn't.

Many outsiders (all those living outside the reservation, including Riteños) expected Nambué to be a homogeneous reservation in which all inhabitants accepted their ascribed Indianness and performed it in stereotypical ways. As will become evident, Indianness (and, by extension, Nambueseño-ness) encompassed a variety of preconceived notions and stereotypes to which outsiders held firm. These included contradictory images of simultaneous Nambueseño violence and passivity, poverty and Nambueseños' condition as spoiled recipients of international aid, and "backwardness"—all of which were both constitutive of and constituted by the concept of Indianness. Throughout my research, outsiders often associated the term *feo* (connoting ugliness and generally undesirable or unpleasant qualities) with the reservation. For insiders, though, as the leader of the youth group asserted, the "ugliness of the reservation is due to its borders." In the remainder of this chapter, I address first outsider then insider views of the reservation.

In taped interviews with high school faculty in Santa Rita, I routinely asked those interviewed if they had visited Nambué and what they thought of the town. Teachers and administrators often phrased their answers in terms of what they expected to see as opposed to what they found when visiting the reservation. The principal noted:

> I expected to see Nambué more [pause] indigenous. I don't know, less advanced. Less transcultured. What I want to say is that Nambué has very few indigenous aspects. I don't know—I thought that Nambué was purely [made up of] *ranchos,* like that, things of their own. And the people—I think

there are indigenous people [there]. I don't know if they're still pure, but really, I didn't see Nambué as an indigenous settlement.

Profesora Natalia, a teacher from Santa Rita, commented on the change in Nambué (which paralleled the changes in its surrounding rural communities as well): "Before, it was more of a reservation. Now it's just a reservation in name. To me, all it has that's reservation-like about it is the name." She went on to explain that years ago it had paths rather than roads. She listed the changes in Nambué that, in her opinion, detracted from its Indianness: "Now it's different. Now it has electricity, all the *ranchos* disappeared. Now all the houses are modern. They [the Nambueseños] are modern. They have electricity and running water."

This quote, not indicative of the attitude of all teachers but also not uncommon among them, exemplifies an expectation that in spite of overall changes in this region of the country, Nambué should somehow have remained static in time, unchanging in response to outside influences. I suggest that this has much to do with Nambué's designation as an area set apart through its reservation label. According to this view, its culture should neither have surpassed its geographic boundaries nor let outside influences in. It ought to have existed isolated in both time and space and thus have remained distinct.

Profesora Natalia appeared to follow this reasoning when she criticized students from Nambué who demonstrated foreign influence in their dress, but she did not extend this criticism to students from other towns whose choices in fashion also followed trends from the United States. She was not alone, as other teachers also looked down on Nambueseño students' preference for North American styles and music.[118] She followed this criticism with the conclusion, "They want to appear that they are not what they are. In other words, they don't accept, on many occasions, that they are an indigenous reservation."[119] The teacher's wording is interesting. It not only displays her view that Nambueseño culture should remain static but also provides evidence of the conflation of place and race at work.[120] She did not note that Nambueseños *live* in a reservation; they *are* a reservation. It appears that in her view, they were overwhelmingly defined by their place of residence.

Other teachers made similar comments lamenting Nambué's change with the times. Profesora Rosaura, another teacher from Santa Rita, opined, "Nambué should have maintained itself as an indigenous reservation in many aspects." She enumerated these as living in *ranchos* and using outdoor adobe ovens "to at least have something representative of the village. But at times I have seen that they want to annul all of this and make their little houses of cement."

Profesora Anatolia, who did not live in Santa Rita but who socialized with those who did, also thought Nambueseños should have continued certain customs. She criticized the loss of their own form of speech (alluding to the fact that Nambueseños were monolingual Spanish speakers). She immediately followed this comment with the observation that "they [had] improved" their way of speaking. This is emblematic of the Catch-22 faced by inhabitants of Nambué. They were chastised for "losing" observable "Indian" attributes, yet it was acknowledged that they were more socially accepted—"improved"—for having done so. This expectation that Nambué should have remained frozen in time is particularly odd given the arbitrariness of Nambué's designation as a reservation and its inhabitants' lack of overt difference from their neighbors outside the reservation's borders. Although place of residence has come to serve as a badge of identity, in the case of Nambué this group identity was perhaps more perceived by outsiders than projected by Nambueseños.

Others have written about place as one definitive factor of ethnicity among several,[121] but in the case of Nambué, place was perhaps the most significant indicator of its inhabitants' ascribed Indianness. Relative wealth and inherited phenotype, however, did not cease to play a role in the way outsiders classified those from Nambué as indigenous. Profesora Natalia alluded to the importance of physical appearance with regard to identity. She lamented, "The race is mixing. Now it is not the original [race]. Before, it was. One only saw Indian people [in Nambué]. Not now. Now they are mixed. Now you have to see what each baby looks like." On numerous occasions I heard similar comments from people inside Nambué inquiring about newborn babies. A common question posed to new parents was "Is [the baby] Indian or light skinned?"

Although relatively few scholars mention physical appearance as a differentiating factor in ethnicity[122] and its importance varies considerably from ethnic group to ethnic group, in the Central American context it is quite common for people to ascribe their ethnic affiliation to physical appearance or phenotype. For others, such a marker is more problematic. Although phenotype can be—and is—used (by both outsiders and group members) to distinguish among ethnic groups in Central America, this is also wrought with problems for those groups commonly considered *desindianizados* (de-Indianized) or mestizo (and thus no longer Indian). Some Nambueseños did consider that their physical appearance denoted ethnic distinctiveness. In the Chorotega reservation, physical appearance topped the list of criteria submitted by a few Nambueseños to the committee charged with deciding which towns would become reservations. When I inquired as to Nambueseños' identities, at least one interviewee looked at the color of his arms and responded, "Of course I'm Indian." Thus, in terms of emic description, phenotype still played a role in defining ethnicity.

According to some scholars of Central America, the use of physical appearance as an indicator of difference is less than apt in that region given the degree of *mestizaje*.[123] One ethnographer has noted that people of the Chorotega region are set apart from the rest of Costa Rican society by their speech and darker skin tones.[124] Although this is sufficient to set them apart as merely "*patriotically* Costa Rican,"[125] it is not sufficient to denote Indianness. Thus, phenotype, like all other traditionally accepted markers of ethnic distinctiveness, is inadequate—perhaps anywhere, but certainly to the lesser-recognized indigenous groups of Central America such as the Chorotega. Still, if individuals consider their physical appearance to be key to their ethnic identity, perhaps scholars should not dismiss the effects of this category so quickly, although it is important to address race as a social condition rather than a biological given and to discuss it with the complexity the topic merits. Many Riteños spoke of Nambué as racially homogeneous. Among them, I often heard the expectation that Nambueseños should not only think and look alike but that they should think and look like good, stereotypical Indians "ought" to. Thus, not only racial homogeneity was assumed for Nambué but also ideological sameness.

Several teachers commented on the political divisions within Nambué, as if a community existed in which all residents agreed at all times. The possible existence of such a homogeneous community, even as a relic of the past, is a concept people find intriguing. One day during my fieldwork, three busloads of students arrived—unannounced and uninvited—from Liberia, a town approximately two hours away. One Nambueseña described the tour as entailing a group of students who came to look at Indians as one would view animals in a zoo. A man from Nambué inferred that they had "come to see loincloths." Presumably, these Costa Rican tourists went to Nambué to view a culture commonly believed to conserve past, quaint, picturesque traditions.

SYMBOLIC REPRESENTATIONS OF NAMBUÉ

Common assumptions of immutable culture were in no way dismantled by popular images of the region. As in the case of the youth's protest of Nambué's photographic representation by a *rancho,* the representation of Nambué has been a sensitive issue for many Nambueseños. Its perceived backwardness was perpetuated and taught through a favorite childhood game called Gran Banco, based on the board game Monopoly. As in the North American version of the game, residential areas are given monetary values and arranged in order from least to most valuable around the board. The four least valuable regions in Costa Rica, according to the board game, are Talamanca (the Costa Rican reservation viewed as the most culturally static and depicted in the game by an Indian in headdress) and Isla del Coco (a little-inhabited island far from shore associated with piracy and represented by a treasure chest). Following these (on a scale of increasing value) are the towns of Majapiñao (the nearest sizable town to Nambué, which is also associated with the Chorotega and is iconized on the game by a pre-Columbian grinding stone) and Liberia (the town in Guanacaste from which the busloads of students came to view culture, symbolized by a marimba). These are contrasted with Costa Rica's wealthy, urban neighborhoods, which occupy prime locations on the game board.

Indianness (especially that of Nambué, from the Riteño perspective) was also represented in a television program filmed in Santa Rita, *La Familia Mena Mora.*[126] In this series—which was fairly popular in Santa Rita during the year of my fieldwork and in which at least two Riteño students (Jaime and Adrián) acted—a character known only as "El Brujo" (the witch[127]) also exemplified (and no doubt furthered) many stereotypes associated with Indianness. Witchcraft itself was very much associated with Indianness in Costa Rica (and in Nambué).[128] The witch in the television program was a dark man with long, black hair (a bad wig) dressed in white shorts and vest made of furs. The character stood silently on the upper beam (just below the thatched roof) of a *rancho*. Hanging from the beam was a *cojombro*—an overgrown relative of the zucchini and a food infrequently prepared in the modern era. Outside the *rancho* was a carved, wooden *pilón,* a large-diameter vessel in which Nambueseños (and others) used to hull rice with a carved wooden pole.

Within Nambué, the community was symbolically represented on a crest painted on a sign in the middle of town. The crest included artifacts (a grinding stone and a ceramic vessel) and a stereotypical depiction of an Indian (bare chested and wearing feathers on his head) with a white mare. The sign was vandalized by youth from Nambué on more than one occasion. Shortly after I left Nambué in 1999, the crest was painted over one night by protesters or vandals (depending upon whom one asks). On the flip side, as noted earlier, Nambueseños selling goods in the market of Majapiñao drew upon their ascribed identity (based on residence in the reservation) to attest to the authenticity of the traditional foods they sold.

Nambué is represented in museums through the artifacts found in Nambué and surrounding areas. It is represented on tourist maps (whereas nearby towns that may have greater populations are not) along with biological reserves, national parks, and other exotic points of interest. Nambué (as opposed to surrounding towns) is also represented in early anthropological/archaeological sources as the place where the "real Indians live."[129]

The first four of these cases—that of Gran Banco, a popular television show, a school crest, and museum exhibits—associate Indianness (which in the show from Santa Rita was, in turn, associated with Nambué specifically) with artifacts from the past. In keeping with (and likely constitutive of) common opinion, indigenous cultures were not assumed to be dynamic but rather were suspended indefinitely in past time. The fifth example (of tourist maps) associates Indianness with nature rather than with humanity in general and in particular with tourist destinations as opposed to everyday communities.

In contrast to these examples, where representations of Indianness were seen as negative, in Majapiñao—a stop along tourist routes destined for the Pacific beaches—merchants and other businesspeople commercialized the Indian image to their benefit. The town had businesses such as the Hotel Chorotega and a real estate agency named with the original Mangue word from which Majapiñao was named—but whose sign was in English, indicating that it might have catered to tourists considering a purchase of beach land or to North American retirees for whom Indianness might be something positive or marketable. The Chorotega Pharmacy, Chorotega Photocopies, and Nambué Bar were other businesses that used allusions to Indianness as a draw for local clientele. This would not be successful in Santa Rita, where Indianness connoted negative attributes such as backwardness, violence, and fear, as I discuss shortly.

As is evident in the preceding examples, stereotypes of Nambué and of Indianness abounded in the region. Some accorded negative stereotypes to indigenous identity, whereas others sought to cash in on that identity in a way that upheld it as a positive image. As we will see, this simultaneous existence of negative and positive stereotypes is not uncharacteristic of indigenous identity. Numerous stereotypes existed in Santa Rita regarding Nambué. This became starkly evident when I began my fieldwork and responded to students' and teachers' questions regarding where I lived. When I replied that I lived in Nambué, my interlocutors' reactions spoke volumes about their impressions of or associations with the reservation.

Stereotypes of the Reservation

Student responses to my residence in Nambué included statements such as "Aren't you afraid to live there," "Why did you go live over *there*" (the Riteña student who said this wrinkled her nose as if in disgust), "Aren't there Indians there," "What, are you Indian," "It's haunted there," and "Nambué is the ugliest part of [this township]." At times, students asking me this question appeared tongue-tied, and their responses took the form of gestures or facial expressions. Several people dropped their jaws, as if in disbelief or shock. Others gave wide-eyed, darting glances toward their equally incredulous Riteño friends nearby.

Teachers' responses were usually more reserved, and most were not so judgmental, but Profesor Teodoro, a teacher not from Santa Rita but who socialized with the Riteño veteran teachers, stated frankly, "Nambué is as ugly as it gets." This usage of the word *ugly* (*feo*) was common in the region and referred not only to aesthetic aspects but also to a general environment of negative, undesirable ways of being. Rude phrases or inhospitable living conditions were also labeled with this term. A teacher-in-training at Nambué's elementary school crossed paths with me one day as she headed home to Santa Rita and I to Nambué. She exclaimed as she passed by, "You must love your husband a *lot* to come *here*," assuming that my residence in Nambué had only to do with my spousal devotion and that I lived there in spite of Nambué being "ugly."

Some of the high school staff, however (primarily non-Riteño members of the faculty), were willing to concede to Nambué a margin of difference, heterogeneity in thought and appearance, and influence by outsiders for which other communities were less frequently criticized. The superintendent of schools noted, "To find oneself in Nambué is equal to being in any other part [of the county] other than central Santa Rita." Three teachers not from Santa Rita commented that Nambué was just like any other small rural town. Another agreed that Nambué was not so different from other places. At least four (of thirty-six) teachers (both Riteño and non-Riteño) acknowledged that with regard to their learning capacity, students from Nambué were the same as those from elsewhere. Profesora Aracely, from Santa Rita, admitted that when she first visited Nambué she expected to see more *ranchos*. She acknowledged, however, that Nambueseños had as much right as anyone to want modern comforts. Visiting students from the local branch of the National University, who arrived on the high school campus one day to talk to me about Nambué, said their professor told them Nambueseños were "Indians with jeans." Such views allow for cultural changes without implying a watering down of ethnicity.

Others, however, attributed only "positive" stereotypes to the Nambueseño population on the whole (although such broad generalizations can always have negative effects). Among these characteristics were "tranquillity," "good behavior," "willingness to serve," being "well mannered," "friendliness," "simplicity," "hardworking," "enthusiasm," "struggling to meet goals," "willingness to succeed," and "sincerity." Still others associated Nambué with a certain economic status but did not accompany this view with a value judgment.

Several teachers interviewed included the assumption of widespread poverty in the reservation in their described impressions of Nambué. Profesora Remedios (not from Santa Rita but associated with the predominantly Riteña clique) noted that "Nambué is a difficult town because [there are] few economic resources. There are still no sources of employment, there isn't much economic solvency." Profesora Alba (not Riteña but accepted by a group of teachers mainly from Santa Rita, although she also associated with the younger traveler teachers[130]) said that when she thought of Nambué, she thought of "a lot of poverty" and an "uncomfortable place." Profesor Adán (a young Riteño) associated Nambué with hunger. Interestingly, Profesor Ramiro (Riteño, but he associated mainly with young traveler teachers) and Profesor Teodoro (not Riteño but accepted in that teachers' clique) expressed the opinion that Nambué had been spoiled by international aid. It was unclear how both perspectives could exist simultaneously. Relative to Santa Rita, Nambué was indeed impoverished. Other stereotypes of the reservation and its inhabitants, however, held less true.

One of the most common stereotypes I encountered about Nambueseños regarded violence.[131] Profesora Delia (not from Santa Rita) recounted that the first time she went to Nambué she "went with much fear because one hears that people in Nambué are fierce, that they like to fight a lot, that they are very impulsive." After her visit, however, she decided that rather than being fierce, Nambueseños were merely on the defensive. Profesor Ramiro commented that once, years ago, he went to Nambué to attend a dance. He saw individuals fighting outside (by no means a behavior unique to dances in Nambué), however, so he went on by. A student who overheard this discussion supported him by agreeing, "Nambueseños are fighters." Profesor Raúl (not Riteño) said Nambué's residents had a reputation for causing harm.

Unfortunately, during my fieldwork a violent episode of domestic abuse (as shocking to Nambueseños as it would be to anyone when unexpected violence occurs in one's town) took place. The result was the near death of and permanent injury to a woman who resided in Nambué. The woman was the mother of a high school student. Many students associated this violence with Nambué's culture. Unfortunately, in this case a solitary occurrence no more usual in Nambué than elsewhere reinforced many people's stereotypes of ferocity and violent tendencies among Nambueseños.

In contrast, when a student from Santa Rita was raped and otherwise abused in that town, it was spoken of as an aberration. The incident did not affect Santa Rita's image as stereotypically serene and safe. In fact, it was kept quiet and shrouded in secrecy for some time—to the point that at a high school staff meeting administrators announced that the incident had occurred and ordered silence surrounding the issue. The high school considered it of utmost importance not to let journalists get wind of the happening. This was in stark contrast to the widespread discussion by students, teachers, and Riteños in general (sometimes in front of the victim's daughter) of the equally alarming attack in Nambué.

Oddly, given the commonly believed reputation for violence in Nambué, one of the other stereotypes of Nambueseños was that of passivity or timidity. Profesora Delia, the counselor who had described being fearful when visiting Nambué, commented on Nambueseño parents' passiveness, so reliable that administrators knew they could assign Nambueseños to classes they did not want to take without risking parental intervention (discussed in more detail in Chapter 4). She admitted, "One knows that these parents are not going to come to fight, to complain. They are students that if you put them there, there they stay. They are passive. When it's time to stand up for their rights, they stop themselves." Thus, the school's manipulation of Nambueseño students was explained in terms of Nambueseños allowing themselves to be manipulated.

Similarly, Profesor Manuel explained the marginalization of Nambueseño students as resulting from these students "letting themselves be called cholos and indios." Several students taught me that those terms were cruel nicknames, since to call someone an "Indian" was an insult. In spite of this, Profesora Delia told me the students called Nambueseño classmates "Indian" and "Cholo" as terms of endearment, but the Nambueseños took being called these names as an insult because they had not "gotten accustomed to it."

Whereas Nambueseño students sometimes felt excluded or looked down upon by students from Santa Rita, several teachers and students from Santa Rita interpreted this as Nambueseños excluding themselves, interacting only with others from their town, and failing to be social. Profesora Alodia (Riteña) said, "They isolate themselves on their own." Profesora Soledad (also Riteña) explained, "They tend to isolate themselves." Profesor Raúl (a traveler teacher) noted, "They go around apart from the others." Profesora Anatolia (a traveler who associated with veteran Riteño teachers) called them "cautious" and noted that they "keep their distance." Jaime, the seventh grader from Santa Rita quoted earlier, explained, "They [the Nambueseño students] are strange. They separate themselves." When a Riteña student chose not to appear in a photograph of her class, her brother teased her by comparing her timidity to that of an Indian. Others, too, used the words *timid, reserved,* and *fearful* to describe the residents of Nambué. Still others used the term *docile* with regard to Nambueseños.

Although these characterizations of Nambueseños appear to contradict one another, they are similar in that they are all negative descriptions. They all point to shortcomings on the part of Nambueseños and ascribe culpability to reservation inhabitants for being marginalized. According to the dominant perceptions of Nambueseños, they were either fearful or to be feared, either aggressively violent or passive to the point of allowing themselves to be wronged.

Not only were the stereotypical associations many people have regarding Indianness negative, students pointed out that merely to be called or to be Indian was an insult. Students reported that in 1998, the year prior to my fieldwork, when the transportation from Nambué arrived at the high school, other students shouted "Indigenous Reservation" and "the Indians from Nambué!" Merely residing in Nambué was seen as deserving of ridicule. It is noteworthy that several teachers (among them Profesora Alodia, Profesora Rosaura, and Profesor Teodoro—all affiliated with the Riteño veteran teachers' clique) commented critically that Nambueseños "don't like you to point out that they are Indian. They don't like you to tell them they are from Nambué."

Profesora Natalia (who resided in Santa Rita and who remarked that Nambueseños "are" a reservation, as discussed earlier) noted that Nambueseños got mad when people called them Indians. She criticized them for "being ashamed of their origin." She followed that statement with an acknowledgment that students' teasing them may have had something to do with Nambueseños' reluctance to accept their ethnicity. Profesor Adán (a young Riteño) remarked that Nambueseño students "tend to not say where they are from. Perhaps they feel like they are worth less—maybe because of the indigenous situation" (meaning they are indigenous).

Often this offense was implied in judgments of Nambué or in well-intentioned descriptions. A prominent Riteño once told me, discussing the legitimacy of Nambué's reservation status, that in Nambué "there are well-proportioned, very pretty girls, so they are not pure Indians but third- and fourth-generation Indians." In a casual conversation, a ninth-grade girl from Santa Rita learned that I was married to a Nambueseño. Her immediate reaction was "Well, love is blind," implying that Nambueseños were considered ugly in Santa Rita. Only after Amanda, her classmate (also Riteña), looked at me, turned red, and slugged the speaker did this girl realize her statement's offensive implication.

Profesora Rosaura, talking about interracial relationships, mentioned a girl who was enamored of a classmate until she learned he was from Nambué. The teacher summarized the girl's reaction: "God forbid they should find out in my house that I like a boy from Nambué." An eighth-grade girl from Santa Rita, who had just told me how much she disliked Nambueseños, explained that the difference between Riteños and Nambueseños was that Nambueseños had darker skin. Profesor Efraín (a young traveler) repeatedly asked me to respond to the question "Isn't it true that there [in Nambué] there are people with indigenous features, protruding cheekbones?" Two ninth-grade Riteña girls pointed out that Riteños' discrimination toward Nambué occurred "surely because they are Indians or because they are black." An eleventh grader from a prominent Riteña family suggested that people in Santa Rita discriminated against Nambueseños because Riteños had more money (connecting discrimination, place of residence, and class). Another eleventh grader explained, "Since in San José they discriminate against

Guanacaste, here in central Santa Rita they discriminate against Nambué."

Profesora Delia said the label *Indian,* used to insult classmates, was applied to people with "straight hair and dark skin," thus directly related to race. It was linked to place as well, however. A girl from Nambué explained that her classmates called her "la Nambueseña" (literally, the girl from Nambué) to tease her. In a separate interview with the same girl, I asked what made a person Indian or not Indian. She replied, "The neighborhood they live in." Classmates teased a Riteña who rode the Nambueseño bus from the entrance of Santa Rita to the school, joking about her being a Nambueseña. The student took considerable offense at the joke. Two eleventh-grade girls from Santa Rita explained that the mere "mention of Nambué provokes ridicule." An eleventh-grade boy from Santa Rita suggested it was an "unconscious discrimination."

It is significant that these stereotypes of Nambueseños were not common to the region in general but specific to Santa Rita. Several Riteños admitted this was the case, as did observers from outside Santa Rita. The vice principal (not from Santa Rita) spoke critically of many Riteños' prejudicial view of Nambueseños. She noted, "They [Riteños] see [Nambueseños] as strange beasts . . . with a lack of education." Jacobo, a tenth-grade boy from Santa Rita who was teased as being Indian (perhaps because of a combination of factors such as his dark complexion, his family's poverty, his affiliation with a religion other than Catholicism, and the fact that he lived with one parent only), expressed disgust with dominant Riteño society. He said Riteños saw Nambueseños as "vulgar and backward" but that in Nambué they were, in fact, "more advanced than here. The ones from here are more vulgar. They think they are the most everything [of everything good] but they are the most vulgar."

Teachers from the town of Majapiñao tended to view Nambué differently. Many Nambueseño vendors went to Majapiñao daily to sell traditional foods. In Majapiñao they were considered the experts on such things. Surely, this, too, resulted from their Indian label (as the "most" Indian people around, they must be the best at making "Indian" foods). In this case, however, stereotypes perhaps worked to Nambueseños' advantage. I saw Socorro, a Nambueseña vendor who told me on numerous occasions that she abhorred being classified as an Indian and did not consider herself as such, change her projected identity when she was at the marketplace.[132] Profesora Belisa from Majapiñao claimed she only bought tortillas from Nambueseñas, as they were known for making the best ones. This teacher (and others who shared her opinions) described Nambué as a tranquil place, full of respectful, honest people, where she felt safe—a marked contrast to many Riteño descriptions of Nambué as violent, yet also distinct from other Riteño comments that equated "tranquillity" with excessive meekness and passivity.

Majapiñao's more accepting atmosphere led Nambueseños to conduct business there in spite of its greater distance from the reservation. Not all Riteños, however, seemed aware of the reason for this choice. Profesora Eugenia (a Riteña who was critical of Nambueseño tendencies not to embrace their ascribed Indian identity) observed that Nambueseños did not attend dances in Santa Rita—"They prefer to go to Majapiñao." Profesora Rosaura asked how Riteño attitudes toward people from Nambué could possibly affect their identities if Nambueseños only wanted to interact with people from Majapiñao. These "preferences" (paralleled by a preference to attend the clinic in Majapiñao rather than the one in Santa Rita) in fact resulted from discrimination Nambueseños faced in Santa Rita.

This discrimination against Nambueseños (seemingly unique to Santa Rita) on the basis of their skin color, place of residence, social class, assumed backwardness, and assorted other stereotypes had profound repercussions in the school setting. Just as certain teachers placed students in categories with regard to personality type and customs based on their place of residence, some categorized students with regard to academic capability on this basis. One Riteño teacher (of agriculture) stereotyped students from Nambué as "always extraordinary" in his classes. Others, however, had less positive things to say with regard to the talent of students from the reservation.

Profesor Teodoro, who told both me and a student from Nambué (on separate occasions) that "Nambué is as ugly as it gets," had this to say about Nambueseño students generally:

> They are not good. They are mediocre. They are lazy. It's not that they can't be [good students], it's that they don't want to [be]. They are lazy. Their problem is that they don't want to work, to sacrifice themselves. There exists a subestimation of themselves. They don't like [any]one to tell them that they are a reservation or that they are Indians.

This teacher was not from Santa Rita, but he socialized with the Riteño teachers. Profesor Arturo, a young teacher from Santa Rita, commented, "They are—I don't know if it's coincidence—they are [students] of lower quality. They have problems. It's hard for them." Profesor Adán, also a young Riteño teacher, said, "They're good, but they could be excellent." Profesora Rosaura, also from Santa Rita, remarked that "excellent elements [in the student body] have not come out of Nambué." Profesora Anatolia (one of the travelers who associated with Riteños) assumed that good Nambueseño students were not common because in the elementary school there, two grades occupied a classroom at a time (which was not the case).

REPERCUSSIONS OF COMMON STEREOTYPES FOR NAMBUESEÑOS

The preceding opinions show that several teachers saw a correlation between students' place of residence and their ability to succeed in school. Most of these teachers considered Nambueseños Indian on the basis of unfounded stereotypes and also gave credit to the negative qualities erroneously (or prejudicially) associated with Indianness. As I discuss in later chapters, these biases had a profound impact on evaluations of Nambueseño students' work and on their ethnic identity. Given many Riteño teachers' underlying biases—from the criticism that Nambueseños did not maintain their culture to the assumptions that students from Nambué were still sufficiently Indian to merit the application of derogatory and offensive attributes to them—it is not difficult to see how a dominant message to Nambueseños in the high school was formed. I will illustrate in later chapters how identity (positive and negative, non-Indian and Indian) was taught to students in Santa Rita's high school, so here it suffices to say that one of the principal messages Nambueseños learned in school was that the maintenance of an Indian identity was incompatible with school success. Another lesson learned by students from the reservation was that Indianness was defined by where they lived. Thus, placism was a prominent part of the high school experience for students from Nambué.

As exemplified earlier, "ugliness" was a concept many Riteños associated with Nambué. Within Nambué, however, it was not Nambué itself (as a geographic setting and a relatively close-knit community) that was deemed "ugly" but rather the imposed identity and all its corresponding stereotypes based on the town's political designation as a reservation. To explain this, one individual from Nambué noted, "*Lo feo de la reserva es por las fronteras*" (The ugliness of the reservation is because of the borders). As I demonstrated earlier, a link between place and race underlay many derogatory Riteño comments on and expectations of Nambué. This connection was rarely problematized, however. Rather, it appeared to be an unconscious conflation. In Nambué, outsiders' discussion of place and race, as if it were a causal relationship, was recognized consciously and theorized at a deeper level. Both the way residence in Nambué defined Indianness (for many people) and what outsiders' impressions of Indianness entailed were frequent topics of my conversations with Nambueseños throughout my fieldwork.

As noted in the Introduction, in 1997 a thirteen-year-old boy explained to me that he was discriminated against "not because of the race but more because of the name. I'm from the indigenous reservation, and for that reason they discriminate against me." This boy's older sister, in 1999, expressed a similar opinion. She noted that the residents of Nambué faced discrimination "because of the name [of the town], nothing else." Sara, a Nambueseña graduate of Santa Rita High School (SRHS), recalled her experiences with prejudiced classmates. She said Riteño peers "made fun just because one is from a place called Nambué." She continued, "They make one feel really bad for being from a place called Nambué."

One form of ridicule this former student recalled was classmates' pronouncing the word *Nambué* in an accent supposed to indicate Indianness (but that this young woman either could not or would not demonstrate to me). Samuel, a boy beginning high school at the time of my fieldwork at SRHS, had the same experience in which the name of his town served as a label with which to taunt him. He said one classmate began to address him as "Nambué" rather than by his name. A girl from Nambué, also in her first year of high school (who dropped out a few months into the year), said other students ridiculed her frequently for being from Nambué. When I asked what kinds of things they said to tease her, she responded, "They said I was a Nambueseña." A man from Nambué who graduated from high school in 1982 remembered, "Nambueseño" (and, by association, Indian) "was the label we carried."

A Nambueseño boy in ninth grade said that when he first got to high school, other students danced around him and made a gesture reminiscent of stereotypical Indians in old western movies in which they intermittently covered their mouths while hollering. Other Nambueseño students recalled similar experiences. One of these students clearly stated that people discriminated against students from Nambué mainly because of their place of residence.

These students' experiences demonstrate several Nambueseño students' motivation to avoid letting others know where they were from. Martín, a ninth grader from the reservation, told me he planned to move as soon as he turned eighteen and was a legal adult. In high school, peers knew where he was from. When he visited other towns, however, he always said he was from Santa Rita rather than Nambué. Martín explained, "It's embarrassing to say you're from Nambué. Everyone responds, 'Nambué, the Indian reservation.' Just with the name 'Nambué' and you're Indian—even though there is no race anymore. Now it's just the name." A young woman from Nambué who did not attend high school but who was familiar with the assumptions outsiders had of Nambueseños noted, "We all know that only the name [of Nambué as a reservation] remains of the indigenous reservation because I think the people who inhabit it now are not like the people who were here before." Several Nambueseños agreed with this definition of Indianness. When I asked a Nambueseño boy in seventh grade at the time of my research what made a person Indian, he replied, "Well, if they call you Indian, you must be Indian [pause] if you're from here." A seventh grader from the reservation responded "the place" to that same question.

Just as knowing a person resided in Nambué led many people to believe they knew that resident's ethnic identity, many outsiders also assumed they knew what it meant to be Indian—although these opinions were often rife with stereotypes. A ninth grader from Nambué noted that her classmates assumed that being from Nambué meant one was "stupid" or "dumb." Numerous people told me a popular expectation of Indians in Nambué was that they wore loincloths and feathers.

INSIDER VIEWS OF THE RESERVATION AND ITS STEREOTYPES

Many inhabitants of Nambué recognized that their town's reservation status had made the Indian label stick only to those from that community rather than to all those who shared their ethnic heritage. One young man (who had attended high school briefly years earlier) explained that he did not like the fact that Nambué was a reservation because "many people criticize us and call us Indian and Cholo, and because of that I don't agree [that Nambué should be a reservation]. I consider myself pretty Indian, but I don't like that people point us out as if we are worth less than the rest of the society here. . . . People point us out and they put us down."

This viewpoint had many proponents as well. Numerous residents of Nambué remarked that they did not resent being indigenous or, necessarily, being labeled as such. What they resented was that they were labeled as the *only* indigenous community in spite of the fact that they were not recognizably different (either in appearance or culture) from other people from the province of Guanacaste (excluding Santa Rita—which Riteña profesora Alodia described as "an island in Guanacaste"). A high school graduate from Nambué expressed on more than one occasion that he considered that he was not indigenous, since other Guanacastecos with similar lifestyles, customs, and language were not labeled as such. He reasoned (at a youth group meeting in 1997), "I think the customs that exist here are not unique to the community but [are] regional. They are from Guanacaste. We are a part of Guanacasteco tradition."

Still, as discussed earlier, the reservation has had its supporters as well. As is to be expected of any community, not all members thought alike. Rather, all of them had their own separate identities, often based on how they fit into the place that defined them or how that place had affected their lives. People construct place differently and according to different experiences and agendas. This is particularly apparent in contested places. When it was named a Chorotega Indigenous Reservation over twenty years ago, the physical properties of Nambué did not change. The variety of experiences tied to being from that place, however, changed drastically. In Nambué, upon its designation as a reservation, political and geographic boundaries were drawn into sharp focus, setting the community apart from the otherwise indistinguishable communities (with the exception of Santa Rita) surrounding it. At that moment more than any other, its place-name became a marker of identity, and place became inextricably linked to ethnicity. As indicated earlier, several inhabitants of Nambué claimed, independent of one another, that the name *Nambué* and its corresponding reservation status have served as a fence that has limited their opportunities, lumped its inhabitants into a seemingly bounded community, and distinguished them from those outside the reservation's border. According to one resident cited earlier, the reason the reservation's borders connote ugliness is that "[t]hey limit us." This man's brother expressed a similar view on a different occasion, while speaking to government officials about his distaste for the reservation:

> As you can see we don't deny that we're Chorotega, we're Chorotega just like everyone else from the province of Guanacaste, in [the town of Majapiñao], [in the town of] Santa Cruz, but I think that you can't limit that, we can't say we're going to enclose them. Personally, I'm not in agreement with their enclosing us in a reservation because we all have the same rights as any Guanacasteco.[133]

The discrimination at hand is not exactly racism, since it often occurred between people of the same ethnic and cultural heritage, but is more a "placism," if you will. The stigmatized, ascribed Indian identity came from residence within a politically defined geographic area. This discrimination formed a considerable portion of the debate surrounding Nambué's reservation status. The variety of lived experiences within Nambué (including those dominated by discrimination) account for the variety of opinions surrounding Nambué, its reservation status, and the ascribed definition of its inhabitants.

As several scholars note, it is not unusual that a place and the people who reside therein come to be mutually defined.[134] It was this dynamic at work when students noted that people discriminated against them as a result of the name of their town, as opposed to their race specifically. And it was perhaps this dynamic that Socorro, the woman who greeted me with an enthusiastic "Hello! You know there's nothing indigenous here," understood when she left Nambué and moved to Cartago—the town whose name has come to be synonymous with white settlers among Nambueseños. An interpreter of this event also referred to this dynamic when he responded (in a play on words), "*Ahora sí la india se hizo cartaga*" (Now the Indian woman did make herself white/an inhabitant of Cartago).

Although Nambueseños were not confined to the reservation by law, as has been the case elsewhere,[135] many complained of the law that required that non-Indians not own land in Nambué or any other reservation in Costa Rica. Unlike the Burakumin of Japan, Nambueseños were never obligated by law to enter certain professions. As I discuss at length in Chapter 4, however, given the discrimination against them and their limited access to higher education, they often did get channeled into certain occupational areas. These class-related limitations, also linked to racist limitations, make the Nambueseño case similar to placist situations in North America as well.[136] Although these other cases of discrimination based on place of residence are similar to that experienced by Nambueseños, Nambué's case is still fairly unusual. Unlike the Burakumin of Japan, Nambué's low castelike status was a result of place of residence, whereas for the Burakumin, caste status led to a prescribed place of residence. Nambué's case is similar to those studied by Peter McLaren and Jay MacLeod in North America with regard to the relation between social class and place. Social class, however, although significant in Santa Rita's discrimination toward Nambué, was of less importance than the connection between place and ethnicity. These were the principal boundary markers pointed to in people's efforts to naturalize the socially constructed distinction (expressed as racial) among Nambueseños, other Guanacastecos, and Riteños.

This chapter has sought to examine how ethnicity and race have been construed both by and for the inhabitants of the reservation. Also, I have aimed to demonstrate the variety of opinions that exist both within and without the reservation regarding the identity of Nambueseños and opinons of the community's reservation status. Of particular importance is the nature of "race" in Nambué as inextricably linked to place of residence. In Chapter 4 I will address the consequences of place-based identity in the school setting.

NOTES

1. "Neither Chicha nor Lemonade."
2. Barth 1969: 15.
3. See, for example, di Leonardo 1984: 23; Oboler 1995; Wade 1997.

4. Eriksen 1993: 21.

5. These ethnic groups are the Chorotega, Bribrí, Cabécar, Huetar, Guaymí/Nobegue, Maleku/Guatuso, Térraba, and Brunca.

6. See Stocker 1997 for further elaboration of this concept.

7. Adams 1991: 203.

8. Matamoros Carvajal 1990: 69; emphasis added, translation mine. Although it may seem odd that reservations would be created for assimilationist purposes, that was the case in Costa Rica. The motivation for this appears to have been to create a homogeneous, national identity. The details surrounding this history are murky and difficult to come by in Costa Rica. For further information on this history, see Stocker 1997.

9. James C. Scott 1990: 21 notes, of the threats of violence in unequal power relations, "whether or not they occur to any particular subordinate, the ever-present knowledge that they might seems to color the relationship as a whole." This comment seems particularly apt to the relationship between Nambué and CONAI.

10. Schaller 1998: 22, 25, 27, 30, 109; see Schaller 1998 for a more detailed account of the process of *consultas* alluded to here.

11. This situation changed in 2000, when various homes had telephones installed, but until then there was only one telephone for the whole town.

12. This and the following details were either recounted to me by participants in this process or are evident through the transcript of the meeting that took place in Nambué, as documented by the Asamblea Legislativa 1997: 7–9, 12, 15.

13. Susanna Schaller, personal communication, 1997.

14. See Stocker 1995.

15. Asamblea Legislativa 1997: 29.

16. Eriksen 1993: 90; Field 1999; Friedlander 1975: 193; Gould 1993: 394; Wade 1997: 80. See also Clifford 1986; Díaz Polanco 1997; Rosaldo 1993; Taussig 1984.

17. See also Yon 2000: 132 for how theory of identity gets lived by individuals.

18. Gagini 1917: 72.

19. The same is also true for noted Costa Rican historian Carlos Monge Alfaro 1960.

20. Peralta 1893: xvi–xvii; translation mine.

21. For a similarly critical perspective on indigenous peoples in Mexico, see García Canclini 1990: 277.

22. Field 1999 and Gould 1998 describe a similar phenomenon for Nicaragua.

23. Costa Rica is by no means the only country whose indigenous communities have been treated in this manner. See Dolby 2001: 54 and Luykx 1999: xxxix for similar dominant views of African students in a South African high school and of Bolivian peasant communities, respectively. See also Jackson 2002: 92 with regard to Colombia and Ramos 1998: 71 for a discussion of the Brazilian case.

24. Bonfil Batalla 1972 outlines a similar dynamic in Mexico.

25. As I have asserted, there was no stark cultural difference between Nambueseños and the dominant population in the 1970s. Thus, assimilation was not necessarily the focus of efforts within Nambué. It was the goal of the law that governed a variety of reservations, however, some of which did contain vast cultural differences from dominant Costa Rican society.

26. Davis 1988: 85; Horowitz 1975: 139–140. See Rival 1996: 153 for an account of how Ecuadorian schools with an assimilationist goal may actually spur heterogeneity.

27. Salguero 1991: 170.

28. See Levinson 2001: 147 for a link between rural residence and ascribed identity.

29. Bozzoli de Wille 1969, 1986.

30. Bozzoli de Wille, personal communication, 1994.

31. Although it may seem unlikely that any one scholar would have the final word on such issues, social scientists in Costa Rica hold tremendous respect for Bozzoli de Wille and are unlikely to disagree with her openly. I have found Costa Rican anthropologists to be defensive of her, and those who even mildly questioned her scholarship requested anonymity from me. It is unclear whether this is out of respect for her thorough and thoughtful research on the Bribrí, her contributions to anthropology in Costa Rica, or the fact that she holds a powerful position at the University of Costa Rica, where others are or may hope to be employed.

32. For a similar perspective, see Bonfil Batalla 1990: 200.

33. See Ramos 1998: 76–77 for a discussion of a similar situation in Brazil.

34. See Wade 1997: 114.

35. Asamblea Legislativa 1997: 22–24; translation mine.

36. Ibid.: 26; translation mine.

37. See Stocker 1997 for more about identity politics in Nambué.

38. Barth 1969: 79; Schermerhorn 1996: 17.

39. Barth 1969: 24; Eriksen 1993: 11.

40. In this consideration, I follow Jenkins 1997: 61.

41. See Banks 1996: 13; Ramos 1998: 7.

42. Adams 1991: 193; Alonso 1994: 395; Geertz 1973: 262–263; Grosby 1996: 51; Nagata 1981: 94; Nederveen Pieterse 1996: 30–31; Wade 1997: 18.

43. Membreño Idiáquez 1992: 125. See also García Bresó 1992: 26.

44. Horowitz 1975: 133–134.

45. See Barrientos et al. 1982: 251 for one such example.

46. Gould 1993: 396.

47. Membreño Idiáquez 1992: 126.

48. Among these are Casey 1993; Feld and Basso 1996; Relph 1976; Tuan 1977.

49. In this assertion, I follow Casey 1987: 186.

50. See Yon 2000: 11, 104 for more on this conceptualization of race.

51. See also ibid.: 103 for a discussion of race as tied to popular culture, social status, and location.

52. With regard to the concept of race as a socially constructed category, I follow Omi and Winant 1986 and others. See Dolby 2001: 112; McCarthy and Crichlow 1993: xix; Ng 1993: 51; Yon 2000: 10.

53. See Dolby 2001: 112; Pinar 1993: 61; Warren and Crichlow 1993: xxi; Yon 2000: 83. Yon 2000: 5 calls race "elusive" as a result of this shifting character.

54. For further reading regarding identity as a process, see Dolby 2001: 13, 15, 115; Levinson and Holland 1996: 11, 13; Luttrell 1996: 94; McCarthy and Crichlow 1993: xvi; Ng 1993: 51; Yon 2000: 12–14.

55. See Jenkins 1997; Pinar 1993: 61.

56. See McCarthy and Crichlow 1993: xvi; Pinar 1993: 61.

57. See Kondo 1990: 16, 31–32; Luykx 1999: 170; Ng 1993: 51; Pinar 1993: 61; Rosaldo 1993: 166; Tsing 1993: 53; Warren and Jackson 2002: 8.

58. See Jenkins 1997: 44; Kondo 1990: 24, 257; Stephen 1991: 20; Tsing 1993: 53; Yon 2000: 13.

59. Jenkins 1997: 44. See also Warren and Jackson 2002: 8–9.

60. Wade 1997:109.

61. Jenkins 1997: 47. See also Alonso 1994 for a similar critique of fluidity in matters of identity and Warren and Jackson 2002: 7–8 for more on the dangers of "deconstruction" in anthropological study of indigenous ethnicity.

62. Eriksen 1993: 27.

63. Ibid.: 33.

64. Knight 1990: 75.

65. See di Leonardo 1984: 22–23; Wade 1997: 66 for more on this concept. Authors who specifically address labeling in the school context include López, Assáel, and Neumann 1984: 309, 362; Oboler 1995.

66. See Sharp 1996: 87 for a compelling discussion of the danger in deconstructing primordialist discourses. See also Wade 1997: 116; Warren and Jackson 2002: 7–8.

67. Castile 1981: 180.

68. Jenkins 1997: 57; Wade 1997: 110; Wilmsen and McAllister 1996: viii.

69. Friedlander 1975: 83–84, 100.

70. Alonso 1994: 397–398; Eriksen 1993: 127; García Canclini 1990: 221.

71. Bonfil Batalla 1989: 13; translation mine.

72. Banks 1996: 128; Eriksen 1993: 103. See also Frye 1996: 10; Nagata 1974: 332 for comments on this unidirectional view of cultural appropriation that recognizes "assimilation" but not national appropriation of ethnic groups' cultural practices.

73. See Hendrickson 1991: 290.

74. Bozzoli de Wille, personal communication, 1994; Marcos Guevara Berger, personal communication, 1996.

75. Alonso 1994: 392; Barth 1969: 38; Jenkins 1997: 52.

76. Guevara Berger and Chacón 1992: 18.

77. Bozzoli de Wille 1969: 4–5; Bozzoli de Wille 1986: 75. See Hobsbawm and Ranger 1983 for a more thorough discussion of reinvented tradition.

78. Oboler 1995: xv.

79. García Bresó 1992: 333.

80. Eriksen 1993: 51; Jenkins 1997: 60; Ramos 1998: 7.

81. Yon 2000:56.

82. Castaneda 1981: 131; Guevara Berger 1993: 226.

83. Eriksen 1993: 21.

84. García Bresó 1992: 16; Marroquín 1975: 750; Rivas 1993: 157.

85. See Bonfil Batalla 1972: 110; Marroquín 1975: 752.

86. Castile 1981: 178, following Spicer.

87. Bhabha 1990: 310.

88. Ibid.: 311.

89. Weber quoted in Alonso 1994: 391.

90. The *encomienda* was a colonial institution, semifeudal in nature, that existed throughout Latin America. Through this system, colonizers to whom royalty granted *encomiendas* exacted tribute in the form of forced labor from indigenous peoples.

91. Eriksen 1993: 35; Geertz 1973: 263.

92. Green 1981: 75, 77; Spicer 1971: 797.

93. Arroyo 1972: 13; Barrientos et al. 1982: 251; Bozzoli de Wille 1969, 1986; Guevara Berger and Chacón 1992: 38; Palmer, Sánchez, and Mayorga 1993: 27.

94. Marroquín 1975: 758–759.

95. Bonfil Batalla 1972: 119.

96. Comaroff and Comaroff 1992: 64; Crumrine 1981: 109; Eriksen 1993: 7; Friedlander 1975: xv; Frye 1996: 63; Mallon 1996: 292.

97. Among these are Field 1999: 191; Friedlander 1975; Frye 1996: 63.

98. Jackson 2002; Ramos 2002: 273.

99. Ramos 2002: 274; Warren and Jackson 2002; Williams 1989. For further discussion of the nexus between class and ethnicity, see Roosens 1989. His discussion focuses on the use of ethnic identity as a tool for political mobilization or for economic gain. Given that indigenous ethnic identity did not bring favor to Nambueseños and in light of Roosens's explicit assertion that his work focuses on "ethnic groups that do not stand in a hierarchical or ranked position to one another," this source is less relevant to an analysis of ethnicity in Nambué (Roosens 1989: 15). Still, it provides an interesting contrast to the Nambueseño case.

100. See Chapin 1989: 11; Field 1995: 792; Gould 1993, 1998; Luykx 1999: 265 for further discussion.

101. Bozzoli de Wille 1986: 75.

102. Marroquín 1975: 751. See also Luykx 1999: 145–146, 149–150 for a discussion of how attempts to disassociate indigenous, peasant identities from the stigmatized term *indio* have resulted in ambiguity surrounding the true meaning of what it is to be Aymara in Boliva.

103. Ramos 2002: 274.

104. See Abercrombie 1991: 98.

105. See Stocker 2002 for a more complete analysis of this situation, contextualized within a greater body of linguistic theory. See also Graham 2002: 189 for a discussion of the expectation that "'real' Indians should speak Indian languages."

106. Spicer 1971: 799. See also Fishman 1972: 4; Gumperz 1972: 219.

107. Chapin 1989: 15, referring to the Salvadoran case, states that the Spanish spoken by these groups differs to some degree from the dominant variety: "It's not an indigenous language, but not Spanish [either]." Rizo Zeledón 1992: 64, speaking of ethnic groups in central and Pacific Nicaragua, states that the Spanish spoken by some elderly women in the community of Matagalpa includes "a large quantity of Matagalpa words and a unique linguistic rhythm in sentence structure"; translation mine.

108. See Stocker 1995.

109. Although I recognize that Nahuatl is spoken in other parts of Latin America, it is not recognizably spoken in Costa Rica.

110. See Fernández de Oviedo y Valdés 1959.

111. Bonfil Batalla 1990: 200; translation mine.

112. Lienhard 1991: 270; translation mine.

113. Guillermo Rodríguez, personal communication, 1993.

114. The transcript of this meeting is documented by the Asamblea Legislativa 1997.

115. Asamblea Legislativa 1997: 18. The idea of kinship is frequently related to ethnic labeling. Some people emphasize the importance of "blood" (Eriksen 1993: 35; Geertz 1973: 261), whereas others cite a more general view of common ancestry or descent (Alonso 1994: 391; Eidheim 1969: 44; Eriksen 1993: 35; Fishman 1996: 63; Weber quoted in Alonso 1994: 341). Some scholars emphasize that it is not so much the biological ties of kinship or genetic connections as the "presumed" blood ties that are important (Nash

1996: 25; see also Spicer 1971: 796). Whether seen as "blood" or through other tropes of kinship, some ancestral relationship is often key to group identity, for many indigenous peoples in particular (Castile 1981: 187).

116. Warren and Jackson's (2002: 28) comment on the nature of symbols is appropriate to this discussion: "Symbols utilized in indigenous representation and self-representation have a kind of polymorphous perversity to them; they are portmanteaux for other symbols, or, chameleonlike, they take on and shed meanings in quick succession."

117. Although I did go to the National Library to seek out this document and confirm the publication of this photo and caption, the issue of the journal that focused on the town of Santa Rita de Cascia was missing from the national collection.

118. For more in-depth analysis of style of dress as an indicator of subgroup status, see Hall and Jefferson 1975; Hebdidge 1979.

119. See Yon 2000: 15 with regard to how globalization has affected student identities and how notions of identity as static do not allow such incorporation into identity. See also Dolby's (2001: 54–55) finding in South Africa involving school staff's views of Zulu students as fixed, although these students tied their own identities to modern and global interests.

120. Although I have defined race and ethnicity as distinct, I am using the terms almost interchangeably here because they are generally seen, in Santa Rita and the surrounding area, as the same phenomenon. Although I perhaps mean ethnicity, Riteños and others talk about this concept in terms of race and see it as marked on the body.

121. See Horowitz 1975; Wade 1997.

122. Among these are Isaacs 1975: 39; Nash 1996: 25–26; Schermerhorn 1996: 17.

123. *Mestizaje* is the process of racial mixing resulting in the mestizo population. See Knight 1990: 74; Marroquín 1975: 749; Wade 1997: 37 for sources that argue against the use of physical appearance as an ethnic marker.

124. Bourgois 1989: 185.

125. Ibid.: 186; emphasis added.

126. The literal translation of the show's title is "The Mena Mora Family." It includes two common surnames from the region and at the same time contains a play on words of the phrase *Me enamora* ("It enamors me").

127. This particular witch was male. The word *witch* did not necessarily imply femaleness in Costa Rica.

128. See Stocker 1995, 1997.

129. Hartman 1914: 9.

130. Like students who lived outside of Santa Rita and traveled to school by bus, teachers not from Santa Rita also bore the label *traveler*. As I discuss in Chapter 4, teachers' cliques were divided largely (but not entirely) on the basis of traveler versus Riteño status.

131. See also Yon 2000: 12 on links among discourses of race, crime, and violence.

132. See Warren and Jackson 2002: 9 for a similar account. See also de la Cadena 1995: 331.

133. Asamblea Legislativa 1997: 13; translation mine.

134. See Blu 1996: 223; Casey 1993: 23.

135. Although some accounts exist of place of residence defining the Chorotega of Nicaragua (see Castegnaro de Foletti 1992; García Bresó 1992; Gould 1993), perhaps more closely tied is a case from across the world. A similar, although longer, history of

discrimination based on place can be found in literature regarding the Burakumin of Japan. In sixteenth-century Japan, lowly castes were confined to particular geographic areas without the possibility of mobility (Shimahara 1971: 17). Like Nambueseños, the Burakumin are viewed as a racial group in spite of the fact that this perceived race does not necessarily correspond to physical difference, skin color, or other markers usually taken as indicative of race (Shimahara 1971: 18). Rather, the Burakumin "form a race only in the sense of an 'invisible race,' a race visible only to the eyes of members of a certain cultural tradition" (Price 1966: 12).

136. For the working-class Canadian girls with whom Peter McLaren 1982 worked, as for the youth interviewed by Jay MacLeod 1987, residence in an impoverished area became an emblem of lower status that carried over into schools.

4

"Aquí son cuatro o cinco que valen la pena"[1]

MECHANISMS OF BOUNDARY MAINTENANCE

ON THE LOCAL LEVEL, THE EFFECTS OF ETHNIC CATEGORIZATION WERE MANY. IN spite of the assimilationist motivation behind the creation of indigenous reservations in Costa Rica, a principal result was to set Nambué (and the other reservations) apart from their surrounding towns. Thus, as noted in earlier chapters, the ethnic identity of Nambué's inhabitants hinged on place. Although place of residence was the most commonly used marker of difference between Nambueseños and those outside the reservation, other lines of division were also drawn to distinguish among individuals who came together in the high school setting, where lines of distinction were marked among students. These divisions were drawn in a variety of ways, and their effects are noteworthy.

This chapter demonstrates the ways people distinguished between "us" and "them" in the absence of stark differences (in terms of the traditional ethnic markers outlined in previous chapters). Mechanisms of distinction included, but were not limited to, teaching strategies, gossip, stereotypes, and ridicule. All of these were means by which students' asymmetrical social and political positions were played out at the levels of community opinion, school policy, teacher technique, and student interaction. Subsequent chapters will address the ways in which divisions were made on an institutional level.

THE MAKINGS OF STATUS:
RACE, ETHNICITY, SOCIAL CLASS, GENDER, AND PLACE

The distinction between Nambueseños and Riteños and between Nambueseños and all others present in the high school has been commented upon. Residence inside the reservation provided a label and an indicator of status in relation to nonreservation towns. This hierarchical relationship, in the case of Nambué vis-à-vis Santa Rita, was related to a racial and ethnic hierarchy that pitted Indianness against whiteness while elucidating a class relationship. Access to education and equality were significantly tied to this hierarchy derived from place of residence as well, but they were by no means the only distinguishing factors between the two groups. Distinctions based on race and class—and, in a more elusive way, gender—were among those that affected the more malleable social divisions and hierarchies both within the reservation and across its fixed geographic border. Profesor Sergio, not from Santa Rita, recognized these various lines of social division. He commented that discrimination at Santa Rita High School (SRHS) "does not have to do only with geography but also with so-called race, if they are Indians, if they are black, if they are mestizos, and it is, in principle, their social status, if they're poor, if they have money, and also the aesthetic concept of physical beauty, which is very important. In sum, all of these elements mark difference."

Indeed, race was not only about physical appearance but also about status and place of residence.[2] Although in some cases (as noted previously) culture change was perceived as culture loss, in Nambué no amount of cultural change was likely to affect its inhabitants' social status based on an ascribed ethnicity as a result of place of residence. The connection of race to place has been discussed with regard to students from Santa Rita who physically resembled Nambueseños but whose place of residence and class status lent themselves to honorary "white" status.

Profesora Delia, in a lesson on drugs and the distortion of reality, explained to a class of seventh graders, "I can't say that I am from Santa Rita if I am from a family of limited [economic] resources." Thus, class was also tied to place in complicated ways. In 1999 Nambueseños had no sources of employment within the reservation and had to depend on the economy of neighboring towns such as Santa Rita and Majapiñao for their income. Given the racist bias against Nambueseños in Santa Rita, Nambueseños rarely found work there. Thus, the class hierarchy was perpetuated.

Although it seems that in many cases Indianness was equivalent to residing within Nambué, which in turn implied a lower-class status than that of most Riteños, class, too, was a malleable category. Status was the product of an elaborate mix of class, ascribed ethnicity, and place of residence—all of which fed one another. The convoluted tangle of mutually defining categories did not end there, however. Gender, too, came into play. In Nambué and Santa Rita, fairly strict gender roles all but dictated the social and economic locations of women and men. Women in this society were less likely to be economically independent and more likely to be held responsible for household roles rather than influential political ones.[3] This, too, affected status.

Some parents of Nambueseño students told me the prejudice and discrimination faced by Nambueseños in high school were even worse for girls.[4] In addition to having offensive racial nicknames, girls often had ones that constructed them as sexualized objects as well, thus adding another layer of categorization and scrutiny to the mix. Furthermore, if ascribed Indian identity was dangerous to one's social status, feminine Indian identity was the kiss of death. Indeed, ethnic identity, escapable for some (as I discuss in detail in Chapter 7), was not so for many women. To the contrary, female cultural behavior was often taken as emblematic of the culture as a whole.[5] Women in many cultures are often seen as the transmitters of culture.[6] Furthermore, the feminization of Indians is a common trope in accounts of colonialism and conquest.[7] As I will discuss toward the end of this chapter, one of the mechanisms of boundary maintenance among different social groups was assignment of nicknames to all students, although students from the reservation had racial nicknames. Some girls from the reservation had racial nicknames with an added layer of sexual innuendo, as just mentioned, and some boys—seemingly following this pattern of the feminization of Indians in a setting where the feminine was seen as inherently inferior in many ways—had feminized racial nicknames. Gendered categories were evident in the divisions among students in the high school setting. Before addressing further the mechanisms by which these divisions were maintained, however, other categorizations were also significant to the mix that were themselves crosscut by race, ethnicity, class, and gender.

STANDARD STUDENTS AND RITEÑO PRIVILEGE

One of the other key divisions of this sort, dividing the valued students taken as the standard versus those who were measured against them, was based on place of residence: not Nambué versus Santa Rita but rather Santa Rita versus everyone else. Edward Spicer notes that the mere presence of terms for "us" and "them" suffices to prove that a cultural boundary is being maintained.[8] One of the most common distinctions heard regarding students was whether they were *viajantes* or *del centro*—whether they traveled to school or were from the center town (Santa Rita).[9]

In school documents (such as those provided for a study carried out by PRODAPEN, a local development agency, and in the school's informational materials) the student body was described as 80 percent travelers versus 20 percent from the center. Having heard this from day one of my research (from administrators and teachers), seen it in written reports, and heard it in Santa Rita's annual radio address to the bishop, I took it for granted. It was not until I tallied the numbers of students from each town that I realized the number was drastically skewed.

Counting the number of students from each town listed on the class rosters at the beginning of the year, I found that of a total of 453 students who began the 1999 school year at SRHS, 185 (41 percent) were from central Santa Rita and 268 (59 percent) were from other towns. When I analyzed the lists further, it appeared that the 80:20 ratio listed so frequently for travelers: Riteño students more closely reflected the ratio of students who were not from important, white, economically well-off Riteño families to those who were. This reinforces my assertion that being Riteño implied wealth and whiteness, inextricably tying race to both place and class.

The division between traveler students and those from the center was discussed frequently, and the division described, to some extent, students who mattered versus those less important to the high school. Those from the center, in spite of constituting the numerical minority, were the standard against which all others were measured; they provided the level of expectation to which all others tried to measure up, and they were considered synonymous with "the students." All others—the travelers—were qualified as such when spoken of. Just as the term *American,* with no hyphenated prefix, often connotes Euro-American in a Eurocentric world whereas all other national, racial, or ethnic minorities must be qualified with a prefix, Riteño students constituted the unmarked category, taken as the standard.

The week of Independence Day, each morning began with pledges of allegiance to the nation and province, anthems were sung, and speeches were made regarding the nation's central values. Almost invariably it was students from the center of Santa Rita and from its most prominent families who carried out these acts. I inquired about the reasons behind this, and the teachers in charge of signing up student "volunteers" (although all were hand selected by two Riteña teachers) told me that for the most part, it was because of the proximity of their houses to the school. Students from the center of town could be counted on to arrive on time, unhampered by unreliable road conditions or transportation. Also, those chosen were known to be good public speakers. One of the teachers in charge of selecting student participants for civic acts noted that sometimes the traveler students were ashamed to participate, whereas those from Santa Rita had more confidence.

Shortly after I began to ask questions about this matter, several traveler students were chosen to officiate one morning's flag raising. I stood, watching the event, with the student body and teachers. Beside me stood a student (Jaime, the self-proclaimed racist seventh grader described in Chapter 2) who was descended from two prominent Riteño family lines. He commented on the fact that all student participants in the day's civic activities were travelers—"purely travelers." On the previous days, in which student participants were exclusively Riteño, I heard no comments on the matter. It was, presumably, what was expected.

Student elections were held yearly and were, in theory, open to all students who wished to participate. Teams of students formed different parties, announced their platforms, and campaigned. For portions of two days, classes were canceled so students could hear their peers' platforms and decide for whom to vote. In one of these sessions, students gathered to ask questions through anonymous inquiries written on slips of paper and passed to candidates, who answered them in front of the student body.

In the 1999 student government elections, four parties sat before the student body to answer their peers' questions. Among the questions was why one party had so many members from the town of Puerto Sereno. Another asked why so many members were from another small town outside Santa Rita. Nobody asked why Riteños dominated most parties, but one student did ask the only team considered to have no Riteño candidates why they were lacking. The team's vice presidential candidate responded that there was indeed one Riteño in their party and begged students not to think the absence of more Riteños was because "we don't like them." One anonymous student asked why none of the parties included any Nambueseños. One party's candidate explained that they had invited one Nambueseño to contribute as a campaign manager (not a candidate), but the student refused. When the election results were in and it was evident that the winning party was that made up of all but one Riteño, Jaime manifested his lack of surprise. He noted that this party had won by a landslide and added "*era de lógica*"—that this was logical and to be expected.

Another process whose outcome could have been predicted was the selection of the most beautiful girls in school for a fund-raising beauty pageant. In this case of Riteña students serving as role models, it was not only ideal student status being upheld by Riteñas but standards of beauty and femininity as well. For the pageant, homerooms elected a female student candidate, or teachers chose one from their homeroom. Of the original candidates nominated from each homeroom, only three were travelers. After a meeting with these young women, at which the event's teacher-organizers told the girls it would be costly and that they would need parental permission as well as appropriate clothing, some candidates dropped out and were replaced. At the final pageant, fourteen candidates showed up to compete. Of these, ten were from Santa Rita. Three were from other towns considered white but perhaps less economically well-off than Santa Rita. Amelia was the only dark-skinned candidate, and she was eliminated in the first round.

My final example of Riteño students being presented as the finest at SRHS is tied to the choosing of the best students from each homeroom class. They were known as *abanderados,* a term indicating both "flag bearers" and, coincidentally, "flagged ones"—a telling term indeed. They were known as such because their selection allowed them to lead their classmates in the Independence Day parade, carrying Costa Rican flags. They were also marked, or flagged, if you will, however, as the cream of the crop—the students who made Santa Rita proud. Not surprisingly, the percentage of flag bearers from Santa Rita did not reflect the proportion of those students to the rest of the student body. Forty-eight percent of flag bearers (twenty-six individuals) were from Santa Rita. Six were from the neighboring town. The rest of the towns were represented by one or two students each. This appeared to show a disproportionate number of "smart kids" from Santa Rita as compared to all other towns.

Several students talked to me, prior to the announcement of the *abanderados'* identities, about corruption in the selection process. Many students alleged that the chosen ones were not the smartest but the favorites. This implied their status as Riteños. Various teachers, on the other hand, asserted that the process was done on the basis of grades, thus suggesting that the basis for selection was academic merit.

Profesora Natalia, a teacher from Santa Rita but not associated with choosing the flag bearers, explained that the discrimination that took place in the school had nothing to do with race or place but instead targeted the undisciplined and the less intelligent. I would add that this "lack of discipline" sometimes had to do with one's relative skill at navigating the high school setting, considerably different from the smaller, sometimes one-room, remote elementary schools attended by those outside Santa Rita. Thus, "the less smart" students were often considered to be from outside Santa Rita, from small towns with small schools.

I propose that although the flag bearers were indeed chosen on the basis of their grades, those grades were not entirely based on academic merit (as I discuss in greater detail in Chapter 5). Two phenomena came into play here. One was Riteños' confidence that they would not be caught or held accountable for cheating, thus enabling them to obtain high grades—a fact I observed on numerous occasions. At times, this confidence was made clear by Riteño students asking me or other teachers, in front of other students, to help them cheat as I proctored their exams.[10] Other times it was evident as I observed certain teachers turning a blind eye to obvious cheating by Riteños. Once, I witnessed traveler profesora Marielos provide answers to the last student left taking an exam. On another occasion I heard a conversation between a Riteña teacher (Profesora Natalia) and a Riteño student in which the latter told the former of a classmate from Santa Rita who cheated so much that her classmates called her "the butcher" because of the cheat sheets, referred to by the word *chuleta*—also the word for pork chop—that she used frequently. The Riteña teacher, not visibly concerned about the student's cheating, simply laughed. The other phenomenon had to do with Riteño students' greater access to schooling.

ACCESS TO EDUCATION

INSTITUTIONALIZED BARRIERS

To begin with, I will address access in the most basic sense: the ability to arrive at school consistently. The rainy season, a seemingly endless stretch of torrential rains capable of washing out roads and creating mud pits like one I personally encountered (see Chapter 1), generally lasts six months. During this time, students from the farthest towns missed weeks of school because of impassable roads; the bus simply did not run. A handful of these students arranged to stay with godparents or friends in Santa Rita during part of this time, but most simply could not get to school. This meant missed lessons, homework, and exams and lower grades. Most teachers took this into account, providing lenience with regard to grading. It was impossible to compete gradewise, however, with those who attended school daily if one was from a far-off town. One teacher in a vocational class told her students to pass on the day's material to the students who were absent because of mudslides that prevented their bus from arriving. The teacher acknowledged that it was not the students' fault that they could not attend classes but that she could not have the rest of the class fall behind for their sake, either.

Students from far off were also impeded from participating in extracurricular activities. Profesor Efraín, a physical education teacher, noted that students were selected (not by him) to play on the volleyball team based on their residence near the school. The proximity to school facilitated training. This policy translated to superior grades because all participants on the extracurricular team received extra credit in their physical education class. Thus, residence in Santa Rita paid off in terms of grades. This, in turn, fueled the stereotype that the smart kids came from Santa Rita.

Furthermore, transportation could lead to absences even when students from far away could get transportation to school. One student explained to me that he did not attend classes one day because he had only one lesson with the guidance counselor (a class frequently canceled at the last minute), as individual teachers had canceled his other lessons for the day (a common occurrence). His coming to school for one lesson would have meant staying at school all day with nothing to do. Therefore, he stayed home, but he was marked absent, which could have affected both his class grade and his conduct grade.

Apart from hindering travelers' arrival at school on a daily basis, the transportation issue affected traveling students and those from the center of Santa Rita differently. For the students farthest from school, their day began as early as 3:45 A.M., when they had to get up to prepare for the bus that picked them up at 4:30 to get them to school by 7:00 A.M. (when the first class of the day began). They did not get home until 6:00 P.M., at which time they had to take care of household responsibilities and do their homework.[11]

Many teachers acknowledged that this schedule took its toll on students. Profesora Marielos, a guidance counselor, remarked that these students got to school and home again tired. Profesora Remedios (a traveler teacher who associated with the Riteño clique) commented that getting home late affected students' academic success and said she took this into account in their grades. She added that those students "make a huge effort." The superintendent also recognized that students from far away had little time for study. The vice principal noted that many students from far away had no time for homework and little time for rest. She asked, rhetorically, "With what kind of enthusiasm can they come to receive classes?"

A student from the farthest town served by the high school noted one more way in which her time-consuming trip to school affected her schooling. She explained that she awakened at 3:45 A.M. and tried not to turn on any lights so as not to disturb her still-sleeping mother and siblings. One morning she came to school in a panic and confided in me that she could not concentrate because of her nervousness. That day she was scheduled to have class with Profesora Eugenia, a Riteña teacher infamous for her strict uniform checks. Profesora Eugenia was known for having students pull up their pants legs to make sure their socks were in keeping with the dress code. Elena, who prepared for school in the dark, had selected a pair of socks that appeared in darkness to be navy blue. She arrived at school by daylight to see, to her horror, that her socks were green. If her most demanding teacher detected this, Elena would be marked absent from that class, thus affecting her grade in the class as well as her conduct grade. Profesor Teodoro noted, in defense of travelers, that in spite of "the sacrifice required by traveling," these students were more dedicated to their schooling. He explained this as a result of their understanding the economic sacrifice posed by attending school—a fact widely considered to be unappreciated by the wealthier Riteño students.

Transportation, or the lack thereof, also affected students who dropped out of school. Guidance counselors noted that there was little they could do, because of a lack of funds and transportation, to bring dropouts back to school if they were not from Santa Rita. For students from Santa Rita, counselors could walk to visit the students at home and encourage them to return to classes. Riteña profesora Alodia recognized that "many of those who drop out are travelers." She added, "There are many who don't like to travel by bus because they have to get up early. They give all of these excuses [for dropping out]." The superintendent commented that many students from small towns had less money and felt bad in school as a result of their economic status. He remarked that for a student like this, "there is no other remedy than to drop out, to later go to a night school, because that is what they do."

SOCIAL CLASS AND RELATIVE SCHOOL SUCCESS

As noted earlier, residents of Santa Rita were considered to have more money than families who lived in other towns. This, too, came into play in sundry ways with regard to school success. In a class period in which the teacher was absent and class was canceled by default, one homeroom section of eighth-grade boys left campus to go to the river. They were reported by townspeople who called the school, subsequently caught by the guidance counselor, and punished through notes to their parents and threats of suspension. Two students were not punished, however, because they told the counselor they had permission from home to go to the river. Profesora Delia called the boys' homes to confirm this, and they were exempted from punishment. Not coincidentally, they were the only two boys in the class—both from Santa Rita—who had telephones in their homes. Such an excuse would have been impossible for students from other towns.

Economics also affected traveler students in more severe ways. The vice principal remarked that many students from small towns came to school without eating breakfast. In contrast, she noted that students from Santa Rita got three meals a day. Students who came to school hungry would not have the same ability to focus in class as those with full stomachs. Whether a student's home had electricity also affected his or her ability to study after school. Those students without electricity at home were travelers (although this was not true for all travelers).

Profesora Natalia (who resided in Santa Rita) noted that because of their limited resources, both parents worked in some travelers' families (a relatively uncommon occurrence in Santa Rita). Such a situation might have increased a student's household responsibilities, providing less time for study, as well as limiting parental help. A young traveler teacher noted that the economic difference between travelers and those from Santa Rita was one of the main divisions among students. I asked her if this was reflected in each group's relative academic success. At first she responded that it was, but she soon changed her mind. She concluded, "No, academic performance depends on each student's effort or the sacrifice that one makes as a student." At least on some level, school staff was aware of the problems posed by the transportation issue. In fact, this was taken into account in the selection of parent representatives from each homeroom and in the appointment of school board members. The vice principal noted that school board members were chosen very deliberately from individuals from Santa Rita so they could attend meetings without transportation problems. If this were not so, the travelers' situation might have been more likely to have been addressed.

Limited financial resources hindered students' access to materials, proper uniforms, and tutoring sessions—all of which could result in lower grades. In spite of the fact that Costa Rica boasts a free and compulsory education for all, attending school was expensive.[12] Students had to attend school in proper uniform (or risk lower grades at best and expulsion at worst), buy their books (or be unable to do their lessons), pay for photocopies (or go without class material, including the pages a test was printed on), and pay for lunch (although many lunch scholarships were given). Not being able to afford these things would likely be evident in students' grades.

Vocational classes required even more money (depending on the class). Students had to bring wood for woodwork, fabric and thread for sewing, disks for computers, and more. Few vocational workshops required no monetary contributions from students. Some vocational teachers took this into account and provided materials from their own pockets. Others found donors of materials. Still, many students suffered academically because of being unable to participate fully if they could not bring all the materials needed for a class. The grandmother of Samuel, a Nambueseño student, was told toward the end of the year that her grandson needed to finish paying the equivalent of nearly seven dollars if he wanted to pass his woodworking course.

At times, the connection between money and grades was even more apparent. A Nambueseño student recounted that those who purchased a biology book that cost approximately ten dollars received extra credit for having done so, to say nothing of having gained additional access to the content. At the end of the school year, some students who were one point or so away from a passing grade were able to purchase the points by buying books to donate to the school library or supplying paint for the desks and classrooms. A math teacher provided extra credit to students who bought board games to enrich students' minds during free time. These activities, although well-intentioned, provide more examples of ways in which relative wealth translated to superior grades.[13]

The school uniform was extremely expensive for families with no regular income, especially given the strict guidelines. One could be marked absent for being "out of uniform" (if one's socks were the wrong color, one's black shoes were the improper style, or one's belt loops followed an inappropriate fashion). Prior to entering the first year of high school, students received basic uniform guidelines indicating the appropriate color of each part of the uniform. Two weeks into the school year, however, teachers met to approve more specific uniform guidelines (involving such things as the number of darts to be sewn into girls' blouses, the correct style of pants pockets and belt loops, the cut of pants legs, the number of buttons per shirt, the preferred weave of socks, and other seemingly trivial details). Profesora Delia protested that parents had already bought uniforms that did not meet these exact specifications. A few teachers responded, "Too bad. Who told them to get their pants made according to another style?" Thus, to avoid punishment (by being marked absent), students had to have their uniforms altered, buy new shoes, and take other costly pains to make sure their uniforms were up to par.

The basic costs of school participation (including the purchase of books, notebooks, writing implements, and uniforms) were high enough for most families of traveler students, but in some classes there were even more costs. In one case, Profesor Teodoro (not Riteño but of that clique) required that his students turn in a final project typed on a computer. Extremely few people, even in Santa Rita, owned computers. Equally few were trained to use them. Thus, students' options were to have their own computers (as the school's computers rarely worked and in fact were not working at the time of the assignment), pay someone with a computer to type their projects for them, or, as one student did, request that the visiting anthropologist sequester a computer in the high school's administrative office and type the project for her. Students in the class protested to the teacher, asking, "What fault do we have in being poor?" Profesor Teodoro was unmoved and maintained the requirement.

PLACE OF RESIDENCE AND ACCESS TO SCHOOL MATERIALS AND OPPORTUNITIES

Access to materials was conditioned not only by relative wealth[14] but also by where students lived. School rules dictated that students were not allowed to leave campus during school (other than Riteño students who could go home for lunch). Although occasionally a guard locked students in on the campus to uphold this rule, usually it was not enforced. For students who considered themselves *en la mira* (under the watchful eye) of community members who had them tagged as "bad kids," however, this was more of a threat. Students considered troublemakers by townspeople in Santa Rita were reported to the school if seen in town.[15] This provided a sort of Catch-22 for students not from Santa Rita. They were not allowed to leave campus and could be punished if they did. Many classes, however, required that students bring materials not available for sale in their small towns. Santa Rita was the place where materials were available for sale, and transportation to Santa Rita was provided just before and immediately after school, thus leaving students only school hours in which to buy their materials. For many families, students' ability to do errands in Santa Rita was one reason they were allowed to attend school. Traveling students often had to do errands at the bank in Santa Rita and make purchases at the stores there. Thus, one could either prepare for class by buying class materials in town during school hours and run the risk of being marked down as having "escaped" or one could arrive at class without the necessary materials but maintain respect for school rules about not leaving campus. Either way, a student's grades could be compromised.

Limited transportation for traveler students also affected, to some extent, their access to vocational classes. On registration day, parents got up as early as 3:00 A.M. to secure a good place in the queue and ensure their child's placement in the vocational workshop of their choice. Teachers and administrators asserted that vocational classes were given on a first come, first served basis. To a large extent, that was the case. Given limited public transportation and limited means for those from more distant towns to hire private transportation for the day, however, Riteño parents tended to be in the "first come" category. The result, generally, was that Riteño students got their preferred courses (such as computer, cooking, silk screening, and arts and crafts classes).

Students from farther away tended to get placed in the remaining vocational classes that were less popular among students (such as cattle raising, horticulture, chicken raising, and the porcine industry). This had great implications for the way in which schooling reproduced the status quo and taught students of different backgrounds about their relative lots in life. I will examine this issue shortly. For the time being, however, a select horror story, which demonstrates how this situation worked against Nambueseño students and how discrimination was tied in as well, will be helpful.

The center of Nambué is approximately one hour's walk from SRHS. In 1999 several Nambueseño parents, with prior experience as to how the system worked, got up early and walked to Santa Rita or made the economic sacrifice to hire a car so they could secure a good place in line for vocational workshop registration. Several got there early enough to sign their children up for computer class—the first workshop to fill up. Interestingly, in both the eighth-grade and the seventh-grade sections, all of the Nambueseño students arrived on the first day of classes to find they had been moved out of computer class and into agriculture (in the case of the seventh graders) and cattle raising (for eighth graders). One Riteño student was also in this situation. All of those who had been removed from their chosen workshops went to the guidance office to complain. The Riteño was moved back into computers. With the exception of one, the Nambueseños were not reassigned. Samuel's grandfather went to school to complain, and Samuel was subsequently reinstated in the computer class—where he was treated so badly that he elected to switch back again after a short time.

Throughout the year, each time I inquired about this situation (at students' request) I got elusive answers about not enough spaces in computer class to go around. One guidance counselor explained that the students' parents had not come to complain or even called. I explained the transportation situation as well as the fact that there was only one telephone for the whole town of Nambué, and it could not be relied upon to function on any given day. I got more evasive answers.

Finally, toward the end of the year, a guidance counselor who planned to teach elsewhere the following year admitted to me that the Nambueseños had been deliberately taken out of the computer classes, thus providing room for others. Profesora Delia explained, "One knows that those [Nambueseño] parents won't come and fight, complain." Thus, it was easier to disappoint Nambueseño students than battle with Riteño parents.

The counselor added, "If they lent themselves to knowing their rights . . . [this wouldn't happen]. If they were to have a different attitude, if they came with respect and complained [it would be different]." I pointed out that these students *had* come to complain. She agreed that they came to her office and asked why they had been changed to another class, and she and her colleague told them there was a lack of space. She then said, "But they're passive. When it is time to demand their rights, they put the brakes on."

Several Nambueseños mentioned to me that this counselor had accused them of talking back. Quite possibly, had these students been less "passive" and "demanded their rights," they would have been reprimanded. When I brought this to Profesora Delia's attention, she reverted to a previous argument: "Their parents didn't come, whereas those from Santa Rita either came or called." Evidently, lack of transportation and limited reliance on and access to phones constituted significant determinants to students' educational opportunities.

Catering to the Privileged

The preceding example and others support the idea that, ultimately, the high school catered to Riteños. This was clear when the principal addressed the student body as if the expectation for everyone were to go to the university after high school (although that was a privilege reserved mainly for a select few Riteño students). It became clear once again in a discussion of the registration process. After a day dedicated to busing sixth graders from the local elementary schools to the high school to court them as future students, faculty members realized there was a problem with the pamphlets they had sent home with students telling them what day their parents had to come register them: the pamphlet neglected to mention what documents must be presented to register students. Profesora Alodia said there was an easy solution. The elementary school in Santa Rita was just down the street from the high school. It was only a matter of sending one person there to announce what students' parents needed to bring. She then acknowledged, almost as an afterthought, that this would work only for students from Santa Rita. She added, "*Y los de largo, ni modo*" (roughly, "And those from far away, oh well"). If a Riteño had to return home for proper documentation, he or she would only lose a coveted place in line. If traveler students' parents had to return, they might not make it back that same day in time to register.

Access to help from parents and teachers was an additional difference between travelers and students from the center of Santa Rita that also had repercussions in the grading process and, thus, in the determination of which students were considered intelligent and which were deemed less so. Access to help with assignments and with learning how to navigate the school system—whether from teachers or parents—was limited for travelers. Most Riteño students were not first-generation high school students. If their parents did not teach at the school, at least they or other relatives had likely attended it. This led to an increased (or even an exaggerated) sense of belonging.[16] Some students had the same teachers their parents had had for certain subjects. This allowed for parental help with homework and in knowing how to "do" school, or how to navigate the school setting both academically and socially. This was less true for traveler students. Thus, they were relegated to the social and academic periphery.

In Nambué in particular, many high school students attending secondary school in the 1990s were the first generation in their family to have such an opportunity. This affected their parents' ability to help them in school academically, to complain about their children having been removed from computer class, and to encourage them to study (which in previous generations was seen as an option for lazy people, a soft alternative to hard manual labor). Several teachers and administrators interpreted Nambueseño parents' lack of involvement in the high school as "disinterest." Parents were chided (indirectly, through comments to me) for never showing up to ask how their children were progressing. Parents, however, were never told directly to do this. In fact, the school's metal gates, labeled with a sign forbidding entrance to "particulars" (just anyone), would suggest that parental visits were discouraged. One Nambueseño parent pointed out that my passage through these gates as a white North American was never questioned. Although I had letters of introduction and permission, I was never asked to present them. This Nambueseño thought his passage—as a Nambueseño—would certainly be questioned.

Extracurricular help was available, in theory, to all students in the ninth and eleventh grades who were preparing for national exams. A few teachers (such as young Riteños Adán and Arturo) offered such help during school hours when they knew their students were free (either as a result of a teacher's absence or through deliberate scheduling). Teachers were not required to offer tutoring, however. Most tutoring sessions were held in the evenings in Santa Rita and had to be paid for by participating students. Sometimes, the teacher's transportation to Santa Rita to give the lessons was costly. Sometimes, payment for the teacher's time was too expensive for many. Either way, it was costly for students with little income. Needless to say, transportation here again limited traveler students' participation. For the most part, Riteño students attended these sessions (thus affecting their results on the exams, once again making it appear that Riteño students were smarter than others). At times, entire homeroom classes held fund-raisers to offset the costs of paying teachers for extracurricular help. Here too, however, it was the Riteño students—those most likely to be able to pay for tutoring sessions anyway—who benefited. In no cases were funds raised to provide transportation to tutoring sessions for travelers.

Teachers explained that this was less of an issue than I was making it. They said any students could attend a tutoring session "if they were interested." All they needed to do was arrange to stay at a Riteño friend's house that night. Profesora Rosa María expressed this as a matter of fact or, rather, of symbiosis: "When the traveling students need to stay over, the students from the center of Santa Rita take them home, and then those from Santa Rita go to the travelers' towns to visit on weekends." Given that peer groups were determined largely by students' place of residence and that there were few pairs of Nambueseño-Riteño buddies, this was more an option in theory than a practical one for students from the reservation.

Students who had godparents in Santa Rita utilized that option, thus relying on fictive kinship networks rather than on friendships. A student from the farthest end of Nambué stayed with a friend at the end of Nambué closest to Santa Rita and planned to walk that distance at night. One student, however, explained the humiliation involved in asking a Riteño for lodging, knowing the bad relations between Nambué and Santa Rita. She talked about how bad students felt when they mustered the courage to ask a Riteño classmate for lodging and were laughed at or rejected. Thus, what several staff members saw as a simple solution for travelers wishing to attend tutoring sessions was, in reality, considerably hindered by strained ethnic relations. Given that many teachers saw tutoring sessions as open to all, though, Nambueseños' inability to attend (given their relations with Riteños, limited transportation options, and lack of funds to pay for tutoring) appeared to many teachers as disinterest.

ACADEMIC EXPECTATIONS AND PLACE OF RESIDENCE

Access to knowledge was hindered not only by traveler students' inability to attend tutoring sessions but also by their having had less exposure to schooling as practiced in Santa Rita. The elementary school in Santa Rita, geographically close to the high school, familiarized students with the high school system early on. Students from Santa Rita knew what the "best" vocational workshops were ahead of time and knew to have their parents go early to sign them up. They knew many of the teachers, who might have been their neighbors or relatives. Their parents often had connections to the high school. Various teachers stated that those from Santa Rita Elementary School came to high school better prepared for high school–level work. One teacher considered that as a result, teachers ought to have given additional help to traveler students. The majority, however, did not share her beliefs. More teachers thought it was up to the traveler students to get up to speed and to "go about integrating themselves." One teacher acknowledged that traveler students came to high school more inhibited, whereas Riteños already knew the ropes and felt superior. According to the principal, about 90 percent of students came from one-room schoolhouses. He noted that these students "receive a shock" upon arrival at the high school. There was more stereotype than truth in this statistic, though. Many people assumed Nambueseños attended a one-room schoolhouse. In fact, Nambué had one of the better-staffed rural elementary schools in the area, with a separate classroom and teacher for each grade. Once again, though, the belief that

Nambueseños were less well prepared affected these students' academic success and the expectations many teachers held of them.

Given that Riteño students were seen as academically ahead of traveler students, Riteño parents did not want their children's progress held back by having them in classes with traveler students, who were thought to need more hand-holding. One result of this was that every grade level had a homeroom dominated by Riteño students, with few or no travelers, and there was often a section dominated by Nambueseños and other social outcasts. Riteña profesora Aracely proposed a series of basic lessons to be held free of charge, with volunteered teacher time, to get all students caught up on basic skills and thus break down the divisions that aligned place of residence with school success. Limited transportation, however, nipped this idea in the bud.

SOCIAL BELONGING AND MARGINALIZATION

In spite of the preceding examples of how students from Nambué specifically and all traveler students to some extent were negatively affected by institutionalized barriers to educational opportunities, many educators at SRHS still believed the problem with Nambueseños was that "they marginalize themselves." Riteña profesora Alodia told me they sat apart in the classroom. "It's rare that they integrate themselves," she noted. Later in our discussion, after talking about the "rivalry" between Nambué and Santa Rita, she insisted, "Couldn't it be that they [Nambueseños] marginalize themselves all by themselves?" Profesora Rosaura also presented Nambueseño students' isolation as resulting from their own free choice, claiming that if they did not participate or speak up in class it was because they did not want to. In contrast, a Nambueseña student admitted that when Nambueseño students did speak in class, their classmates cut them off. My own observations generally support this assertion. Profesor Efraín stated the dynamic this way: "I feel that they go around apart from the others. They themselves reject themselves within the [larger] group."[17] A Riteño student told me it was not Riteños who rejected Nambueseños but the other way around. Profesor Manuel, a young teacher from Santa Rita, explained that all students were equal—but that Nambueseños had always been marginalized. He said this resulted from the fact that "they have allowed people to call them [names]."

Not subscribing to the theory that Nambueseños isolate themselves, I will present the mechanisms of boundary maintenance that prevented the lines between Nambueseños and Riteños from becoming too blurred, even in the absence of clear, traditional categories of difference. I have shown that the traditional markers of ethnic difference (such as language, consciousness of kind, "blood," form of dress, and the like) did not distinguish among social categories in this school setting. Rather, class, perceived race and ethnicity, and place of residence were the axes along which identities and their relative values were construed. It is the intersection of these axes that sheds light on when one aspect of identity might take precedence and when another might do so. For Nambueseños and other travelers at SRHS, social marginalization was often interpreted as a matter of choice, although that was often far from the case.[18] How school culture manifested, reproduced, and enforced societal divisions is the topic of the remainder of this chapter.

THE SCHOOL'S MAINTENANCE OF SOCIETAL DIVISIONS
Stereotypes and Schooling

For Edward Spicer, the terminology a group uses to speak of itself and others is key to maintaining societal separations.[19] Various terms are employed by local communities to divide "us" from "them" in specific settings. Around Nambué and Santa Rita these terms included place affiliations and ethnic categorizations such as Cartagos versus Guanacastecos and *blancos* (whites) versus cholos or mestizos and *indios*. In the geographic context that is the focus of this book, these ethnic- and place-based divisions were reinforced through certain cultural practices such as foodways and other customs. Numerous people in both Nambué and Santa Rita spoke of derogatory terms for the opposing group that linked place or ethnicity to practice. Nambueseños chided their rivals with the name *"cartago come-cusuco"* (armadillo-eating Cartago). Some retorted with *"cholo come-camarón con caca"* (crap-covered shrimp-eating *cholo*), a phrase alluding to the practice of catching freshwater shrimp in the river and eating it there without elaborate preparation.[20]

Thus, places and ethnicities, as is often the case, are tied inseparably to certain stereotypes. Many of these stereotypes—such as those espoused by a racist seventh grader against Nambué—have been elucidated in previous chapters. Many (like Jaime's assumption that rain dances were held in Nambué) had no basis in reality. Nevertheless, these stereotypes can tell us much about the situation. Likewise, a group's compliance with stereotypical expectations may shed light on that group's relative academic "success."[21]

This has implications in the classroom setting for students seen to be noncompliant with the stereotypes of their group. Profesora Anatolia, a teacher of vocational classes, noted that discrimination against Nambueseño students had decreased because of a change over time in their manner of speaking. She added that it was lamentable that Nambueseño students had "lost" their form of speech (referring to the speech style typical of the entire province, often erroneously considered to be spoken only by Nambueseños). She lamented this loss because, as she expressed, "I think one should maintain certain customs. They have lost their form of speech, they have bettered it, relatively. Now they speak better than those before. I have spoken and worked here a long time, and I see this. They [Nambueseños], upon interacting with the people [pause] from here, they have become equal in this sense."

It is interesting that although Profesora Anatolia considered that the change in dialect was instrumental to the decrease in discrimination against Nambueseños, she lamented that change. A Nambueseña dropout recounted that in her first and only year of high school, a Spanish teacher (no longer employed at the high school in

1999) asked groups to write about how their communities had lived before. The group, containing only Nambueseño students, received a zero on the assignment for not describing and affirming stereotypes of Indians.

The same teacher, on a different occasion, was talking about the Apaches. The teacher suggested that the Nambueseño students might be able to tell the class more about them, given their common Indian classification.[22] When Nambueseño students refused to do so, out of a combination of offense and understandable ignorance regarding the Apaches of North America, the students were sent to the guidance counselor's office for punishment. Thus, stereotypes—whether based in reality or nonsense—did guide the ways in which students were judged for approximating or failing to uphold stereotypical expectations of them. Similar to what Bradley Levinson found, Nambueseño students at SRHS also "had to contend with both material limitations and the dominant, city-based construction of them as rural dwellers, or Indians."[23]

Nambueseños were not the only students subject to judgment based on stereotypes, however. One other set of students was equally limited by negative stereotypes. There was a community served by SRHS whose inhabitants may have enjoyed the same degree of relative wealth as Riteños but who had nowhere near their level of prestige. Puerto Sereno (also known as Sereno) was the only town in Santa Rita County not supported by an agricultural (primarily coffee-based) economy. It was a beach town popular among both international and local tourists. Numerous teachers criticized the students from the town for being affected by North American tourist culture. For some teachers, just a few students from Sereno fit the stereotype. For others, all students from Sereno were shadowed by a reputation for drug use and disorder.

Profesora Rosaura specified that the previous year (1998), certain students from Sereno had come to school with dyed hair and a different vocabulary—both of which she attributed to interaction with tourists. Many teachers, however, did not limit this reputation to specific students or one particular year. Profesora Rosa María, a teacher not from Santa Rita but tied more to the Santa Rita teachers' peer group than to the traveler teachers' group, explained that the most problematic students came from Sereno. She noted that Sereno had a "party" environment characterized by *pachangas* (loud, boisterous celebrations) and drugs "because many foreigners go there, and the students from Sereno want to do what they do." The librarian, another traveler teacher who identified more with the Riteño teachers' clique, said the students from Sereno had influences from the beach culture that typified their town. She elaborated on what constitutes beach culture: "They have adopted another personality because they relate more with foreigners. They [male students] have earrings and different hairstyles. They play at being plastic people. They have access to dollars."

Profesor Adán, a young teacher from Santa Rita, explained that students from Sereno were experiencing what he called "transculturation" and that this process "doesn't permit them to excel. They aren't interested in studying. Most have drug problems. Here in Santa Rita there were no drugs. They were introduced by students from Sereno. They're more interested in the beach." Another Riteña teacher, Profesora Eugenia, also used the term *transculturation* to explain Sereno students' alleged inferiority, noting "they are receiving a complete transculturation." She elaborated on this idea, commenting on the students' desire to imitate foreigners, who were "more careless. This has brought us big problems in the high school [in terms of] discipline. There is talk of their introducing drugs from there. It is a town that has been affected by the arrival of so much tourism. It makes one feel unsafe in that town. I felt fear [there]."

Other teachers, in discussing Sereno, brought up the common presence in the town of surfing, prostitution, fashion, birth control, and gringos—as if all five were equally dangerous and undesirable. Some mentioned that even mothers worked in hotels in Sereno (as opposed to most Riteña women who did not work outside the home), and students were allowed to attend dances freely. In a highly xenophobic town such as Santa Rita, outside (especially North American) influence spelled danger. Interestingly, only one of the numerous teachers who attributed drug use to North American influence acknowledged my connection to that region or seemed to note that I might take offense at the implications.

Profesor Arnoldo—neither a Riteño nor a traveler connected to the Riteño social group—explained, "The environment [in Sereno] is different because it is near the beach and has a great deal of foreign influence." He added, "Let me clarify," and he laughed nervously. "[Influence] of bad foreigners—because there are foreigners who behave themselves. Not all foreigners come here to misbehave. Some come to teach us many proper things." His next comment, "Don't blush," suggests that my unintentional reaction may have inspired this "clarification."

Several teachers, however, made an explicit connection between North American tourism and the consequent "bad environment." Profesora Marta Iris specified, "What we most need to improve in the high school, generally speaking, is to not permit the arrival of foreign influences . . . so that the students don't get off track." (Interestingly, the word she chose for "foreign" was not *extranjero* but *extraño*. Although both terms imply foreignness, the latter word also connotes strangeness.) The treatment of students from Sereno based on their approximation to these stereotypes could be severe. For some, it was merely a stigma. For others, according to Profesora Greis, a traveler teacher, it became a self-fulfilling prophecy. One seventh-grade girl from Sereno decided to drop out of school after being wrongly accused of drug use on campus. Teachers who knew her beyond the stereotypes convinced her to stay in school. A Sereno boy's suicide the year prior to my fieldwork was attributed to the stereotypical behavior considered true of students from that town. Profesor Ramiro, who knew the boy well, however, alluded to the possibility that the motivation for his death was linked more to his stereotypical categorization than to the validity of the stereotypes.

Several teachers describing students from Sereno noted their tendency to follow fashions that were different from those of other students. The verisimilitude of this stereotype seems doubtful, given the enforced use of uniforms at SRHS. Some staff members and students, however, noted the failings of the administration's attempts to erase such cultural boundaries. To begin with, the uniform guidelines specified, "Male students should have short, well-groomed hair, avoiding strange and extravagant hairstyles." Although I never heard teachers comment negatively about the practice—common among elite girls of Santa Rita—of dying blond highlights into their hair, boys from Sereno with blond highlights were criticized frequently.

TRACKING

One additional administrative practice also exacerbated the societal divides already present in the high school setting: placing students in the same grade level into separate sections. In theory, this was no reflection of place of residence, economic status, or any other social dividing force, given that it was tied to students' choices of vocational classes. (Each homeroom class was divided into two "blocks," determined by the vocational classes "selected" by students.) As we have seen, however, Riteño parents were more likely to be able to put their children in the preferred vocational workshops, whereas traveling students tended to get the dregs of workshops, and Nambueseño students—more often than students from other places— were sometimes removed from the classes of their choice and placed in less desirable workshops.

One principal result of this set of circumstances was that within every grade level at least one homeroom class was dominated by—if not exclusively constituted of—students from Santa Rita (in spite of their numerical minority in the earlier grades) and one was made up almost exclusively of poorer travelers, Nambueseños, and other relative social outcasts, such as students from Sereno and those from "respected" towns who for one reason or another did not uphold the image of ideal students. (Classes between these extremes consisted of a mix of Riteño and traveler students.) This practice of channeling certain students into particular classrooms or programs was by no means unique to the Riteño case.[24]

Profesora Rosaura explained that the elementary school in Santa Rita was so large that there were often thirty to sixty students who had been together in school since kindergarten, as opposed to groups as small as two or three students coming from some of the smaller, more rural schools. This gave rise to "teams" of students that ganged up on those from smaller schools when they met in the high school on unequal footing. These classes, dominated by Riteño students, were invariably viewed as containing the best students at each grade level. On the opposite extreme were the classes filled with Nambueseños and other seemingly less worthy students. There was evidence of this practice in various grade levels and years. In this chapter, however, I will focus on the most striking example of this practice that I observed throughout 1999—a seventh-grade class commonly thought by both students and teachers to be the worst class in school.

This homeroom class was known as section 7-5. The numbering system indicates that it was the fifth of five seventh-grade homeroom classes to fill up. Not coincidentally, it was the section with the least desirable vocational workshops. The section contained one Nambueseño student who had been removed from computer class against his will. Profesor Arnoldo, the class's homeroom teacher, acknowledged to me that in filling the class it seemed as if students had been chosen according to the criterion "this one is bad, this one is bad, this one is bad, we'll put them in this section."

Profesor Agustín commented, "These are a bunch of kids with a bunch of problems." He added, "And social problems at home." He did not specify the nature of those problems, but the class consisted of four Nambueseño students (all but two in the seventh grade), two girls from Sereno (out of four total in seventh grade; one of the two dropped out early on, and the other was accused of drug use and considered dropping out), only three Riteños (out of forty-two in seventh grade), and several poor students from other towns. Those from Santa Rita—coincidentally or not—were considered by peers or teachers homosexual, non-Catholic, poor, overweight, or some combination of these socially stigmatized characteristics. Teachers, however, did not always speak of them in these terms.

Rather, more frequently, the students of section 7-5 were discussed as learning disabled (not necessarily the case), disorderly, unmotivated, and "less good" students in general. Profesora Genofeva said to me mid-lesson, within the first few weeks of school and in front of the students of section 7-5, "Here there are only four or five [students] who are worth the effort." Later in the semester, however, she admitted that those few were the best students of all her seventh graders. The class was referred to, by both students and staff (including teachers not directly involved with these students), as the lowest end of the spectrum in terms of academic potential. One day the students in another seventh-grade classroom asked to be let out early (a common—and often effective—practice, especially by students from Santa Rita). The teacher refused, noting that the class was behind others and could not waste time. Jaime asked sarcastically, "What, and 7-5 is way ahead?" Sometimes staff members excluded section 7-5 altogether. Profesora Eugenia, responsible for teaching one subject to seventh graders, elected to teach all the sections of seventh graders except 7-5. In a meeting held with beauty pageant candidates, the director announced that representatives of all the sections were present. He then added "except 7-5 [pause], well, the whole high school." The implication was either that section 7-5 was not an integral part of the high school or that it contained no girls worthy of potential beauty queen status.

Early in the semester, students in 7-5 began to fulfill the teachers' prophecy about them—perhaps because of a lack of motivation or because of teachers' underwhelming efforts to cater to them. In any case, later in the semester 7-5's homeroom teacher, along with Profesora Marta Iris—a generally understanding Riteña teacher—gave students from 7-5 a pep talk in which they encouraged students to prove the stereotype wrong. This took place after the dropout rate from the class was recognized as unusually high. By the end of the semester, eight of the original twenty-three students who arrived the first day of class (34 percent) had dropped out. One other had considered doing so and was convinced to stay. At least one other decided not to return the following year, as she would have had to repeat the seventh grade.

Although section 7-5's poor academic performance was most often attributed to individual student failings, teachers clearly did not hold the same expectations for these students as they did for others from the start. This is not surprising, in light of the fact that students in 7-5 were those most "different" from the ideal student image. In a well-known study, George and Louise Spindler describe "Roger Harker," a teacher who considered himself, and was viewed by others, as a fair teacher who did not engage in preferential treatment and who taught students of various ethnic backgrounds.[25] The researchers found that Harker knew more about students most like himself (in terms of ethnic and class background) and paid more attention to them. Unwittingly and without overt racist intent, Roger Harker tended to reinforce dominant (and biased) notions that the white, middle-class students were "better" students and that students of color were less worthy of his attention. The tendency of teachers to direct their efforts toward students most like themselves was evident at SRHS during my year of fieldwork there. It was not limited to Riteño teachers aiming lessons at students from their community but was paralleled by traveler teachers, who at times favored traveler students. The disproportionate power of Riteño teachers in the school, their greater number of years of experience there, and a lower turnover rate for Riteño teachers, however, entrenched them as the standard against which all teachers were measured, just as students from their town played an analogous role among the student population.

SOCIAL DIVISIONS AMONG TEACHERS

The division between traveler teachers and those from Santa Rita was as marked as that between student groups. Animosity between the two subsets of teachers was high, and moral judgments about both groups resulted in the view that traveler teachers were liberal and those from the center of Santa Rita (as well as a few who no longer lived there but whose past residence in the town lumped them with this peer group) were moral and religious pillars of the community. The same transportation issues limiting traveler students limited traveler teachers' participation in extracurricular activities, thus leading many to believe they were less dedicated to the school's efforts. Profesora Rosaura, talking to Profesora Belisa, a traveler teacher, expressed her hope that a graduate of the high school would fill the position then occupied by Profesora Belisa so more Riteño teachers would be on staff. She did not appear to realize the offensiveness of her statement (which revealed her desire that the teacher she was speaking with be replaced by a local), although Profesora Belisa certainly did. Three of the more experienced Riteña teachers (Profesora Eugenia, Profesora Rosaura, and Profesora Marta Iris) individually reflected with nostalgia upon the halcyon era, years ago, when all teachers at the high school lived in Santa Rita.

Profesora Eugenia explained to me, "We, the older teachers, the old staff that exists here, are the best element of this high school [because of] the affection we have for the institution." She asked, rhetorically and fearfully, what would happen when they retired (an impending reality for most of them). She explained that she saw this group as "one of the strongest pillars [of SRHS]. It will fall down on us with the new staff not tied [personally] to the school. Most of us are from town. The young people [teachers] that are arriving are not of the community. Otherwise, [the high school] could pick itself up again." She concluded that the traveler teachers were the reason for the high school's deterioration. The retirement of the "pillars," which this teacher feared, was eagerly awaited by some traveler teachers. Some noted that nothing would change with regard to discrimination in the school until some of these "pillars" of the institution retired. Interestingly, this group of "pillars" decided among themselves to wear uniforms to school. Not all teachers adopted the uniform—it was mainly the self-proclaimed "pillars" (and two others) who set themselves apart in this manner.

The divisions between these groups were spoken of in terms similar to those used to describe student divisions. Those in power talked about others "separating themselves," "not integrating," and alluded to their self-marginalization from the larger teachers' community. Some labeled the division as one of experienced teachers versus newer ones. Given the high turnover of traveler teachers, however, these categories easily corresponded to those of place of residence. Only in the travelers' group (of which I was considered a member, for the most part), in my experience, was the relationship between exclusion and gossip by the Riteño teachers and the high turnover rate of travelers made explicit.

This division between traveler teachers and those from Santa Rita was by no means the only division among staff members. It was, however, one of the most salient and that which most greatly affected students with regard to the "Roger Harker effect."[26] Which students were most directly taught was very much tied to which students most nearly approximated the "pillars" in terms of class, race, ethnicity, and place of residence. This dynamic was observable in terms of which students were called on in class or spoken to directly, which teachers chatted with which students outside class, and in the nature of teachers' other interactions with students from prominent Riteño families as opposed to those with students from less privileged positions.

Preferential Treatment Inside the Classroom and Out

One student in section 7-5 was considered a shining star. This student—whom I'll call Wilmer—was tall and fair-skinned, hailed from a town near Santa Rita also considered a fairly white town, and had a non-Spanish, European first name. Teachers spoke to him often, directing their gaze specifically at him as they taught section

7-5. This happened especially in Profesora Genofeva's classroom; she also often left Wilmer in charge when she left the room. Wilmer's leadership soon became customary even while the teacher continued to preside over the class herself.

Once, Profesora Genofeva (a white European immigrant) was explaining that student groups would be required to give oral presentations. She gave the instructions, speaking to Wilmer and naming him directly: "Look, Wilmer, these are the presentation topics." Twice I observed Nambueseño students (Samuel and Marco) volunteering answers at the same time Wilmer offered a response. In both cases the teacher only acknowledged Wilmer's reply. In one case she responded, "Is Wilmer the only one who studied?" thus acknowledging that she did not notice the other volunteered responses. Samuel ceased participating verbally in class shortly thereafter. Marco continued, not visibly discouraged by the teacher's preferential treatment toward Wilmer, and he became one of the flag bearers for his class.

I witnessed a similar occurrence in another teacher's class. Profesora Alba (a white woman not from Santa Rita but who chose to wear the uniform characteristic of the Riteña teachers' clique) solicited examples of the literary topic being discussed. Marco and Samuel offered examples, as did Wilmer. Neither Nambueseño's response was commented upon or recognized in any way. The teacher also looked directly at Wilmer as she taught and requested that he give summaries of what they had studied, asking other students to pay attention to his response.

This same teacher provided the most striking examples of Roger Harker–like behavior that I saw. In various classes with seventh graders, Profesora Alba called on individual students to read aloud. All those called upon were from Santa Rita. Once the supply of Riteño students was exhausted, I expected her to turn to other student readers. She did not. Instead, she asked the Riteño students to read aloud one or even two more times each. On another occasion, this teacher requested volunteered responses. The students she called upon (by acknowledging their raised hands) were almost invariably from Santa Rita. At one point a Nambueseño volunteered and accompanied his hand raising with an enthusiastic "me, teacher, me, me, me." Profesora Alba did not acknowledge him.

Such behavior was standard for Profesora Alba's interactions with her five seventh-grade classes. With other levels, however, the dynamic was slightly different. There I did see her encourage participation by students from various towns, although she still called upon students from Santa Rita with greater frequency. Profesora Alba was not the only teacher to exhibit these behaviors. Two other teachers from Santa Rita also called on students from their town with greater frequency than they called on other students.

In addition to watching which teachers acknowledged which students' responses, I studied where they directed their gaze with regard to where students from different places chose to sit (in most cases) or where they were assigned to sit (in others). Several teachers' gazes did include the entire classroom. The times I saw this comprehensive gaze by teachers who habitually called on Riteño students, it occurred in sections dominated by Riteño students. Profesor Agustín, a teacher usually good at including the whole class, during one class looked at each student at least once, except for the row containing only two students—both from Sereno. Profesora Eugenia, known for assigning seats, rarely looked up from her lesson material. When she did, she stared at a row filled entirely by Riteño students. Profesor Adán, a Riteño teacher, stared disproportionately at one student: the daughter of the province's representative to the National Legislature. Two non-Riteño teachers (Profesores Sergio and Belisa) also followed the Roger Harker pattern in terms of looking more frequently at students of color who were not from Santa Rita. Interestingly, these two teachers were the subject of a controversial meeting between Riteño parents and two Riteño teachers (Profesoras Rosaura and Eugenia), which resulted in complaints being made to the director about the two traveler teachers' methods.[27]

Teachers' greater identification with students more like themselves was also visible in their unofficial interaction with students, whether outside of class or during group work in the classroom. At these times it was telling to focus on which teachers chatted with which students. Profesora Alba frequently spent time chatting with girls from Santa Rita, arranging for the class to acknowledge their birthdays, allowing them frequent "bathroom" breaks (rarely used for this purpose but rather for walking around school and conversing), and otherwise involving herself with them socially. This teacher once commented that a particular group of girls was her favorite in one section of seventh graders. She did not refer to them as Riteñas, although they were, but rather as "that little group of little girls that always sits in front and answers questions" (as if the girls' frequent participation was unrelated to the teacher's pedagogical style). I observed the same sort of casual behavior with Riteño students by Profesoras Natalia and Eugenia—both of whom lived in Santa Rita. Once, outside school, I witnessed Profesora Eugenia talking to Jaime about who the smart kids were (invariably Riteños) from other sections.

Other actions also betrayed Riteño or white teachers' greater familiarity with Riteño students. Profesora Alba reviewed student homework during class and commented on it aloud. She gave only positive comments on Riteño work, whereas mestizo or *moreno* students' work tended to be criticized aloud. Sometimes in class she pointed to the latter students and asked others what their names were, even several months into the school year. In contrast, she knew the names of her Riteño students. In one such incident she addressed a Nambueseño student as "you [singular] in the corner" and then added "excuse me. I don't know your [plural] names." It was unclear if the plural "your" referred to students from Nambué, students in the corner, or students of color, as the students in the corner fit all three descriptions.

Profesora Alba talked about how preferences for students from important or prestigious Riteño families ran rampant in the school, adding "although I may not have [these preferences]." She noted that such favoritism, evident in her colleagues, was based on whether a student was the child of a fellow teacher or from a wealthy or prominent Riteño family. I talked to Jaime about the general preferential treatment toward such students. He openly admitted that a student from one of these families was less likely to get in trouble for being out of uniform, not having a shirt tucked in properly, or committing some other infraction.

Although my view of which students received more favorable treatment is a privileged one (in that it is from the perspective of a person who observed numerous classes and teachers with an eye for this dynamic specifically), students also noted differential treatment by teachers. They talked about this in terms of "preferences" of certain teachers for particular students. After several students brought this issue up on their own, I began to ask specific questions about where they noted evidence of such preferences. A student from Nambué explained that when there were extracurricular activities such as raffles, traveler students were not informed of them. A student from Sereno said teachers preferred sections that contained more Riteño students, as well as students who were prettier or more handsome than others. Amelia, the only *morena* beauty pageant candidate, also noted beauty as a reason for preferential treatment, although she did not specify if this was a comment about herself or about a classmate. Another student noted that the "most popular" students (and those named were Riteños) were given special treatment. Numerous students brought up the preferential treatment accorded to teachers' children.

Certain teachers commented on being pressured by other teachers to give a colleague's failing child a passing grade. Profesora Anatolia noted that she had been pressured to raise grades for children of prominent Riteño community members and teachers' children, sometimes to the point that the priest tried to convince her to do so. In another case, the regional representative to the National Legislature pressured a faculty member to raise his child's grade.

Evidence of favoritism with regard to teachers' children's grades was striking, given several Nambueseño students' allegations that they had failed a class (and sometimes, thus, a whole year) by one point or a fraction of a point. At least three Nambueseño students had this experience. In contrast, one day Profesoras Natalia and Eugenia invited me to wait for the bus with them. One said to the other, matter-of-factly, that her son got a 38 (out of 100, where 65 was the minimum passing grade) on the first quiz in her class and that he believed he had also failed the most recent one. The other teacher said she did not recall the boy's grade on the recent quiz but assured his mother—her colleague—that "he won't fail my class."

Profesor Antonio noted that Profesora Marta Iris's daughter tried to pressure him to raise her grade (without seeking her mother's backing). He commented, "A teacher's child can pressure more." Indeed, a Nambueseña mother told me of a teacher failing to count fifteen points in her daughter's final test score. The girl brought the math error to the teacher's attention, and the teacher corrected her grade. The mother, however, wondered aloud what would happen if a student felt uncomfortable pointing out a teacher's error. This was a common fear, given that many teachers were thought to hold grudges against certain students—including those who pointed out errors.

In a situation I discuss further in Chapter 5, the posters on a classroom wall offended some Nambueseño students. They did not want to bring their indignation to the teacher's attention, however, for in doing so they might risk being disliked. Another Nambueseña student (who had dropped out prior to my year of study in the high school, citing discrimination as her reason) told me about a different set of offensive, racist posters students from Santa Rita (according to her analysis of the situation) had put up in the girls' bathroom. She recalled that she and some friends tore them up and threw them out—and were consequently punished for vandalism. Evidently, the term *vandalism* did not encompass the placement of unauthorized, offensive materials but included only their removal.

This same student told me of an incident in which two students—the daughters of two different teachers—stole items from the truck delivering soft drinks to campus. She noted that had any other students done this, it would have been grounds for expulsion. School officials let these students off the hook, however. Although numerous people (among them parents, students, and teachers) complained of favoritism such as this, some teachers with relatives in school insisted they were stricter with students who were their family members.

At an early staff meeting (one month into the school year), teachers urged the director to apply the same rules to all children. The director commented, "When it's your turn [implying when it happens to your child], everyone jumps. But when it's another's [it's] 'apply all the rules.'" Profesora Natalia, whose son was in the school at the time, stated that she preferred that all the rules be applied to her child as well. This was, however, the same teacher who was concerned that her son would not pass a class when he was twenty-seven points below a passing grade.

One of the most revealing events in terms of favoritism was a staff meeting held toward the end of the school year whose purpose was, in the words of the principal, "to see if there are students who can be helped—to see who has a chance." In other words, the meeting was held for all teachers to declare which students were in danger of failing their classes, which students would be likely to fail the year, and—most significant—which students would be spoken for by teachers willing to pass them in spite of their failing grades. In addition to noting which students were failing and which ones were given a second chance, I noted the quantity of racial descriptors attached to students with failing grades.

A transfer student from the Atlantic Coast was listed as failing. Profesora Eugenia clarified, "That little black girl." The name of a *moreno* boy from Santa Rita was listed, and the same teacher explained that he was failing, "but I took him out of the oven" (meaning she had decided to pass him). Profesor Agustín joked, "He burned!" (In the end, this student failed.) When the name of a white student from Santa Rita whose family was prominent in the Catholic Church was called, Profesora Eugenia called out in surprise, "What's that about?" The student passed in the end.

Certain students from prominent Riteña families were announced to "have been passed" (seemingly anonymously). One Riteño student mentioned as failing was defended by a teacher who noted that he was "helpful" and "obliging" and that his family was of limited means. In the end, this student was still on the list of those who failed the year without the chance of taking makeup exams (posted for all to see). Although of all the students in school fifteen Riteños were listed as failing at the time of the meeting, in the end only four did so. Only one was from a known Riteño family. Another was Jacobo, the student who noted "I won't stay Indian. I'll keep studying."

When Jacobo's name came up at the meeting, he was failing seven classes. Following guffaws, Profesora Aracely noted that he had dropped out (because he had been told he would fail conduct) and later was convinced to return to school. When he realized he was still failing four classes (as a result of having dropped out temporarily), however, he decided not to take his other exams. Profesora Aracely explained, "Why kill himself [studying] anymore?" Nobody else expressed sympathy.

One student from Santa Rita who would have been on the list of students in danger of failing was saved by a teacher who agreed to repeat his grade on a first trimester exam for a later one he missed because of medical reasons. Carmen, from Nambué, was in the same situation, but the teachers were unwilling to let her make up exams—in spite of her documentation of having had surgery and permission from the principal to miss school—unless a committee of teachers approved it. She had me, the anthropologist, deliver her letter of explanation and doctor's documentation to a teacher on the committee. Later, however, she found out that the committee had not informed teachers that she had permission to make up exams. She talked to Profesor Arturo, a teacher on the committee, who realized that Profesora Remedios, the teacher who had the letter, had withheld it from the other committee members.

In the end, the Nambueseña student was allowed to make up her exams. It appeared at the meeting, however, that such rigmarole was not required of the Riteño student, whose teacher merely repeated a prior grade. The previous year, five students had failed math class for the year. Four of them were passed on to the next grade in spite of this. Carmen was the one who was not. The next year, students turned in a group project to Profesor Teodoro. Carmen's grade was over twenty points lower than the other students in her group who had done the same work. She mentioned that Profesora Remedios as well as Profesor Teodoro had grudges against her.

Many students talked about teachers' grudges. Some talked about feeling they were under the surveillance of teachers waiting for them to make mistakes. Others felt certain teachers *se les llevaban clavo* (held a grudge). Profesor Miguel acknowledged that some of his colleagues acted on grudges, to students' detriment. Whether through preferences toward certain students or grudges against others, SRHS was by no means a level playing field. For some, it was even considered a battlefield.

This became apparent from the first day of classes, as teachers talked in war metaphors about preparing for battle, about conduct grades that could be considered "arms," and about parents of students as "double-edged swords." Some teachers feared student retaliation (toward their cars, motorcycles, homes, and, in one case, a teacher's pet parakeet) for disciplining students or reporting misbehavior. Some feared parental retaliation through lawsuits. In many ways, opposing forces between teachers and students and between teachers and parents were drawn into focus. Nowhere were battle lines drawn more clearly, however, than among students.

STUDENT DIVISIONS

Spatial Territory and Peer Groups

Students maintained divisions among themselves through numerous mechanisms, including the maintenance of spatial territories both within and outside the classroom, violence (verbal and physical), gossip, stereotypes, ridicule and teasing, and, above all, the use of nicknames and labels. Jacobo, always an insightful student, noted certain spaces on campus where teachers gossiped about one another and others where they gossiped about students. Different factions among teachers seemed to have spaces on campus that served as home bases, or places somehow owned by each group. Some teachers would peek into the teachers' lounge to see if it was being "owned" by the group associated with it. Depending on who was present, they would or would not enter. The administrative office and the family-owned café across from the school served as spaces that were in theory open to any staff member but that were in practice places of comfort for different teacher cliques.

Students used space in a similar fashion. The "bad kids" owned one part of the cafeteria. Some students from Santa Rita would never eat there. Others ate there together out of necessity, since they received lunch scholarships, but they left that stigmatized space as soon as they finished eating. Profesoras Rosaura and Alodia noted that students from Nambué generally sat apart from others in the classroom. Both suggested that this occurred at the beginning of the year, before students got to know one another, and that it changed by the end of the year. My observations and careful charting of where students sat suggest otherwise. Nambueseño students, especially boys, tended to stick together inside the classroom (usually toward the back). Nambueseño boys, regardless of grade level, hung out together outside of class. Nambueseña girls tended to find friendships within their homeroom sections, as was customary for most students at SRHS.

Some Nambueseña graduates noted that they did spend free time in school not only with fellow Nambueseñas but also with relatives, especially outside of class. I did not notice this in 1999, however. In questioning students about their closest friends from school, most Nambueseños noted that their best friends were other Nambueseños or students from small towns other than Santa Rita. There was little overlap between the Nambueseño and Riteño peer groups, generally speaking.

A few Nambueseño boys talked about resorting to violence to put an end to Riteño teasing and ridicule. Most, however, fought back with similar strategies. As is common in all high schools with which I have had any connection, gossip, rumor, stereotypes, and name-calling played a large role in defining all-but-permanent cleavages between social groups.[28] At SRHS, however, name-calling was taken to new extremes.

Nicknames: Origins and Implications

From studies I conducted prior to my year of fieldwork at SRHS in 1999, I knew Nambueseños tended to be labeled with stigmatizing, offensive nicknames that came to replace their actual names among classmates. After a short time of observation at the high school, however, I realized that practically all students, regardless of place of residence, had nicknames. These nicknames fell along a continuum from ridiculous or embarrassing at best to offensive at worst. This became clear early on, as I asked students if they liked their nicknames. One student replied, "Who's going to like a nickname?" I soon found that teachers had nicknames as well. I began to solicit lists of nicknames from students, and from these lists several trends became manifest.

Many students' nicknames were drawn from comments made in class that became embarrassing, from words that were mispronounced, or from names that stuck with classmates for one reason or another. A student who referred to the school's white pigs with black spots as "Dalmatian pigs" was stuck with that nickname: Chancha Dálmata. A student who sang the national anthem, mistaking the word *prestigio* (prestige) for *prestiño* (a flaky pastry), inadvertently provoked both his own nickname and that of his female twin. He was Prestiño and she became Prestiña.

Some nicknames were born of plays on words from students' given names. A girl named Clareth (pronounced with a silent h) was called Cloret after the name brand of a breath-freshening gum. Others were named for cartoon or television characters or singers they resembled physically. Often, these nicknames were innocuous. Larger girls, however, were often given names of Worldwide Wrestling Federation personalities, thus commenting on a body type not in keeping with the societal ideal. Sometimes this tied into race, as darker-skinned children were named for famous black television or literary characters. A favorite was Cocorí, the Afro-Caribbean child protagonist of a Costa Rican children's book from the Atlantic Coast,[29] thus proving that multicultural materials alone do not make for antiracist education.[30] In the case of certain students called Cocorí on campus, the nickname—considered cruel by students—proves that if not taught with a deliberately antiracist message, multicultural readings may only provide fuel for the fire.

Sexuality came into play in the imposition of nicknames for boys deemed homosexual and girls with reputations for sleeping around. Some heterosexual boys were given nicknames for *not* sleeping around, thus elucidating a common double standard. One girl considered experienced beyond her years was known as La Periférica (the name of a bus that makes many stops) and Vaso de Agua (Glass of Water—*porque todo el mundo la toma* [because everyone drinks/takes her]). Another girl's nickname was less explicit. This girl, not considered promiscuous per se but known to be sexually active with her longtime boyfriend, was known sarcastically as Monja (Nun). Two promiscuous female students from prominent Riteño families, however, had nicknames that did not reflect this promiscuity, although graffiti on desks and talk around campus demonstrated that it was commonly thought to be the case. Another girl considered prudish had the English word *freezer* for a nickname, displaying yet another double standard.[31] Many students also had nicknames based on adaptations of the name or nickname of their significant other.

Salient physical features provided inspiration for many nicknames. Kids with big eyes were called Buho (owl). A tall skinny boy had the name Tubo Pevecé (PVC tubing). Most often, these names did not pass judgment on the pronounced feature but merely drew attention to it. That was not the case, however, for girls who were named La Tule or La Segua, after renowned ugly, malevolent female antagonists in local lore. Students with blue eyes were called Gato, Gata, or Felino (Cat or Feline).

Whether racial nicknames were an extension of names based on salient features or whether they belonged to another category is unclear. They existed for both white students (although few in number) and *moreno* students. When I asked students which names were considered mean, however, students often responded only to names about sexuality and race other than whiteness, such as "Indio." Some of these included Cocorí, Mono Jamaiquino (Jamaican Monkey), Cara de Mono (Monkey Face), Pocahontas (a girl not from Nambué who was considered to "look Indian," named such by Jaime), Cholo (meaning mestizo or acculturated Indian—for a boy not from Nambué), and Chola (for a darker girl from Santa Rita) as opposed to India (Indian) for her classmate from Nambué.

The girl known as India once asked me the difference between Chola and India. I suggested the explanation given previously, and she did not have an alternative one. I asked if the Riteña known as La Chola got upset when she was called this. "La India" replied, "Surely they call her that out of affection." I asked if she is called La India out of affection as well. She responded, "I don't care, but supposedly it is ugly." Profesora Delia assured me that students called Cholo or Indio were called such out of affection. Most students with names that reflected their Indianness took their nicknames to be offensive. Whether each individual who called them by a nickname had racist intentions is not necessarily the issue here. It makes sense that these labels, with their long-standing history of negative connotations, would hold negative meaning for their targets regardless of the name-caller's intent.[32]

In one instance, Profesor Teodoro approached Carmen, a Nambueseña, in front of her peers and asked her to take some fliers "to the Indians" (to Nambué). She felt offended by his statement, although he later insisted he meant no offense. The incident led to a debate between Profesor Teodoro and myself. Later, Profesor Teodoro took his anger with me out on the student's grade and threatened to fail her for the year. He was unwilling to consider that, despite his intent, enough people at SRHS had used the term *Indian* in a derogatory way to ensure that it was taken as offensive. He considered that being careful with his usage of the term was tantamount to babying Nambueseños.

Nambueseños tended to have a disproportionate number of race-based nicknames. Often these were combined with other offensive elements as well. Some Nambueseño boys had feminized racial names, such as Negra (Black Girl).[33] I asked one boy's fellow students why he was called this. They said, "Because he's *moreno.*" I then asked why they used the feminine form, and they replied that they did so merely to add insult. A girl who dropped out because of discrimination was called Sexy India (Sexy Indian Girl). One Nambueseño's nickname invoked the stereotype of Nambueseños' poor speech. Classmates said his nickname, Gorila (Gorilla), came from the fact that he talked like a gorilla. Federico, a boy from a white family that lived in Nambué, was known as Carne Garrobo (Carne [de] Garrobo—Iguana Meat)—likely an allusion to the stereotypical foodways of Cartagos.

Some of the nicknames that referred to whiteness included Pan Blanco (White Bread) for a boy from Santa Rita, Chancho Blanco (White Pig) for a boy from a small town far from both Nambué and Santa Rita, Chisa Gringa (Gringa Squirrel) for a white, hyperactive Riteña, and Morenazo (Big Moreno) for a very pale, white, skinny Riteño.

A few students had no nicknames (or none that were relayed to me). They tended to be white, popular Riteño students. Interestingly, given the sexualization of nicknames for sexually active girls, a thirteen-year-old girl who missed the first few weeks of school after giving birth had no nickname. In providing me with the list of their classmates' nicknames, a class dominated by Riteños did not know the actual name of their classmate from Nambué. One had to ask another, using the boy's nickname, "What's Michael Jackson's name?"

Teachers' nicknames were most often based on salient physical features, as well as teaching style (in the case of Sentinela—Sentinel—for Profesor Sergio, a teacher who never let students get away with cheating on exams). Again, those without nicknames (eight according to some counts and ten by others) were white teachers from Santa Rita. One of these, however—Profesor Eugenia—who had no nickname according to two lists, was called "Hitler" on another list. This is interesting, given her status as one of the "pillars" of the institution and a teacher responsible for discrimination in her class. I asked some students if teachers without nicknames lacked them because they were well liked. Students responded, unconvincingly, "No, they just don't inspire any."

The mechanisms discussed here for maintaining social divisions are varied. Some were intentional, although many were unconscious. Some were meant to provoke pain, and some that were hurtful were assumed to be innocuous. At any rate, the ways the communities involved—the administration, teachers, and students—marked boundaries between one group and another were effective. Through these mechanisms, students learned where they were assumed to belong within the social hierarchy. Most of the ways in which teachers let students know which of them were considered deserving students and which were not were unconscious. The following chapters address more direct teaching of identity and items of curriculum within the classroom.

NOTES

1. "Here there are only four or five that are worth the effort."
2. See Bourricaud 1975: 351. Levinson 2001: 150 also explains how the category of "rural dwellers" is linked to accent, skin color, dress, taste in music, and place of residence, thus noting that status is tied to place of residence in a variety of ways.

3. See de la Cadena 1995: 333 for a similar situation in Peru.

4. See Luykx 1999: 165–166; McCarthy and Crichlow 1993: xix for further discussion of gendered experiences of education.

5. Di Leonardo 1984: 218–219.

6. Anzaldúa 1987: 16; de la Cadena 1995; Parsons 1975: 66; Silverblatt 1987: 198–199; Wade 1997: 103.

7. Wade 1997: 103. See also Ramos 1998: 164–166; Silverblatt 1987: 67 for additional comments on the feminization of colonized peoples.

8. Spicer 1971: 799.

9. See Dolby 2001: 35; Luykx 1999: 119 for similar school divisions revolving around those who come to school from farther away and those who live nearby. In Dolby's work, the rurality of those who traveled to school from farther away also led to problems with access to schooling, similar to those I discuss in this chapter.

10. See Luykx 1999: 238 for a similar anecdote.

11. See Dolby 2001: 38 for a similar situation.

12. See Luykx 1999: 146 for further comments on the expense of "free" education; see Arnove 1986: 3 for a similar critique of Nicaraguan education.

13. The costs mentioned here are high for families of limited means. Still, these examples are considerably less extreme than what Luykx 1999: 249 found in a normal school in Bolivia, where sexual favors were allegedly traded for grades.

14. See López, Assáel, and Neumann 1984: 8 for additional commentary on school success and economic status.

15. See Luykx 1999: 82 for another account of the surveillance of students off campus. See also Scott 1990: 3 for critical comments on the role of surveillance in power relations.

16. See McNamara Horvat and Antonio 1999: 333 for a similar case.

17. The implication of this and previous comments is that Nambueseños isolated themselves because of an inferiority complex; in contrast, Levinson 2001: 206 claims some students at the school in which he conducted his research saw other students as separating themselves out of aloofness.

18. See Cousins 1999: 299 for a similar analysis.

19. Spicer 1971: 799.

20. See Yon 2000: 82 for comments on the racialization of cultural practice.

21. See Sibley 1995: 18, 100 for additional commentary on the value of studying stereotypes.

22. See Dolby 2001: 53 for a comparable situation in which South African teachers taught about an "imagined Zuluness" based on stereotypes.

23. Levinson 2001: 149.

24. See MacLeod 1987: 113 on the role of U.S. schools in the perpetuation of inequality.

25. Spindler and Spindler 1982.

26. Ibid.

27. These two teachers also tried to incorporate more innovative pedagogical strategies in their classrooms to encourage students to relate to the material individually and to make them think rather than simply memorize. This may also have influenced parents' evaluations of their teaching ability. López, Assáel, and Neumann note that the pedagogical techniques of rote memorization, copying, and dictation result in "a vertical and

authoritative relationship between the teacher and the students" (1984: 360; translation mine). Both these pedagogical techniques and the resulting authoritative role of teachers were common at SRHS and were perhaps preferred, given that ultimate "success" (passing the national exams) was dependent upon memorization and a strict adherence to the national curriculum.

28. See Cazden and John 1971: 267 for the role of teasing as social control; Oboler 1995: xvi for the power of labeling. López, Assáel, and Neumann 1984: 309, 362 discuss labeling as both a form of discrimination and as integral to the danger of forming self-fulfilling prophecies.

29. Gutiérrez 1918.

30. See Luykx 1999: 148, 308; McCarthy 1993: 293–294; McCarthy and Crichlow 1993: xxi; Sleeter 1993: 157; Yon 2000: 20 for additional discussion of how multicultural curricula are not necessarily antiracist. See also McCarthy 1993 for a more extensive discussion of what multicultural education must encompass to be effective.

31. See McLaren 1982: 22 for more on the double bind of high school girls with regard to sexual activity and social status.

32. See Allport 1974: 112.

33. Ann Arnett Ferguson 2000: 173 also discusses femininity as an insult for male schoolchildren.

5

"Nada más de estar usando la lógica"[1]

CURRICULUM AND TEACHING METHODS IN SRHS

JOAQUÍN, A RITEÑO SEVENTH GRADER, BROUGHT ME HIS RECENTLY GRADED English exam and asked me to look over a section he got wrong. The instructions called for students to arrange the disconnected parts of a dialogue taken from their workbooks in a logical order. The "correct" answer involved putting the dialogue in the order it was presented in the workbook, although the teacher had assured me she would accept other valid arrangements as well. I ordered the parts of the dialogue in a way that made sense to me as an English speaker. My ordering of the phrases matched Joaquín's exactly.

As the teacher, Profesora Eugenia, reviewed that section of the exam, Joaquín asked if there might be other perspectives on how the parts of the dialogue could be ordered. Profesora Eugenia responded, "Look, you all have the workbook. Had anyone done it in a [different but] logical order, I would have accepted it as correct." As he called out the "correct" answers with his classmates, Joaquín asked Profesora Eugenia if a given phrase could be placed elsewhere in the dialogue. She responded curtly, "One would have to see about that"—although she did not do so. When Profesora Eugenia had finished reviewing the entire test and left students to work in groups, Joaquín took his test to her and declared that I found his ordering of the dialogue reasonable. She replied, "It doesn't sound right to me." Then she announced loudly, "I'll accept it. This time I'll accept it but not next time, OK? This time I'll take it." She said to the entire class, "Look, Joaquín's is an exceptional case. In Joaquín's case I accepted it, but only this time. No more using logic. You need to study."

Profesora Eugenia's wording, placing "using logic" and "study" in opposition to one another, is telling in light of the dominant teaching methods used in Santa Rita High School (SRHS). In a system that revolved, with few exceptions, around rote learning and memorization, thinking excessively about the curriculum—much less questioning the teachers' authority—was not encouraged, to say the least.[2] This chapter examines the explicit teachings at SRHS and the ways they were conveyed to students, in a country in which citizens pride themselves on their educational system. In addition, the chapter will illuminate the extracurricular teachings students received, what teachers perceived their roles to include, and how the school's physical condition provided other limitations to learning. Ultimately, I question how well SRHS served its students.

Costa Ricans often brag about having more teachers than soldiers.[3] Very infrequently do they acknowledge that this means little, given the country's lack of a military. The seventh-grade civics textbook used at SRHS boasted that "since the beginning of its history as a State and, later, as a Republic, Costa Rica has . . . invested more in books, classrooms, and chalk than other nations have dedicated to weapons."[4] Another point of pride is the constitutional guarantee of free and obligatory education for all, from preschool through high school, although this guarantee was not evident in practice. According to a 1994 United Nations study, the average Costa Rican adult had not completed elementary school.[5] Economic limitations were in part responsible for this. Attitudes surrounding education beyond elementary school also played a role. Particularly in Santa Rita, where Catholicism was all-important, schooling was at times equated with self-centeredness. Both Father Sánchez and the bishop who visited Santa Rita annually gave sermons criticizing those who claimed to have no time for Mass yet were quick to allocate time to higher education rather than spiritual development. Just as the popularly stated pride in the state of education in Costa Rica was overstated, given the reality of limited educational opportunities, the general description of secondary educational offerings exceeded Riteño reality.

The first nine years of schooling (six in elementary school and the first three years of high school) are considered "basic general education." The first three years of high school are referred to as "the third cycle." In theory, students can choose between a strictly academic track and a vocational track as a fourth cycle.[6] In the region where I conducted my research, the first option was not available. There was no secondary school reasonably near that was geared solely toward an academic track. Students with the economic means to pay for transportation could attend a vocational school nearby whose course offerings included ecotourism, secretarial skills, accounting, and mechanical skills. Most, however, had no choice but to attend SRHS, which had a primarily agricultural focus. There, academic courses are combined with vocational ones throughout the students' mandatory five years of high school education. After that, students can choose to take an additional year of vocational courses to earn a certificate in addition to the diploma earned after the fifth year of high school, provided they pass the standardized tests administered across the nation by the Ministry of Education.

CURRICULAR OFFERINGS

Three noted scholars of Costa Rican society note that in public schools, "twenty-four hours a week are devoted to Spanish, English, French, social studies (with emphasis on Costa Rica), math, general science, religion, civics, family life, industrial arts (shop), plastic arts, music, and physical education."[7] Furthermore, Mavis, Richard, and Karen Biesanz contend that in the tenth and eleventh grades, subjects such as philosophy, psychology, physics, chemistry, and biology are added, as well as a choice of English or French and a requirement of community service.[8] Once again, the reality of school in Santa Rita was somewhat different. Schedules were arranged to allow for twelve academic lessons (forty minutes each) or three to four vocational lessons (up to two hours each) per day, but frequent teacher absence, conflicting meetings, and classroom time spent on uniform checks and classroom cleanliness resulted in a far-reduced quantity of time spent on the curriculum. The topics outlined by the Biesanzes were for the most part relevant to the curriculum at SRHS, with the exception of French, community service, family life, and philosophy. Furthermore, as discussed in Chapter 4, whether students could take industrial or plastic arts depended on their opportunity to "choose" these vocational workshops, which, in turn, depended largely on their status and place of residence.

The courses taught to all students at SRHS were Spanish, English, math, physics, social studies, civics, music, religion (unless students were exempt[9]), physical education, physics, and "guidance" (occasional group meetings with the guidance counselors, scheduled as regular weekly classes). Students in the tenth and eleventh grades also received psychology, chemistry, and biology classes. The vocational workshops offered were "creative minds in search of automated solutions" (computers), "let's reproduce our plants," "the exploitation of lesser species" (raising chickens), "manual food production techniques," "the food industry," "the construction of small furniture," "cutting and crafting" (sewing), "let's produce in the garden," "techniques of textile artisanry," "food preparation" (cooking), "the industrialization of meat and milk," "drafting," "production of meat and milk," "techniques in leatherwork," "sustainability of natural resources," and "silk-screening." These workshops were considered "exploratory workshops" from which students could choose their area of specialization in tenth and eleventh grades, focusing on carpentry, the textile industry (sewing), agroindustry ("*agroindustria*"—the business end of agriculture), and farming ("*agropecuaria*"—courses in zoology and botany).

The content of some academic courses (such as math, physics, chemistry, biology, and physical education) was fairly straightforward. The content of other courses, however, merits a more detailed discussion, given that the curricula followed by public schools generally say a great deal about what is worth learning in a particular culture, as they form the basis of what every adult national subject "ought" to know. Dominant or hegemonic social biases are inherent in what has been selected as curriculum and how it is taught.[10] The seventh-grade civics textbook explained schooling as the "process by which a community transmits its culture with the object of assuring its existence."[11] The text's authors note the role of school in community and vice versa and how the bonds created therein may hinge on such things as ethnic belonging:

> The manner of being of a community determines, to a large extent, the principal features that mark the high school. The physical, social, economic, political, and cultural space[s] where it is located put their stamp on the life within the institution. . . . In this case, we refer to [community] as the physical, social, economic, political, and cultural space where the high school lives and is located. The term *community* presupposes the existence of ties among people that form it and that make them feel part of the group. The types of ties that are established depend on many factors: the place where it [the community] is located, the ethnic origin of its inhabitants, their socio-cultural condition, and the activities they practice, among others.[12]

Indeed, issues of ethnic origin and place did relate to a sense of belonging in the community in question. In this chapter I examine what exactly was presented as "cultural memory" and what was omitted from it, in the interest of elucidating just how this particular school made its students feel like "part of the group" (or not) and on what bases.

Vocational workshops offered at the school taught different processes or stages integral to production and marketing in various industries. Students in agriculture classes unloaded sacks of feed; raised chickens, pigs, and cattle; castrated and butchered pigs; made milk and meat products; learned business techniques to market those products; and sold them on and around campus. Sewing courses taught basic pattern making, sewing, ironing, and embroidery techniques, as well as business skills to market sewn products. Food industry courses taught the composition, production, use, and preservation of certain food products; the preparation and cooking of foods; and the sale of cooked, baked, or pickled goods. Students in carpentry classes went from learning the basic use of various tools to building small items such as towel racks to building and finishing furniture such as armoires and beds that were sold locally or used in students' homes. Arts and crafts classes studied line drawing and made items that could be displayed in students' homes or sold as souvenirs.

Spanish classes at SRHS aimed to teach grammar, oral and written skills surrounding language use, and literature. The variety of Spanish grammar taught included forms not generally used in Costa Rica (but that are characteristic of Castilian Spanish). The literature studied in these courses (following the Ministry of Education's mandates) included works by national authors, as well as classics such as *Don Quixote* and works by Gabriel García Márquez and Isabel Allende. The teachers of these classes—Profesoras Rosaura and Alba (a Riteña and a traveler, respectively)—discussed the ways literature allowed them to teach other concepts to students.

Profesora Rosaura spoke of the capacity of García Márquez's works to open discussion on issues such as virginity, gender equality, and sex education. Profesora Alba taught students that the stories they read were related to reality in numerous ways. She related the messages from class readings to the ways we, as humans, enclose ourselves within limits and to common social situations such as abandonment and adultery. Students in the class also read *Marcos Ramírez,* an autobiographical novel by Costa Rican author and activist Carlos Luis Fallas in which Costa Rica's educational system is critically described as wrought with favoritism and pedagogical downfalls such as a focus on rote learning, thus providing an accurate criticism of these students' actual learning environment.[13]

English classes, taught by speakers with limited English proficiency, focused on grammar and vocabulary but also included other topics addressed through reading comprehension sections and translations. Profesora Yolanda, a young traveler teacher whose class involved slightly more focus on speaking than Profesora Eugenia's class, noted that among the topics addressed in her class were sports, daily routines, environmental issues, tourism, and other "things for daily use."

Profesora Eugenia's English class centered on written translation and memorization of vocabulary. Topics such as AIDS, abstinence, women's rights, and violence against women were among those presented in translation practice and reading comprehension. Profesora Eugenia often interjected her own opinions on these subjects, such as "we all know there is no weaker sex," "mothers are the principal culprits in machismo," and "we [women] should respect ourselves" and not accept sexual harassment in the workplace. The topics listed for her final makeup exams were "morals and valves [sic]" and "women's and valves [sic]." Her grammatical errors and misspelling of the word *values* demonstrate her own limited English proficiency. A graduate of the high school recalled of this teacher, "She demands a lot from her students but not from herself." Her curriculum also included the translation of numerous prayers, many of which are most frequently associated with the Catholic Church. Thus, in her class the hidden curriculum of Catholic values and beliefs was made overt.

Social studies classes, taught by two travelers (Profesor Sergio and Profesor Arnoldo) and one accepted immigrant resident of Santa Rita (Profesor Agustín), centered on Costa Rican history and culture. Other topics included medieval European history, the Crusades, cartography, anthropology and the origins of humanity, wars throughout the world, women's suffrage, and political systems, including democracy in Costa Rica and elsewhere. A lesson on the opening of universities in Europe included the opinion that this was a turning point in history in that it changed education from something accessible only to a few to something now seen as the right of all people. I found this lesson ironic, given that in Santa Rita higher education is a privilege accorded to relatively few people. Every three weeks these teachers took time from their social studies curriculum to focus on civics, which covered some of the same topics, such as Costa Rican history and democracy.

Music classes—taught by Profesor Tadeo, a traveler teacher who was often absent—included lessons on the history of music and types of music around the world and involved frequent singing. Guidance counseling sessions (scheduled once weekly for each homeroom class) rarely met. When they did, topics included self-esteem and drug awareness. Science classes covered numerous topics ranging from ecology, advances in technology, and cell structure to more controversial topics (in Santa Rita anyway) such as reproduction and evolution. In Profesor Arturo's introduction of evolution, the Riteño teacher noted that it was a controversial topic and that "there are always different points of view." He told students they needed to respect and value the opinions of others on this topic.

Psychology class (the primary area of instruction for Profesor Arnoldo) involved a list of the different branches of psychology and dictated information regarding psychological theory, such as Freud's developmental stages. The way this subject and others were taught—through dictation, with little to no explanation—resulted in many students being unclear about their purpose. At times students voiced this concern, and at times I imagined students held such criticism silently. I especially thought the latter to be the case as I observed students taking a psychology exam covering decontextualized topics dictated or read as homework from photocopies. During the exam, a shy student with a broken arm had to dictate his responses to questions on the exam to Profesora Soledad, the religion teacher who proctored the exam. I supposed he resented the unclear purpose of these "teachings" as he dictated to his catechism teacher his response to the essay question "What is masturbation?"

NATIONAL REPRESENTATION AND THE MARGINALIZATION OF INDIGENOUS EXISTENCE IN THE COSTA RICAN CURRICULUM

Michel Foucault states that discourse is key to relations of power.[14] The discourse provided through the curriculum and textbooks at SRHS was one that addressed students as Costa Rican national subjects. That is, they presented students as fitting into a classless, unified society of European descent with a strong work ethic. As noted earlier, Costa Rican history has practically erased all records of an indigenous past and denies an indigenous present. Thus, the dominant image of Costa Rica is that of a white, homogeneous society that buys into the rhetoric of a Costa Rican democracy that upholds education as a fulfilled right for all citizens. We can look to curricula to see what sort of knowledge (and from whose perspective) is legitimated in a society.[15] The culture legitimated through the curriculum at SRHS is that of the "pillars"—white, European, Catholic society. Culture related to any minority group, including indigenous populations, was generally excluded.

Although civics classes and school assemblies regularly praised Costa Rican democracy, the curriculum in general did not provide equal representation for all. The civics textbook used by seventh graders at SRHS discussed public education in

Costa Rica as upholding the principles established by the Universal Declaration of Human Rights.[16] Groups contributing to such legislation, however, such as the United Nations committee that produced the *Study of the Problem of Discrimination Against Indigenous Populations,* have produced guidelines for these principles of public education that are not upheld in the national curriculum in Costa Rica. Article 449 of the study demands that

> systematic, persistent and wide-ranging campaigns must be developed and conducted against all forms of misconceptions, ingrained prejudices, and mistaken or distorted ideas regarding indigenous populations. Textbooks for non-indigenous populations must place the necessary emphasis on the need to respect the rights of indigenous populations in everyday life.[17]

Article 450 of the document states, with regard to the curricula of dominant cultures, that

> efforts must be made to eliminate inaccurate, prejudicial and distorted information and to replace it by accurate and verified information on the history, traditions, customs, arts and crafts of the indigenous populations and on their contributions to the cultural environment of non-indigenous populations in present-day societies.[18]

Likewise, International Labor Organization Treaty 169 (Convention Concerning Indigenous and Tribal Peoples in Independent Countries, 1989), ratified in Costa Rica, demands similar guarantees for equal access to education for indigenous persons, as well as equal representation in curriculum. Specifically, Article 27 of the treaty requires that education directed toward indigenous populations "should include their history, their knowledge and techniques, their systems of value, and all other socioeconomic and cultural aspirations."[19] Furthermore, Article 31 of the treaty states that

> educative measures should be adopted in all sectors of the national community, especially in those that are in [the] most direct contact with the interested [indigenous] communities, with the objective of eliminating the prejudices there might be with regard to these communities. To this end, there should be efforts to assure that history books and other didactic materials offer a fair, exact, and instructive description of the societies and cultures of the interested communities.[20]

On a more local level, the Ministry of Education contains a token Department of Indigenous Education that promotes a program called "intercultural education"—akin to multicultural education in the United States—which has received little support from ministry higher-ups. The department also supports the use of a curriculum in "indigenous schools"—schools vaguely defined as and roughly correlating to those inside the country's reservations (thus excluding SRHS). This curriculum consists of three axes, which the representatives of the department explained to me as pertaining to "culture" (which a representative described as "daily life" as opposed to "folklore" and which, for example, might address agriculture in Nambué), "language" (although this would not be carried out in Nambué, the representative noted), and "environment." In spite of the fact that SRHS serves an allegedly indigenous population, its location outside a reservation results in its exemption from the curriculum of intercultural education. Indeed, these—or any other—aspects of indigenous culture were rarely addressed in the high school's curriculum. When they were, it tended to occur in stereotypical ways.[21] Thus, the marginality of indigenous existence to the curriculum appeared to reflect its marginality to issues of curricular or national import as well.[22]

STEREOTYPICAL REFERENCES TO INDIGENOUS PEOPLES IN THE CURRICULUM

A music lesson involved a discussion of the invention of music by aboriginal peoples and its performance on instruments made of reeds, clay, skin, and other natural materials. Profesor Tadeo claimed that the musical staff was a relatively recent invention. He also discussed local styles of music with roots in indigenous tradition and required students to investigate this as homework. The assignment was met with more loud student protests than usual. One of Profesora Rosaura's Spanish classes studied a story classified as "realist" in which the partners in an Indian couple were unable to communicate their feelings to each other. Their inability to express feelings, ultimately ending in their separation, was explained as a result of how they were raised.[23] Profesor Manuel, a vocational teacher, explained the process of smoking meats and noted that this is how "the ancestors" preserved them. These are but a few examples of how a generalized, unspecified "Indian"—whether stereotypical or not—was interjected (albeit infrequently) into the curriculum. Other classes addressed indigenous culture or history more specifically, although not necessarily more accurately.

Profesor Agustín, the young social studies teacher who had been accepted as a resident of Santa Rita, had his fifth-grade class (containing no Nambueseños) make various maps. One map students made was of the country's reservations. I was not present in the class when this map was presented to the students. When Profesor Agustín showed it to me, I asked if any comments about Nambué came up at that time. He said that of course they did, but he did not readily elaborate. When I insisted that he explain the resulting commentaries, he noted that a student said there was a mix of privately owned and communal lands in Nambué. I informed him that there were lands that were purchased for community use, just as any other local community would have a public meeting hall or a soccer field, but there were no lands in Nambué that have retained communal ownership through time, as the stereotype of reservations suggests.

Another social studies class—taught by Profesor Sergio, a young traveler teacher—addressed indigenous history and contributions fairly frequently, although not necessarily with regard to Costa Rican indigenous groups. In one lesson I observed, the teacher asked students to recall from their textbook which indigenous groups inhabited Mesoamerica. Students listed the Mayas, Aztecs, and Incas. A student from Nambué added, "The Bribrí and the Chorotega" (both ethnic groups from Costa Rica). Profesor Sergio commented that the Incas had not lived in Mesoamerica, but he did not respond to the comment on local indigenous peoples. Federico, a white student from Nambué, added "the Nambueseños." He and another (nonwhite) Nambueseño laughed. Federico noted "it's a joke" and high-fived his Nambueseño classmate. Neither the teacher nor any other students commented on or reacted to these comments in any way visible to me. Profesor Sergio continued the lesson, noting that he would focus on the Mayas, Aztecs, and Incas in his lecture since there were too many indigenous groups to cover them all. He listed a few others that existed. Among them were the Chibchas, Chichimecas, and Olmecs. He then listed the Bruncas, Huétares, and Bribrí—"which still exist" (all of which are Costa Rican tribes).

Profesor Sergio asked students to list contributions of the Mayas and Aztecs. Among those students listed were numerical systems, architecture, and roads. Federico jokingly added "and the chain of Tikal supermarkets" (which uses a stone pyramid as its logo). There was no response to his clowning. Profesor Sergio drew a conical-style house on the blackboard and asked what it was. Federico responded, "It's a typical *rancho* from Nambué," following which he made the stereotypical "war cry" with which Nambueseño students are taunted and which Profesor Sergio had once listed as stereotypical of Nambueseño "speech." Again, Federico was ignored. Profesor Sergio asked why *ranchos* were made (using past tense) of biodegradable materials. Federico replied, "So that when they fall down on you, it doesn't hurt so much." Finally, a Riteña student scolded him, shouting "Federico!" Another Nambueseño answered that *ranchos* are cool in the day and warm at night. The teacher acknowledged this as the correct response.

Profesor Sergio went on to discuss corn and natural dyes as legacies of indigenous peoples. A Nambueseño brought up crop rotation as another contribution. Profesor Sergio asked for ideas on what corn was used for (again, using past tense). A third Nambueseño student offered "for *chicha* and *chicheme*" (two beverages made from corn in Nambué and elsewhere). Profesor Sergio added that these beverages were used for ceremonial purposes (although they were—and still are—made in Nambué for celebrations as well as for general consumption). The teacher changed the topic slightly and talked about shamans, noting the popular song titled "Chamán" (Shaman) by the Mexican rock group Maná.

A Nambueseño student asked which of the three groups in question (Aztecs, Mayas, and Incas) had disappeared. Profesor Sergio said that in all three cases they had disappeared as a result of the arrival of the Spaniards. He listed five explanations for the "extermination" of these groups: the arrival of Columbus and firearms; sicknesses; wars among indigenous groups and with the Spaniards; lack of political unity within indigenous groups, which permitted the assassination of political leaders; and religions that considered death a stage of life and thus not something to be avoided at the hands of the Spaniards or by any other means. He did not discuss *encomienda* service, nor did he acknowledge any current existence of individuals from these groups.

I found several aspects of this classroom interaction interesting. To begin with, it promoted various stereotypes (such as the extinction of indigenous peoples and the validation of existing indigenous groups based on which ones have shamans). In spite of a Nambueseño's contributions to the discussion, noting ways indigenous groups were still practicing cultural traditions (such as *rancho* building and the production of *chicha* and *chicheme*), Profesor Sergio did not use these examples to discuss present indigenous influence in society. Rather, he tended to use past tense in the discussion. He did acknowledge the continuing existence of three Costa Rican indigenous groups, but the Chorotega were not among those listed.

Finally, the clowning antics of Federico, the white Nambueseño student, are of interest, although their meaning is difficult to decipher. Federico frequently joked in class and had a reputation for being a class clown. This day, however, all of his joking interruptions were about Nambueseños or Indians and were posed in a way that took neither of these categories seriously. At the same time, his comments disrupted the teacher's "official discourse" on Indians. The person who rebuked him for his antics was a peer from Santa Rita rather than a Nambueseño who might take offense or the teacher who might want to control the classroom. It is possible that my presence—as an advocate and resident of Nambué—in the classroom affected other students' reactions to these comments (or lack thereof), as well as the teacher's response to the situation.

The only other occasion on which I witnessed local indigenous peoples mentioned in a class was on a reading comprehension section of an English exam given in Profesora Yolanda's class on September 3, 1999 (likely copied from the Costa Rican English-language newspaper, *The Tico Times*). The text and three relevant test questions read as follows:

> Fireworks explode, the band plays, and crowds gather to watch the "little mare" dancing to ancient Indian music of flute and drum, while leading the procession, [were] altar boys, priests, and the statue of a dark skinned Virgin Mary dressed in brilliant satin robes.
>
> When the Spaniards arrived in 1519, they discovered to their horror that the Chorotegas not only worshipped the sun, moon, fire, water, and wind, but also they celebrated the Festival of Corn.
>
> The man representing La Yegüita [the little mare] wears a hoop with a horse's head and small reins. Another man carries a small doll dressed in bright pink clothes, the Indian Princess. The two men dance to the music of a wooden flute and drums.
>
> 1. Who participated in the procession of the Festival?
>   a. Indians
>   b. Spaniards
>   c. Chorotegas
>   d. Altar boys
>   . . .

3. What did the Chorotega Indians worship?
   a. Virgin Mary
   b. A small doll
   c. The Festival of Corn
   d. The sun, the moon, and the wind

4. What did the small doll represent?
   a. La Yegüita
   b. Virgin Mary
   c. A little mare
   d. The Indian princess

The festival described in this reading comprehension exercise is one celebrated annually in Majapiñao on December 12 (the Day of the Virgin of Guadalupe) and one in which many Nambueseños participate. It honors the Virgin of Guadalupe and commemorates a miraculous occurrence in which two Nambueseños, headed to Majapiñao for the festival in honor of the Virgin of Guadalupe, started a sure-to-be fatal machete fight. Nambueseño onlookers, according to narratives about the happening, called upon the Virgin of Guadalupe to intervene. A white mare, kicking and rearing, appeared between the two men, stopping the fight. It is considered that the mare was sent by the Virgin of Guadalupe or was the form she herself took to prevent the deaths of the fighting men.

The present-day celebration involves priests and parishioners carrying the statue of the Virgin of Guadalupe from the contemporary local church around town and back to what is known as "the Colonial Church" (no longer used by parishioners but which stands as a historical monument) of Majapiñao. During the procession, in front of the statue of the Virgin of Guadalupe a man wearing a cloth-covered hoop with a mare's head (representing the "little mare") dances with a man holding a small doll, whose symbolism is open to various interpretations but is often seen as representing the Virgin of Guadalupe. The procession ends with participants feasting on traditional foods such as *chicheme* and *tiste* (a beverage made of cacao ground with rice, cloves, and sugar) served out of hollowed gourds, Guanacastecan tortillas, *rosquillas,* and other local delicacies. Women from Nambué are invariably encouraged to help prepare these foods, and many Nambueseños participate in the procession.

This information is relevant to the present discussion, given that students from Nambué taking this exam had experiential knowledge of the event (it is significant that I did not see students from other towns participating in it). The knowledge of this event, which Nambueseño students had from their own experience or from their grandmothers' participation in the food preparation (or their great-grandfathers' participation as past *mayordomos* of the festival), conflicted with the information provided in the text of the exam. A student who was an excellent student of English (and who, in fact, accompanied me to the festival in 1999) told me she had no problem with these contradictions because it was clear from the text which were the "correct" answers. Nambueseño students whom I observed taking the test, however, had more difficulty.

Question one asked who participated in the procession. Those who had attended it knew that altar boys (the "correct" answer according to the text) were in the minority among procession participants and that most people there were considered Indians, if not Chorotegas—both of which were "incorrect" responses on the exam. Indeed, both Nambueseño students in the homeroom section I observed taking this test answered that Chorotegas participated in the event (although one of the students had underlined the "correct" part of the text, noting that altar boys participated).

Although question three asked about past religious practices of the Chorotegas, Nambueseños and other participants in the festival knew it was a religious one sponsored by the Catholic Church. Although both Nambueseño students in the class answered "correctly" that the Chorotegas worshipped the sun, the moon, and the wind, I wondered how many Nambueseño students in other sections would answer "Virgin Mary" out of spite or anger at the perpetuation of these stereotypes. Question four asked about the symbolism behind the small doll. According to the text, it represented an "Indian princess." According to those I had interviewed on the matter, it represented the Virgin of Guadalupe. The students in the class did answer the question "correctly" according to the text.

This contradiction between what students knew from experience about their culture specifically and what was taught to them in school was cause for confusion. The promotion of stereotypes and the presentation of inaccurate information must also have been frustrating.[24] Certainly, it was contrary to the legislation that seeks to promote indigenous representation in the curriculum. As Greg Sarris found in a classroom utilizing published Kashaya stories to teach reading to Kashaya students, the selection used in the English class I observed served to further "otherize" the Chorotega students rather than include their history and culture in the curriculum in an adequate way.[25] In Sarris's words, "The story was about them in a way that was not them."[26]

I read students' civics books looking for mention of indigenous peoples as part of Costa Rica's national population. I found some mention of them in a seventh-grade civics book; but these, too, were homogenizing and inaccurate, and they represented indigenous peoples as a thing of the past. The book upheld indigenous peoples of Costa Rica as having laid the foundation for democracy prior to the arrival of the Spaniards. It noted, "[T]he local indigenous societies gave a civil example: they lived in harmony with nature, which they considered to be a living being. In them, there was not the marked individualism of the European conquerors. To the contrary, among the aborigines there triumphed a sense of belonging to a community and to the nature that surrounded them."[27]

The text named no ethnic groups in particular but rather promoted stereotypes for this homogenized, generic "Indian" presence. The text then discussed local indigenous peoples using past tense. It discussed one individual cacique, upheld as a hero, who resisted conquest but who ultimately failed. The text discussed an indigenous uprising in Talamanca, Costa Rica (inhabited by the Bribrí and Cabécar tribes), and the death of its instigator. The textbook explained, "The process of conquest and colonization destructured the indigenous societies, which were reorganized according to the interests of the conquistadors. The indigenous survivors fled to the mountains and regions of difficult access."[28] Finally, this section of the text discussed "profound *mestizaje*" and the "emergence of a new culture."[29] This was the extent of its discussion of indigenous influence in Costa Rica.

There was no mention of indigenous groups in the Pacific northwestern part of Costa Rica (the Chorotega and others). Rather, as with national consciousness, "Indianness" in Costa Rica was tied to Talamanca (the Atlantic region deemed "truly Indian" by social scientists who have doubted Nambué's inclusion in such a category). Thus, local indigenous presence (relative to Santa Rita) was mostly ignored, both in the textbooks and in the classroom, in favor of topics deemed more relevant to national society.

Although a logical solution might be to demand greater and more accurate representation of indigenous peoples in the curriculum, that, too, is problematic. Recall what might be interpreted as Federico's uneasiness (manifested through clowning) when issues of local indigenous influence were mentioned in the classroom. Other Nambueseños I interviewed expressed relief that the Chorotega were not discussed as a curriculum item. Some noted that on the rare occasions when this happened, they were pointed to and ridiculed. Thus, at least some Nambueseño students preferred to have their heritage absent from the curriculum, given the stigma presently associated with being Indian in a country and a county that pride themselves on whiteness. These students preferred to keep the curriculum as it was.

HIDDEN CURRICULUM TURNED OVERT: THE CONDUCT GRADE

In addition to the courses already mentioned, students received grades for what might seem more like part of a "hidden curriculum." At SRHS, however, these items were overt and corresponded to a graded body of knowledge. I refer here to the conduct grade. The year of my fieldwork in SRHS, the Ministry of Education had reinstated a program from years ago. Whereas proper behavior was still considered in grades for all classes, students also received a conduct grade. Thus, what were once tacit expectations of students, perhaps, became standard curricular items. In the capital city (San José) there were organized student protests against this change in curriculum. In Santa Rita there was a mixture of parental support by some and mumbled complaints by other students and parents. Presenting this new curricular item at a staff meeting, the principal explained, "Now conduct is just one more subject."

Each student's conduct grade was evaluated by a guidance counselor and two teachers, as well as by the student government representative of each homeroom, following a handout distributed to teachers and listing ten criteria:

[The student]
1. Behavior: Demonstrates conduct and behavior that dignify him/her as a person and elevate the name of the educational institution to which he/she belongs, as well as that of the community in general.

2. Personal presentation: Dresses with decorum and complies strictly with the regulations established by the institution regarding uniform and personal presentation.
3. Comradeship: Practices friendship. . . .
4. Responsibility: Attends to commitments, responsibility, seriousness, and effort in his/her process of learning. . . .
5. Cooperation: Contributes, in his/her responsible conduct and participation, in the creation and maintenance and strengthening of an adequate learning environment; collaborates and participates actively, in the manner indicated by educators, in curricular or extracurricular lessons or scholastic activities.
6. Respect: Is esteemed by his/her peers; respectful with his/her educators, with all personnel of the institution, and with members of the community.
7. Honesty: Respects the property of his/her teachers. . . .
8. Interest in Study: Complies with his/her scholastic duties. Develops study habits. Manifests constant progress.
9. Takes Care of the Physical Space: Takes care of buildings, installations, equipment, material, furniture, and, in general, all school property.
10. Hygiene, Cleanliness, and Adornment: Complies exactly with the indications formulated by educational authorities related to the habits of tidiness and personal hygiene, as well as with the norms of adornment, cleanliness, and morality which reign in the institution.

I found many aspects of this list worrisome in that many of these criteria are extremely subjective, whereas the existence of this rubric for grading projected an image of objectivity. The "behavior" and "honesty" categories are problematic given that students commonly viewed as "bad kids" were often wrongly accused by authorities. Criterion nine is disturbing for the same reasons. I saw "favorite" Riteño students as well as "bad kids" write on the walls, although I never saw the favored students get in trouble for it. Personal presentation is a questionable category in that potential compliance with the exact uniform guidelines was largely determined by a student's economic situation.

Comradeship might also have been a problem for some students, given the way Nambueseño students were considered by teachers and peers to "exclude themselves." Cooperation required participation in extracurricular activities that was possible only for nontraveler students who did not rely on transportation to and from school. The treatment of community members was considered in one's grade, although no particular community was specified. I witnessed Riteño girls addressing the Nambueseño bus driver in inappropriate or disrespectful ways, with no negative consequences.[30] A Nambueseño addressing a Riteño adult using the same terms would likely have been seen as in violation of the rules of conduct. Finally, cleanliness was more easily maintained in the rainy season by Riteños whose roads were paved than by Nambueseños who walked through mud to get to the bus stop, and by Riteños in vocational workshops like computers than by Nambueseños in agriculture classes. Thus, as with all other grading at the institution, place of residence and economic class may have affected students' "success."

I asked some teachers about the appropriateness of these criteria. In particular, I addressed the issue of cleanliness for students in classes involving labor carried out in mud, manure, pigpens, or cane fields. Some teachers responded that they took place of residence into account and were more lenient with traveler students who had dirty uniforms. Presumably, this recognition of place of residence worked to traveler students' advantage. If it was acknowledged, however, could it not also have worked to their detriment in a place that favored students from Santa Rita?

In the end, few teachers used the criteria for evaluating conduct. I witnessed various teachers filling out conduct grade forms. One teacher told her co-worker, "Just give them all 10s." Then she lowered the scores of the "bad kids" in her class. Profesora Alba said the list of criteria was "idiocy." She said she merely considered who kept their shirts tucked in and who did not litter.

Profesora Belisa noted that she only cared about honesty. Profesora Alba replied that they could not know which students were honest. I agreed, having watched numerous "flag-bearer" honors students cheat on tests. Profesora Yolanda told me she did not go by the criteria. Rather, she pointed out—as she filled out her grade sheet—that a teacher generally knows which students are better behaved than others. One of her colleagues insisted that teachers did need to consider all ten criteria. Just then Profesor Arnoldo recited, "*Yo no fui, fue Teté, péguele, péguele, que ella fue,*" the Costa Rican equivalent of "Eenie meenie miney moe." I was permitted to view the final conduct grades for all homeroom sections. It appeared that cleanliness was not an issue for students from towns with muddy roads, although "bad kids" did tend to be graded down for cleanliness.

EXTRACURRICULAR LESSONS AND VARIATION IN PEDAGOGICAL STYLE

In addition to the subjects they were hired to teach, many teachers held personal agendas that they shared with me. In my interviews with teachers, I asked if they had other lessons outside of their academic or vocational specialty that they hoped to impart to students. Invariably, they did. The range of these extracurricular lessons was wide. Many teachers talked about their role in forming citizens out of students. Others spoke of teaching a strong work ethic; the importance of eating well; respect for others; respect for elders; seeking job satisfaction; values, such as loving thy neighbor, solidarity, forgiveness, prayer; how girls should sit with their legs together; honesty; discipline; virginity and abstinence, as well as birth control options; having goals; and the importance of studying before they had children. Thus, the curriculum at SRHS included many items and topics not usually listed with academic or vocational subjects.

Indeed, many teachers saw the inculcation of certain extracurricular lessons as part of their role. In my interviews with teachers, I specifically asked what they saw their role as educators as encompassing. Profesora Anatolia, a veteran "pillar" teacher, explained that her role was to transmit not only the program of study but also moral and civic values. Various other "pillars" echoed her concern. In contrast, many younger traveler teachers had a different view of the role of an educator. Profesora Yolanda explained this difference of opinion: "Before, to be an educator was to be superior. And that's not the way it is. Teachers eat because students give us a job." She criticized unnamed colleagues for pretending to be superior to students and for being unable to see students as friends: "You have to see your student as a human being—all equal."

This split over how teachers should view the relationship between themselves and their students—whether as a friendship or as a hierarchical relationship—was one of the reasons for the antagonism felt between the two groups. Another point of division was teaching style, which was closely tied to teachers' visions of the proper distance between student and teacher. Profesora Eugenia, who demanded that students discontinue the use of logic in her classroom, based her teaching style on direct translations in student workbooks. Often, she dictated the translation students wrote in their workbooks, leaving students with the sole task of answering reading comprehension questions in their first language. She taught students to search for unfamiliar words in a dictionary or vocabulary list rather than try to make sense of them from the context. She chastised students for writing lengthy responses to workbook reading comprehension questions rather than seeking the appropriate phrase from the text and copying it verbatim in the space given for the response. She told students, "You'll never learn like that, writing more than necessary. I like short answers because I can see that you understood." The goal for her class was not to have students graduate with the ability to communicate in a second language but to prepare students for the Ministry of Education's written standardized test. To that end, her teaching style was effective. Other teachers (often the younger traveler students, but not exclusively so) tried to be more innovative in their teaching methods and to rely less on rote memorization.

Students' opinions of these teaching styles varied. Teachers were appreciated for their ability to explain, for their patience, for their understanding, and for humane treatment of students. Some students appreciated more freedom in the classroom, whereas others preferred strictness. Only a few students complained that high school classes tended to be boring and monotonous. Qualities disliked in teachers included tendencies to meddle in personal lives or to gossip about students, to humiliate them in class, and to hold grudges. Students were resentful of teachers who merely passed out photocopies of information to memorize with no explanation, yet excessive explanation seemed unappreciated as well. Overall, it appeared that teachers' role as formers of morality led to more extreme criticism by students. Teachers' extracurricular roles seemed to overshadow their academic role in students' evaluations of them. Several students, when asked who the best teachers were, had to clarify "the best people or the best teachers," thus indicating that teachers' dual roles were apparent to students.

Sara, a graduate of SRHS who was at the university in 1999, reminisced about effective and ineffective teaching styles. The advice she would give to high school teachers would be "to make [students] have to think—because one gets to the university and doesn't know how to think." She would not have gotten to the university, however, if not for passing the Ministry of Education exams, which require rote memorization.[31] Thus, the solution to this issue may not lie within the reach of high school employees.

THE LIMITATIONS OF SCHOOLING

Ultimately, I came to question just how well the high school prepared students for higher education. In earlier chapters I discussed to whom schooling was directed. I now question how effective schooling was even for students who reaped all its benefits. In the remainder of this chapter, I will examine the limitations of schooling even for students who might have been favored. Apart from larger issues of discrimination and favoritism, numerous limitations were placed on all students at SRHS.

Frequent rain on the tin roofs made dictation (a primary teaching method) intermittently inaudible for approximately six months of every year. Lack of funds led to further limitations. Teachers typically had no equipment other than a chalkboard at their disposal. In my research, I found teachers to be fairly competent at taking advantage of local resources (such as procuring donated leather scraps from a nationally acclaimed leather company for leatherwork class and getting local merchants to donate materials). A scarcity of equipment was more constraining. Years ago, the school had received funding to build a science laboratory, complete with work tables and gas connections. In 1999 it was used like any other classroom. One day I observed Federico clowning in the class. He turned the knobs to the gas and shrieked, jokingly, "Oh no! The gas is escaping!" The joke was that there had been no gas in the lab since long before his time. Yeison, a student in computer class, mockingly ordered a fellow student to "shut the door! The cold air is escaping!" as he nodded toward the hole in the wall where an air conditioning unit used to be.[32]

Given insufficient and inadequate equipment, Profesora Rosa María had to find ways to teach computer class to groups of fifteen students with five or fewer (and usually no) working computers (this sometimes resulted in "theory lessons" involving dictation or copying information from the manual by hand). Profesor Raúl, a teacher of "lesser species," had to occupy students' time and maintain their interest in spite of the fact that they had no chickens (the subject of the class) for the first seven months of the school year. Profesora Remedios, the teacher of a leatherwork course, had to come up with an alternative curriculum until the class received donated leather to work with. Although the school boasted ownership of 71.3 hectares of farmland, it lacked adequate equipment to take advantage of the land.

Even courses that required nothing more than classrooms, books, and a teacher fared little better. The school had insufficient desks for the number of students, too few classrooms for the number of classes held simultaneously, and problems with faulty lights that hindered learning. The scarcity of classrooms resulted in students often not knowing where their class would meet, which often caused them to be marked late or the class to have insufficient time to meet. Absenteeism among teachers was another common problem. Even if students had materials and a classroom, the teacher might not appear. At least two teachers' frequent absences led their students to ask office attendants or the aspiring anthropologist if such-and-such a teacher had arrived, thus to know whether to return to school after lunch or whether to go to school in the first place. Furthermore, many teachers (six academic and numerous vocational teachers) had not completed their degrees. Thus, many teachers who offered classes to students were not fully qualified to teach them. Given these situations, even students who could fully benefit from all the school had to offer were limited.

Memorization of trivia was unlikely to be of service to students who did not go on to the university, where they would need it for the entrance exam. For those able to pursue higher education, that teaching style would help on the admission exam but not in their university courses. For those who wanted a high school diploma to obtain better job opportunities or status, passing the national exam was key. Even a student with perfect grades in all of his or her subjects, however, might fail the year if he or she did not pass the Ministry of Education's standardized tests. Mavis, Richard, and Karen Biesanz report that in spite of the goal to teach students to pass the national exams, less than 50 percent of public high school students in Costa Rica did so in 1990.[33] In SRHS in 1999, 21 of 37 eleventh graders (57 percent) graduated and received a high school diploma. The others failed the Ministry of Education exam.

Those who did not graduate could elect to repeat the school year (most often considered too embarrassing to be a serious option), seek to get the Costa Rican equivalent of a general equivalency diploma (GED), give up, or return to high school for a sixth year to specialize in a vocation and receive a certificate in that vocation rather than a diploma. The relative benefits of these options are the topic of Chapter 6. To conclude this chapter, I will summarize what the lasting teachings of high school might be for someone whose formal education ended there (either successfully, with a diploma, or not). To do so, I return to the seventh-grade civics book that inculcated students on what it meant to be Costa Rican.

Just as a student might be required to memorize mathematical theorems, agricultural techniques, or a particular arrangement of the parts of a dialogue in English, students might have needed to reproduce this information on an exam:

> Communities, like people, also come to have an identity. They aren't born with it, but they go about forming it over time, from years of sharing the same environment, language, customs. And the basis of this identity is history. . . . But the national identity was formed with a base in the first encounter of cultures and later integration of other ethnicities: African, Asian, and European. This coexistence in a single territory, sharing customs, food, beliefs, and difficulties, identifies us today.[34]

In this instance, students were taught about their own national and local identities through direct curriculum. I would argue that lessons of identity were among the most lasting the high school imparted to students. Most frequently, however, these lessons were not taught in such a direct, traditional manner. More often, they were inculcated through subtle and enduring means. In this chapter I have discussed the ways an official curriculum was taught to students at SRHS in accordance with guidelines set forth by the Ministry of Education. Chapter 6 will examine the lessons taught in less explicit ways that demonstrated to students their belonging to or exclusion from the local community identity.

NOTES

1. "No more using logic."

2. Luykx 1999: 172; López, Assáel, and Neumann 1984: 360 note that rote memorization and copying were key pedagogical techniques in Bolivia and Chile, respectively, as well. López, Assáel, and Neumann overtly criticize these tactics as resulting in the instruction of isolated concepts (1984: 360).

3. Biesanz, Biesanz, and Biesanz 1999: 199.

4. Mora Chinchilla and Trejos Trejos 1996: 50; translation mine.

5. Biesanz, Biesanz, and Biesanz 1999: 199.

6. Ibid.: 204.

7. Ibid.: 205.

8. Ibid.: 205–206.

9. Students who were not Catholic could bring a letter from a religious leader of a different sect to gain exemption from this class.

10. See Holland and Eisenhart 1990: 54 for a similar analysis of gender bias.

11. John Dewey quoted in Mora Chinchilla and Trejos Trejos 1996: 50; translation mine.

12. Ibid.: 52–54; translation mine.

13. For a more extensive account of Spanish classes at SRHS, see Stocker 2002.

14. Foucault 1978: 29–35.

15. Aronowitz and Giroux 1993: 140. See also López, Assáel, and Neumann 1984: 361; Luykx 1999: 204; Pinar 1993: 60 with regard to what curriculum says (indirectly) about whose knowledge is privileged in schools.

16. Mora Chinchilla and Trejos Trejos 1996.

17. Martínez Cobo 1987: 35.

18. Ibid.

19. Organización Internacional del Trabajo 1989: 32; translation mine.

20. Ibid.: 35–36; translation mine.

21. See Luykx 1999: 147.

22. Ibid.: 129 addresses how curriculum in a Bolivian normal school teaches students about the place of rural or indigenous students in the society as a whole.

23. See ibid.: 146–147 for a similar example of curriculum teaching ethnic stereotypes.

24. See ibid.: 148 for a discussion of how the Bolivian normal school she studied at times glorified an indigenous past and simultaneously made it clear that professional status demanded a departure from such an identity.

25. Sarris 1993: 257.

26. Ibid.: 260.

27. Mora Chinchilla and Trejos Trejos 1996: 11; translation mine.

28. Ibid.

29. Ibid.

30. In one such example, I heard a Riteña address the Nambueseño bus driver as "*Vos, Güila*" (You [familiar], Kid).

31. López, Assáel, and Neumann 1984: 361–362 found that students who were most likely to succeed academically in the Chilean schools in which they based their research were those who conformed to the schools' routine of passive learning.

32. See ibid.: 350 for a list of material conditions that interfere with education in Chile.

33. Biesanz, Biesanz, and Biesanz 1999: 211.

34. Mora Chinchilla and Trejos Trejos 1996: 68; translation mine.

6

"A qué me va a servir esto en la bananera?"[1]

Teaching Identity and Its Consequences in the Post–High School Realm

Early in my fieldwork, I requested permission from a teacher to observe eighth graders in her classroom. Profesora Rosa María invited me into the room where she taught and graciously offered me a seat at her desk. From there I had a stellar view of all the students in the room. It was not the students who most caught my eye that day, however. On the wall facing me were two posters. One, higher than the other and to the right, depicted a child with straight blond hair, blue eyes, white skin, and a thin curved line as a smile. The caption read *"¡Tú eres mi ideal!"* (You're my ideal!). The other, lower and to the left, contained a drawing of a child with brown skin, black eyes, curly black hair, and pursed, full lips. This one read *"¡Eres diferente!"* (You're different!). At this point in my study I was looking into issues of hidden curriculum, only to find that they were not quite as "hidden" as I had expected.

Through numerous vehicles, including these classroom decorations, lessons regarding the relative value placed on different identities were apparent throughout the high school. This chapter examines the ways students were taught identity—racial, gendered, and otherwise—in the classroom.[2] Whereas Chapter 4 focused on aspects of school organization such as tracking, this chapter focuses on lessons taught implicitly or tacitly, in most cases, with regard to what is often termed the *hidden curriculum*.[3]

HIDDEN CURRICULUM AND HABITUS

Hidden curriculum is as much about learning how to navigate the classroom setting as it is about learning to function successfully within the larger context. Most important, these lessons are not taught overtly but must either be already inculcated in the student (from learning how to "be" in the community in which the school is located) or be picked up along the way. In this manner, the hidden curriculum can be compared to Pierre Bourdieu's concept of habitus.

According to Bourdieu, habitus is internalized, taken for granted, lasting, the "product of inculcation," and—perhaps most important—it "tends to produce . . . the naturalization of its own arbitrariness."[4] It is "history turned into nature," yet it is "denied as such."[5] Habitus was apparent in the unquestioned beliefs perpetuated in the high school setting, as noted in Chapter 2 when I recounted Jaime's lengthy list of attributes that set him apart from Nambueseños: "I was raised to be a Spaniard. . . . I don't play with dirt. I never played with dirt. I don't eat with my mouth open. . . . [To be Spanish is] to be cultured, to be educated, to know. They [Nambueseños] don't know. . . . Because of their culture, they're dirty. They smell bad." Jaime's lessons on his own class habitus likely began in his home community, as they were already entrenched by the time he reached his first year of high school, when I met him. His beliefs, however, dominant in the town of Santa Rita, were rampant in the school as well. Students who were not inculcated with these prejudices prior to attending high school could certainly pick them up there.[6]

I am by no means the first to suggest that identity is intertwined with schools and that schools affect individuals' social realms.[7] One way in which this differential treatment and opportunity occurred in Santa Rita High School (SRHS) was through tracking, as noted earlier with regard to the lack of attention given to students in section 7-5. For those students, many of whom were from Nambué, teachers' racism was not necessarily overt.[8] I will argue that, knowingly or unknowingly, several teachers as well as students at SRHS encouraged or legitimized students' social roles along the lines of gender, class, ethnicity, race, place of residence, and more. I will also address the way students resisted and transformed these ideas. First, though, I will focus on how these ideas were created and perpetuated.

TEACHING AND LEARNING IDENTITY

Schools provide an interesting context through which to view the matrices of power at work and the identities involved therein. These are crosscut by ethnicity, gender, class, and place of residence. Power is constantly shifting and plays out in different ways.[9] Although students may have come to the high school with various of these identities already in place, the high school served as a site in which identity was taught as well. Indeed, the classroom interactions I witnessed taught students their social locations with regard to race, class, ethnicity, gender, and academic status. Some teachers openly discussed the concept of identity. A teacher who noted that it was her job to mold young people described to her class the way in which we all have many faces and at times show one and at times another to those around us. She questioned, rhetorically, which of our selves is *"el verdadero yo"* (the true me). Jacobo, a tenth grader at the time of the study and not a student of this teacher during the year of my fieldwork at SRHS, also acknowledged the concept of multifaceted identity yet insisted that teachers had pegged one single identity on him.

Jacobo spoke of his peers in school and his family not knowing who he really was. In both places he had been cast as a bad kid, but he talked about how he rarely spoke at home, where he spent his time studying and being quiet. Although at times he enjoyed his reputation as a troublemaker, he admitted to me on more than one occasion that he was rarely disruptive in the ways others considered him to be (an admission that corresponds with my observations). Once, Profesora Eugenia, a strict Riteña "pillar" (and the one responsible for naming her clique of mostly, but not exclusively, Riteña veteran teachers "pillars"), scolded him for not being at marching practice in preparation for the Independence Day parade and asked him why he had not been there. He responded with the word *ya* (already), meaning he had already practiced and his group had been dismissed for the day. Profesora Eugenia, however, interpreted his *ya* as it was often used, to mean "enough already." She took his comment as disrespectful. He explained to me that Profesora Eugenia was "punishing us [referring to himself and his cousin, who was present for that exchange] for our ancestors."

Jacobo elaborated on his comment, noting that he meant teachers punished him and his cousin, Ileana, for the ways their older siblings—long gone from the high school—had treated teachers with disrespect. He noted that his brother had been particularly rude to Profesora Eugenia, so she expected the same treatment from him. I found his choice of words particularly telling, as often was the case with Jacobo's comments. As a *moreno* student from a poorer family, considered Indian by some in this predominantly white, racist town, he might indeed have been punished because of his ancestors. His legacy (be it as sibling of a known problem student or as a descendant of a line deemed inferior) predetermined Jacobo's school success (or relative lack thereof).

Jacobo, although not always fitting his ascribed identity, had accepted it long before I met him. In fact, he had come to embrace it. During two separate conversations in which I talked to him about the discrepancy between his ascribed identity as troublemaker and the conscientious student I knew him to be, he specifically asked me not to blow his cover.[10] Jacobo was not the only student who was taught that he was bad. Profesora Rosa María, the teacher whose classroom contained the posters mentioned at the beginning of this chapter, described the quality of her students to me in front of them. She pointed to two and said she had problems with them and with the student seated next to them. In a different class, she separated a student from the others at the beginning of each lesson I observed and throughout the lesson spoke aloud, to everyone and to no one in particular, about how lazy and problematic he was.

Profesora Alba, the white traveler teacher most guilty of Roger Harker–like behavior, called on a student to read aloud, addressing him by his last name and asking him to read "loudly, just like you shout and cause trouble." Profesor Sergio, a *moreno* traveler teacher, told a student at the beginning of a class to "pay attention, just for today—[so I do] not have to scold you." I never saw any of these three students act up in a class I observed. Profesora Greis, a *morena* traveler teacher, commented on the possibility of teachers creating a self-fulfilling prophecy by frequently telling students they were bad. Specifically, she addressed the reputation held by students from Sereno. She suggested, hitting her fist into her hand for emphasis, "So often they tell them and tell them [they are bad]; maybe they come to believe it."

It was not only with regard to behavior that students came to internalize teachings of their inferiority. As noted in Chapter 4, Profesora Genofeva, a teacher of section 7-5, told me in front of the class that only a few students were worth the effort. Various scholars have noted the effects of teachers' categorization of students or lower expectations of particular pupils on those students' self-esteem and school performance.[11] Thus, just as students may have come to believe their categorization as bad kids generally, they may also have come to internalize their ascribed status as bad students. The identity-related teachings did not stop there, however.

Profesor Arnoldo's psychology class taught students (using handouts never discussed in class but that students strove to memorize for an upcoming test) that their respective body types predestined their characters. The lesson was drawn from Ernest Krestchmer's personality types based on body structure and included these predetermined qualities for students of different shapes, as copied from students' notes: "a. Fat, small, round people: communicative, partiers, charlatans; b. Tall, thin people: reserved, communicative, serious, authoritarian; c. People with evident physical problems: mood swings, communicative or noncommunicative; d. Athletes: serious, active, optimistic, disciplinarians, reserved." In this way, stereotypes were taught as fact. A lesson by Profesora Aracely, a Riteña vocational teacher, added to the one about physical handicaps noted in the previous list. In a lesson on occupational safety, the teacher stressed the importance of being careful in the workplace. She explained that even if one lost only a finger, that would be a problem. "You'll be one more burden on society," she warned as she pointed out that the employee's place of business and the entire country would have to pay his or her way from then on. She continued to list the negative effects of such an injury: it would cause upsets in the family and perhaps the loss of the injured person's spouse. "Maybe your wife met you [when you were] all handsome," she hypothesized, "and now you're left without a leg, handicapped. You could lose your family. It is *not* the same thing to come across a blind person as a sighted person or a person on crutches as a person without crutches."

Some teachers were less severe. Profesora Marta Iris, a white woman from Santa Rita and a favorite teacher of many students, told her students that for her, "what is most important is not that you pass this course. For me, the most important thing is that you be excellent people and, second, that you pass all your classes this school year." This teacher, however, who let students know that she accepted them regardless of their intelligence or ability, was in the minority. More commonly, I saw teachers tell me or the class (in front of the students described) that "they don't like to read," "they don't like to work," or "Yeison causes me problems. . . . [So-and-so] hasn't made any progress today. He hasn't wanted to."

In the case of Yeison, he began a computer lesson assigned to a faulty computer and was not allowed to switch. Toward the end of the class, amid Profesora Rosa María's accusatory remarks, he pleaded, "Teacher, I want to spend five minutes [on a working computer], even if it's only five minutes. Teacher, I just want to touch a [working] computer, that's all." In another case, Adrián, a high-achieving student with the goal of following in the footsteps of Costa Rican astronaut Franklin Chang-Díaz, was reprimanded in guidance counselor Profesora Delia's office. Profesora Marielos, the other guidance counselor, explained to me, "It's that he only thinks of the moon, of NASA, not of *today*. Only of the year 2000."[12]

Students who did not fit the image of the ideal student (white, wealthy, and from Santa Rita for the most part) were quickly made aware of the expectations of them as members of a specific class, race, ethnicity, or gender. In an environment in which professed indigenous identity was less than conducive to school success, Nambueseño students at SRHS faced contradictory pressures. The national curriculum—set on producing good, "non-ethnic" Costa Ricans—urged students to fit the national mold, whereas the local society held Nambueseños and others to stigmatized identities.

RACIAL AND RACIST LESSONS

Among the stigmatized identities tied to Nambueseños were those related to race and ethnicity. As noted earlier, in theoretical literature these are two distinct but related concepts. What I might consider ethnicity (e.g., Chorotega indigenous identity), however, was referred to as "race" in Santa Rita and talked about in terms of color (although it might not always have been marked so on the body). Thus, the terms were not easily separated in this context. One way in which racial identity was taught was through examples like that provided at the beginning of this chapter. I viewed the posters as emanating a racist message. To be sure that I was not imposing my own cultural interpretations on the situation, I asked students and teachers whom I knew well about them. Three *moreno* traveler teachers interpreted them as cruel teachings. Four students from Nambué (interviewed together and for whom Federico did most of the talking) felt the posters held no offensive message. Two other Nambueseño students did take offense at them but were reluctant to complain about them for fear of engendering the teacher's possible grudge. The most extensive interview I conducted about the posters was with the school superintendent.

In my general interview with the superintendent, I asked if he thought discrimination was a problem in the high school. He did not. I showed him pictures I had taken of the posters and asked if he did not see a racial message in them. He explained, "No, they may not have any racist meaning. Simply put, these are put on the market for sale. People buy what they want to buy—especially people in Costa Rica. They are very consumeristic. It's a matter of 'hey, I like this little drawing, I'm going to buy it,' and they put it up there." Others explained to me that these drawings were common, and one could purchase any image with any message. Just as one could buy a poster with a white child that said "You're my ideal!" one could buy a poster of a *moreno* child with that same message. Therefore, it was not the posters themselves that were racist. I would still argue, however, that the configuration in which they were placed, and their juxtaposition of races and values, conveyed a racist message. Hegemonic views of race and status in Santa Rita, however, did not allow this to be visible. Once again, one can attribute such blindness to habitus, "which causes an individual agent's practices, without either explicit reason or signifying intent, to be none the less 'sensible' and 'reasonable.' "[13]

In other incidents, racial teachings were more direct. Profesora Natalia, a *morena* teacher residing in Santa Rita, taught a girl reluctant to see herself as Guanacasteca and *morena* (she was the eighth-grade girl who had pulled up her pants leg to prove her whiteness to me) that because she had been born in Majapiñao rather than Santa Rita, she was Guanacasteca. Profesora Natalia added, "You have the look of a Guanacasteca. You are the typical Guanacasteca." Profesora Natalia then said that she herself was also Guanacasteca and proud of it. Another *moreno* teacher, Profesor Isidro, who also lived in Santa Rita, told me on numerous occasions that he liked to tell the Indian students they were more pure because they knew their origin, as opposed to the others who were more like "mutts." Profesor Sergio, a young *moreno* traveler teacher, told students in a class I observed that they should not make fun of Nicaraguans, Indians, or others because "we all carry all kinds of blood."

Carlos, a Nambueseño graduate, in an interview that took place prior to my year of fieldwork at the high school, explained that a teacher had inspired him during the first week of school. The student in question felt dejected as a result of his classmates' ethnic slurs and racist epithets that conflated his ethnicity with stupidity. The teacher pulled the student aside and assured him that he was not as stupid as his peers were making him out to be because he was not truly Indian but mestizo. Thus, the teacher did not decry the stereotype being transmitted. Rather, he affirmed it, but he removed the student's stigma by placing him in a different ethnic category. The teacher still supported the dominant, derogatory mode of thinking that suggested that Indianness connoted reduced potential for success.[14]

SRHS, and the individuals who influenced its culture, taught students that Indian identity was incompatible with school success and simultaneously imposed that identity on students. Profesora Eugenia saw a recent photo of a former student and remarked to a colleague, "You should see the change in [this former student]. When he was here, he was insignificant: a little black boy. Now he's handsome." The teacher seemed to use the words *insignificant* and *little black boy* synonymously. Surely this attitude must have come across to students if teachers admitted such attitudes so freely to a researcher known to be studying discrimination.

ENGENDERING SOCIAL ROLES

School also taught gender roles. Girls were at once taught to suppress and develop femininity. They were likewise taught to discredit ideas surrounding gendered work roles while being placed in classes that reinforced those ideas. The seventh-grade civics textbook used at SRHS taught this regarding gender and education:

> The State has the obligation to promote coed education and to oversee that this is carried out. Furthermore, it has the task of revising educational texts, methods, and pedagogical instruments so that they do not assign men and women roles in society that are different or contrary to social equality or gender complementarity or that maintain women in a subaltern condition.[15]

In spite of this, however, gender differences in education abounded. As in the United States, this might have been, to some degree, unavoidable, given the gender bias evident in percentages of female to male teachers and in school materials.[16]

Teachers of vocational classes at SRHS talked to me about past years when the Ministry of Education enforced girls' participation in certain courses and boys' involvement in others. According to one teacher, this rule had been relaxed in 1995 or 1996. Others suggested it had never been a strict rule set down by the ministry but rather one enforced locally, by teachers and students. Such local pressures—similar to those Dorothy Holland and Margaret Eisenhart refer to as "peer-imposed sexism"— still existed in 1999.[17] Although girls could take vocational classes widely considered to be masculine, such as woodshop and carpentry, the teacher of the course noted that in his thirteen years of teaching he had seen only three girls specialize in that subject. In a conversation I overheard in a sewing class in section 7-5, a girl complained that the agricultural course was "men's work." A boy placed in both sewing and agricultural classes commented that one does not need to learn to do agricultural work anyway. Profesora Rosa María criticized his attitude, asking, "What kind of men are we going to have here?" Her comment seemed to reaffirm the girl's consideration that such a class was only for males.

The courses thought of as boys' classes included "lesser species" (about raising chickens), carpentry, "let's produce in the garden" (involving planting foods for human consumption), and "let's reproduce our plants" (a course on horticulture and reforestation). Classes deemed feminine included arts and crafts, sewing, fashion design, and certain cooking classes (although cooking and arts and crafts were more acceptable for boys than sewing classes were). Other classes—computers, silk screening, drafting, dairy preparation, and pork processing—seemed to be gender neutral.

At the end of ninth grade, students chose a specialty from those offered for the following year, which usually included sewing, carpentry, the business side of agriculture, and the production of meat and milk products. During 1999, all eleven of those specializing in tenth-grade carpentry were boys. All but one of six students specializing in eleventh-grade carpentry were boys. One of sixteen students in tenth-grade sewing class was a boy (who was teased a great deal).[18] All eleven students in eleventh-grade sewing were girls.

Various scholars have noted the role of schools in reproducing gender roles in society by training women for jobs deemed "feminine" or preparing them for future wifely status.[19] In SRHS, at least one teacher encouraged girls to stay in school to avoid such routine labor. Profesora Yolanda, a young, white traveler teacher, told a girl from Sereno (tempted to drop out after rumors of her drug use circulated among teachers) to "not even think about [dropping out]. Forget that stupidity, because it is stupidity. You have to think that you have to study. And remember that now anyone who doesn't study is nobody. Remember that you aren't going to go home now to make tortillas because if you don't make it studying, all your life it will be your job to do that." Some girls talked to me about not having to do housework because their job then was to study, although when they got married their job would be to do housework. Thus, not all girls saw schooling as tantamount to future career opportunities. With regard to gendered vocational classes, two seventh-grade girls studying the chapter on gender equality I copied from their civics book asked, "In [matters of] work, why did they [women] ask for equality?" I asked one girl what she meant. She said that in her lesser species class (which did not have chickens until the end of the year) "there is only men's work: cutting grass [with a machete], cutting sugarcane, washing out pigpens, milking cows, and all that. And the teacher says that is equality: 'Women asked for equality.'" Her female classmate added, "God made the man so he would work and the woman so she would [pause] take care of children." Certainly, these gender roles were also taught in school.[20]

Profesor Arnoldo, a traveler teacher, informed me that "it is the dream of every woman to be a mother." Female students were taught that same lesson. Profesora Rosaura, from Santa Rita, talked about how she liked speaking to girls about "when [not if] they have their babies" and preparing them for that day. As was evident to me at the Mother's Day celebration described in Chapter 2, remaining childless was not an acceptable choice for women in this setting.

Mothering, however, was not the only future role expected of girls. Some teachers also talked about girls' future role as keepers of their houses and saw themselves as preparing girls for this role. Both inside and out of class, I heard Profesora Natalia instruct girls on proper ironing techniques. Furthermore, one afternoon in the teachers' lounge the conversation among three teachers belonging to the "pillars" clique turned to the problem of girls getting out of marching practice because they were menstruating (a common way to get excused from physical education as well). Profesora Natalia criticized such girls, noting, "They think they're sick because they're menstruating." She then commented to her colleagues, rhetorically, "as if one doesn't still have to do housework when one has her period."

Other gender expectations—such as the importance of personal appearance—were also taught to girls in school. Profesora Anatolia, a traveler "pillar" teacher, told me that what she tried to teach students apart from her vocational specialty was the importance of their personal appearance. She noted that she thought this was even more important for girls than for boys. Profesora Rosaura said she would like to have girls only be able to wear skirts as part of their uniform (as opposed to having the choice between skirts and pants) "to differentiate them. Here it appears that all are men. One sees how they sit, how they lift up their feet, and all that. So I think it would be beneficial for the girls. They would keep being girls consistently. I tell them to come to exhibit their legs and they laugh. . . . I think femininity has gotten lost." Still, the view that girls ought to display femininity (not to be confused with excessive sexuality) was clear at SRHS.

Another traditional role taught to girls in high school was to be objects of beauty. Profesor Sergio, a young *moreno* traveler teacher, sat outside in the hall as I interviewed him. Amanda, a white Riteña student, came out of his classroom, and he scooted over to make room for her on his chair. He joked with me, in her presence, saying she was a pretty girl and a good student but that she talked a lot. Profesor Agustín passed by, and Profesor Sergio commented to him that he liked Amanda and that she was pretty. Profesor Agustín replied, "She is also intelligent." Thus, for girls, intelligence was only one important attribute in school, and it was perhaps eclipsed by the importance of their appearance. Still, girls' ideal appearance and presentation of femininity were not equally attainable for all. Beauty, for girls, was very much tied to whiteness.[21]

TEACHING THE VALUE OF WHITENESS

In the class called fashion design, girls made paper dolls, designed outfits for them, and held a fashion show with their dolls. All the paper dolls I saw were white. Many had blue eyes. Although some scholars suggest that beauty standards in school are set by peers rather than by higher authorities[22] and another considers that whiteness is an *invisible* standard against which all students are measured,[23] this was less the case at SRHS where various teachers explicitly equated beauty with whiteness and where girls participated in a beauty pageant that might as well have been a pageant of whiteness.

The value placed on whiteness was visible in many ways. The posters described at the beginning of this chapter constitute one way that value was conveyed to students. Profesora Delia, one of the two school counselors, taught students that self-esteem meant coming to terms with being fat, thin, or *moreno* or with having straight hair. Thus, darkness was specified as a quality to "deal with" or to "get beyond" in order to attain self-esteem. (Given the high school's racist context, this might have been a realistic and useful lesson.) A seventh-grade girl interviewed all of her classmates on various topics ranging from their favorite music to the object of their desire and wrote the responses in a notebook (which a school counselor later ordered her to burn). She asked classmates whether the person they liked was *moreno* or *blanco*. Only one classmate said *moreno*. The girls in school whom boys talked about as the prettiest were invariably white. The male teachers the girls held up as icons of handsomeness were also white. Several girls listed all the white teachers and asked me if I didn't think they were handsome. At once seeking their reactions and trying to avoid gossip, I said no. One of the girls commented that I had very strange tastes.

At a soccer game between Nambué's elementary school and Santa Rita's, I took pictures of the girls from Nambué who cheered for their (all-male) team. Santa Rita's cheerleaders shouted that I would break my camera taking pictures of such ugly girls. The Nambueseña cheerleaders belted out a retort (in a *bomba*, a rhyming linguistic style considered typical of Guanacaste) to their white Riteña rivals that also equated darkness with ugliness and framed the rivalry as one not only of place but also of racial opposition: "*Soy negrita fea, nacida en Guanacaste. Pero en el baile de punto, no hay cartaga que me aplaste*" (I'm an ugly black girl, born in Guanacaste. But in the [traditionally Guanacasteco] *punto* dance, there's no Cartaga that can beat me). Amelia, a *morena* not from Santa Rita, noted, "People don't like dark women. They don't like *morenas.*"

Even within Nambué, the value placed on whiteness was evident. In interviews with parents of Nambueseño students, mothers sometimes referred to the hierarchy of students from Nambué. They tended to use the phrases "the lightest ones" and "the ones that are physically better off" interchangeably. More than one mother told me her daughter had better not marry a Nambueseño.

I do not wish to suggest that the value placed on whiteness was reinforced only among peers. At times it was the topic of teacher-led classroom discussion. In a class led by Profesora Rosaura, a Riteña, students discussed an assigned short story called "The Green Eyes." Profesora Rosaura explained that the story was about the idealization of women. The protagonist was described as having yellow hair—"like the rays of the sun"—yellow eyelashes, and white skin, "so that she looks more like an angel," explained the teacher. A boy in the class commented "Clara" (the name of the student who won the school beauty pageant, who was present in the classroom). I recalled one of my first interactions with Clara toward the beginning of the year. She was lying on a bench during free time, combing her fingers through her hair as several male classmates looked on. The wind carried away a loose blond hair, and she exclaimed, jokingly yet knowingly, "catch that—it's worth money!"

Focusing again on the class at hand, I took notes as Profesora Rosaura—not yet commenting on the boy's comparison of the protagonist to Clara—went on to discuss the way boys tended to idealize the girls they liked. She then looked directly at Clara and noted that boys could say, "She has very dry [skinny] legs. She has no waist. She has ugly hair." Profesora Rosaura turned her gaze away from Clara and explained matter-of-factly that when a boy liked a girl, he wouldn't see those defects. As the teacher listed Clara's defects, one boy's jaw dropped. He looked from Clara to Profesora Rosaura to his classmates, but no other student manifested shock at the teacher's comments—not even Clara, who sat quietly, turning slightly red. Profesora Rosaura continued, explaining that in the story people idealized the woman with green eyes, noting that this character had no other name. A boy again suggested "Clara." The teacher did not respond. She noted that some people considered the protagonist to be of this world while others saw her as an angel.

In a subsequent class, Profesora Rosaura continued to discuss "The Green Eyes." She asked students, "Why did she [the protagonist] have white skin?" Juan Pablo, a boy from Nambué, replied, "Because she was Cartaga." Profesora Rosaura (who self-identified as a Cartaga in our interview) did not acknowledge his response. Instead, she said the protagonist was white because she was a spirit and went on to describe her in detail: "She was more than beautiful. In that time, the fashion was to be very white." The teacher talked about people wearing hats and carrying parasols to protect their white skin. I thought of women in Santa Rita in 1999 who followed the same custom. The teacher then pointed out that current fashion dictated that women should have tanned skin and that men with excessively white legs looked ugly. Although she stated that whiteness was less prized currently and bronzed skin was considered superior, her previous comments in this class and the preceding lesson suggested otherwise. Both the teacher's and the students' comments on whiteness and on Clara manifested that Clara's whiteness was integral to her perceived perfection.

Although Profesora Rosaura's comments on the popularity of tanning might have been true to some degree, many students who could afford them used assorted whitening "remedies." Girls with the economic means to do so lightened their hair or added blond highlights. Profesora Eugenia—one of the principal "pillars"—as well as various students wore thick pancake makeup shades lighter and pinker than their skin tone, resulting in a geisha-like effect. The message that whiteness was valued and could be bought by those in a position to do so was very clear. Once again, whiteness, class, and status intermingled in this school setting.[24]

I will return to the maintenance of this hierarchy of color shortly. First, however, I will briefly reiterate what female students might have achieved through whiteness and provide one more example of the cult of feminine whiteness in SRHS. Profesor Sergio, the teacher who shared his chair with a student as he taught her the value of her beauty, talked to me about beauty and status in our interview. First, he noted that "if [a female student] is considered by her peers and her brutish teachers to be an Indian [pause], she does suffer discrimination." Later in the interview he assured me that he treated students the same regardless of their appearance. He acknowledged, however, that students from Nambué and Sereno who had light skin or eyes would be treated differently—in a less discriminatory manner—by students from Santa Rita than their fellow students from Nambué and Sereno would. Thus, race and attractiveness played a significant part in girls' experience.[25]

The event in which the equation of whiteness with beauty became most clear was a school-sponsored beauty pageant. There, too, femininity and all that it ideally entailed were elucidated. On the day of the pageant, I asked students and teachers who they thought would win. At least one person admitted that we could rule out Amelia, the single *morena* candidate, from the start. Amelia was, incidentally, one of the few traveler students participating. Several students and teachers predicted that Clara, the whitest of the candidates, would win. One teacher described her as looking "like a Barbie doll." Some teachers, however, criticized her body, noting a lack of feminine curves that would be a disadvantage in this event.

Fourteen candidates (of the original seventeen) arrived to participate. When the event began, each girl was introduced by the number of her homeroom section, not her name, and she paraded around the room in a short, formfitting dress until she arrived at the stage of the community meeting hall. As the girls walked around the room, an announcer noted each girl's hair color, eye color, skin color, and height. The announcer described most of the girls as *"trigueña"* or *"blanca"*—terms connoting relative blondness and whiteness, respectively. Eye colors listed included black (for Amelia), "sky blue," and "honey" (light brown). Once on stage, each girl greeted the crowd and introduced herself by name and the number of the homeroom section she represented.

Once all the candidates were on stage, the names of five finalists were read (with no explanation of how they were selected). The girls eliminated from competition left the stage. The remaining five were all Riteñas, and all were white with either honey-colored or blue eyes. After another round of deliberation by the judges, Clara was crowned by the principal and addressed the crowd. She then took a final promenade around the room and the pageant ended, to be followed by a dance. I returned to Nambué, where nobody was surprised at the outcome. The standard of whiteness as an ideal against which all others were measured was anything but invisible there.

Monitoring Whiteness and the Policing of Interracial Relationships

David Sibley writes critically of whiteness both as something to be achieved and as constantly threatened.[26] Evidently, several high school staff members also felt this threat. On numerous occasions the discussion at staff meetings turned from academic matters to the need to control student relationships.[27] Although students were specifically taught certain aspects of femininity, controls on sexuality were strictly enforced. Girls were supposed to at once exude femininity and avoid sexuality.[28] To some extent, peers, too, controlled girls' sexuality. Recall that girls' nicknames implied too little sexual activity (as in the case of "Freezer") but also excessive sexuality (as was true for "Glass of Water").[29] Particular teachers, though, also controlled girls' sexuality. On a religion exam regarding human sexuality (read: reproduction within marriage), I watched Profesora Soledad shake her head in disapproval as she marked a student's response incorrect. The question asked for three characteristics of human sexuality; the one marked wrong was "it is pleasurable." Usually, however, discussions of students' sexuality were based on their experience rather than on curricular items.

Students reported that in the past, girls who became pregnant were kicked out of school. One student reported that the first pregnant student to stand her ground was a Riteña who insisted on being able to stay in school. The year of my fieldwork, one topic discussed at the first staff meeting was two students' pregnancies. Profesora Eugenia announced that they ought to drop out then because they would never be able to catch up. Although the girls began the school year late, both did catch up. They were frequent topics of gossip in the teachers' lounge, however. Girls in relationships where sexual activity was suspected but not confirmed were the topic of staff meetings. This was not true for all girls' relationships, however. Those discussed the most at staff meetings tended to be relationships between white Riteña girls and *moreno* boys.

In one case, teachers talked about Amelia—a *morena*—and a Riteño boy. At the beginning of the school year, a teacher had suggested that these two students were inappropriately involved. It was reported that the two were found leaving an abandoned school building with their classmates standing around, "keeping watch." Over the course of the year, I got to know both of the implicated students as well as Profesora Anatolia, the "pillar" teacher who reported that event. Amelia eventually explained what had occurred. Her class was free, and students were passing the time. She was seated next to the boy in question on a rock outside the abandoned building, and her classmates were nearby. That was the extent of the situation. Nevertheless, after a great deal of hyperbole, Amelia was taken to the principal's office to be reprimanded. Nothing happened to the boy. Amelia remarked to me that a student in such a bind could not do anything "because they are teachers, and they are above one." Amelia's version was more credible to me by this time, both because I knew her well and because I had seen ample evidence of Profesora Anatolia's penchant for often unfounded gossip.

As Foucault describes with secondary schools in the eighteenth century, the question of sex was ever present.[30] In this context, the question of sex was mixed with other elements. As in the larger community context, race, place, and gender were mingled. Irene, a white, non-Riteña girl with green eyes, was involved with a Riteño boy. When she had chicken pox and was unable to come to school, Riteño gossips told her boyfriend that she was surely seeing someone else, and he was warned to end his involvement with her.

Sara, a girl from Nambué with white skin and green eyes, was warned by family members residing in Santa Rita to marry someone white so her family would look like her. A woman originally from Santa Rita, now married to a Nambueseño and residing there, was disowned by her family. Near-constant surveillance in Santa Rita awaited those who crossed the boundaries of place, class, race, and gender. This policing of sexuality also served to guard against racial mixing, given that *mestizaje* was viewed, perhaps, as potentially undermining white privilege.[31] In this sense, the high school and the community in which it was located were comparable to a colonial context. It was a setting in which colonizers (Riteños) confronted the colonized (Nambueseños), and *la rectitud andante* (composed mainly of the self-proclaimed pillars of Riteño society) policed morality and guarded against racial mixing or any other type of "outside," or foreign, influence.[32]

I talked to a member of *la rectitud andante* (the teachers who saw themselves as taking on others' morality as a focal point of their attention) about the policing of relationships that often occurred in staff meetings. Profesora Rosaura admitted that teachers "take care of" Riteña girls (by prohibiting their relationships with non-Riteños) more than other girls. She explained, "One worries because one knows those from [Santa Rita] better. Now, those from the different towns, since they travel, one can't know the details of that place." I asked if she referred to not being able to know about the relationships that existed outside of Santa Rita. She said yes. She noted that one of the girls who began school late because she was pregnant was in a problematic situation, given that her boyfriend's family did not accept her since she was *morena*. She acknowledged, "Yes, sometimes it could occur that one is more inclined toward taking care of the girls from here relative to those from other places."

Profesora Rosaura also noted that it would be very difficult for a Nambueseño boy to date a Riteña girl. She interjected that she did not share this feeling, but she had observed it. Although she initially spoke of this situation in terms of place of residence, she then clarified that it was true for boys "of a dark color." She added that where they came from did not matter; it was about color. She said people from Santa Rita and girls from families with money "look for their partners not like that—not very Indian." She talked about Riteños seeking Nambueseña women for affairs or to use sexually but not for potentially serious partners or marriage.[33] In providing the example (related in Chapter 3) about a girl who ceased being interested in a boy when she found out he was from Nambué (because her family would not approve), Profesora Rosaura's explanation hinged on place. Soon after, though, she added that Riteña daughters not only were forbidden to date Nambueseños. She said this was true of all of Guanacaste, then noted the whiteness of Santa Rita in particular. She added:

> The model is that one's partner, one's boyfriend, be Cartago also. When the mix from outside comes, then they don't like it. Much less from Nambué because if he is from Santa Cruz or Majapiñao, [that's] more or less [acceptable], but if he is from Nambué, it is as if they say, "well, from Nambué—that he is lazy, he doesn't work, so what future will they have," let's say, concepts like that [exist].

I told Profesora Rosaura about Samuel, a Nambueseño student who, for a school fund-raiser, had to sell tickets to a dance that would be held in Santa Rita. Samuel explained that a Nambueseño would have to buy two tickets to take someone willing to dance with him. Profesora Rosaura agreed that Samuel had a valid concern.

Several teachers also policed relationships between Riteña girls and boys from Sereno.[34] I heard teachers' criticisms of two such couples. Both girls were from prominent Riteño families. After one round of criticism, one girl talked to me about being forced to end her relationship with her Sereno boyfriend of a year and a half. She stated the reason as *"habladas de profesores"*—teachers' talk—which had reached her mother, who told her to avoid becoming the object of such gossip. The alternative for many girls was to be pulled out of school by concerned parents.

In another case, the discussion took place in the teachers' lounge between Profesor Teodoro and Profesora Alodia—two members of the Riteño teachers' clique—and the vice principal. Profesor Teodoro reported that he had observed the niece of a Riteña teacher and a boy from Sereno in, as he phrased it, "a love scene." His description was detailed, and Profesora Alodia, a "pillar" known for both decrying student romance and observing and reporting it in minute detail, hung on his every word. Her conclusion was to call the girl's mother (not the boy's) to see if she knew about and permitted the relationship. If so, she added, they ought to tell this couple not to let other students catch them in such scenes, since it would set a bad example for others. She also noted that if the teachers did nothing, students would consider it preferential treatment resulting from the fact that the female student was related to a teacher. (Inasmuch as the student seated on a rock with a boy was not given such benefit of the doubt before being punished, the consideration of preferential treatment was valid.) Profesor Teodoro and Profesora Alodia then described other romantic student interactions in steamy detail. On a different occasion, Profesor Teodoro referred to a boy as a certain Nambueseña's boyfriend. He did not show disapproval or concern about that relationship.

Through hidden curriculum and direct teachings, students were taught their social location within a hierarchy of place, race, class, ethnicity, and gender, as well as which intersections of these categories were acceptable and which were not. Habitus and the naturalization of these teachings obscured the ways they differentially opened doors or shut them to various students' futures. I turn now to the ways school channeled students into particular futures, and how professional options were differentially available to traveler and Riteño students, respectively. I also examine future prospects for those who graduated versus those who did not. In particular, I question whether the high school experience at SRHS is of any value to students from the reservation.

DIFFERENTIAL OPPORTUNITIES AFTER HIGH SCHOOL

David, a tenth-grade student from Nambué, when faced with academic content he felt was inappropriate or irrelevant to his life, had the habit of drawing attention to his opinion in a curious way. From the back of the room, where he routinely sat, he would shout, "*¿A qué me va a servir esto en la bananera?*" (What good is this going to do me in the banana plantation?). This simple comment was at once a critique of the curriculum offered at SRHS and a pointed commentary on students' post–high school job options.

Various scholars have noted that schools channel students into particular fields associated with their class status.[35] The proponents of this social reproduction theory (or cultural reproduction theory) blame the dominant society's goal of maintaining the status quo and preventing minority students from obtaining the cultural capital necessary to succeed in school, thus perpetuating their lower-class positions in society.[36] Earlier proponents of social reproduction theory left little space for human agency, ignored variation within and among different groups,[37] and downplayed the possibility of resistance to the imposition of dominant ideas.[38] Also, this theory has been criticized as being deterministic and overly functionalist.[39] Although these criticisms are valid (and are explored further in Chapter 7), they formed a foundation for scholarship and paved the way for researchers who now address both structural constraints and individual agency.

More recent scholars in education and anthropology have built on this foundation to address the complexities of social reproduction more thoroughly. Bradley
Levinson, Douglas Foley, and Dorothy Holland have written about "cultural production" in part to address "the interplay of agency and structure."[40] Others, too,
have debated the relative strength of the reproductive nature of schooling and that of
subaltern resistance.[41] It is useful to elaborate on the contributions of social reproduction theory in this chapter as it relates to students at SRHS.

In Chapter 4 I demonstrated how the school valued the experience of dominant
students and worked to the detriment of traveler students. This occurred by teachers
taking for granted that students from Santa Rita were better students (i.e., versed in
how to "do" school) upon their arrival at SRHS, whereas travelers had to learn the
ropes as they went along. Thus, the cultural capital of the dominant class was privileged in the school setting. The remainder of this chapter addresses the ways the
results of the practices already described played out in the job market and how the
school's perpetuation of inequality was "rationalized" and made to look like something other than discrimination.

As we have seen in earlier chapters, class and race played significant roles in the
opportunities given to students in the school. By ignoring that these were significant
factors, the school hierarchy was made to look like a meritocracy.[42] Tied to this
concept is what Jay MacLeod terms the "achievement ideology,"[43] which suggests
that a student who studies and tries hard can succeed regardless of factors such as
poverty and the attitudes that surround it. MacLeod, addressing why teachers continue to promote this achievement ideology in spite of evidence to the contrary,
asserts that they intend to motivate students in this manner and that they believe it
works.[44] Professor Miguel seemed to follow this line of thought when he noted, "I feel
that the student, regardless of his/her place of residence, can be as good a student as
he/she wants to [be]."

Another ideology evident at SRHS was one that linked hard work and schooling to future economic success. One teacher appeared to follow this thinking when
she urged students, "If you don't finish school, what is in store for you? Work at home
and that's it." Profesora Yolanda used this logic to prevent a girl from dropping out.
She warned that if the student did not finish school, she would be stuck at home
forever making tortillas. Another teacher told students who wanted to drop out that
schooling "is a once-in-a-lifetime opportunity, and one should not underestimate it,
as one can get benefits from it: personal, social, and economic improvement." A
guidance counselor believed a student who stayed in school would become "a professional who will earn money easily." Profesor Isidro told students, "Quitting your
studies isn't convenient because we live in a changing world, and if a person isn't
educated, he/she will have a hard time finding work and will be likely to let a boss
impose his/her will." Another teacher told students that with a diploma they could
work and have "social and economic mobility." Other teachers, however, had a more
realistic view of the future options of poor traveler students. In going over a list of
graduates of the high school and speculating on what they were doing in 1999,

Profesora Eugenia explained that one girl from a faraway town "must be there. She's from a poor family. Students from poor families get their diplomas and they stay there [in those towns]."

It appeared that the perceived link between school success and economic security, more commonly expressed than Profesora Eugenia's realist view, did affect at least some students. After graduation, one girl from Nambué intended to study sewing at the National Institute of Learning (Instituto Nacional de Aprendizaje [INA]). To be accepted there, she needed to get her high school diploma. She noted, "Without a high school degree, you can't do anything." To some extent, this might have been true. The seventh-grade civics textbook asserts, "High school will better youths' possibilities for integration into the job market. Finishing secondary education marks a substantial difference upon obtaining a salaried job, especially in the case of vocational high schools, where students also learn a vocation and receive a title to back them up."[45] Mavis, Richard, and Karen Biesanz suggest that in Costa Rica a high school diploma is required even for menial labor.[46] Although there is some validity to this claim, later in this chapter I examine just how useful a high school diploma may be to a student from the reservation.

As a result of this achievement ideology, student "failure" was viewed as just that—the result of personal failings rather than of phenomena embedded in the school's structure.[47] When students internalized this view, the achievement ideology became naturalized.[48] Through tracking in the vocational courses and other means, students at SRHS were channeled into unequal opportunities and taught to accept their lot.[49] The structural or institutionalized mechanisms that served this end in SRHS also included biased textbooks and differences in educational identities, as addressed in earlier chapters. As discussed earlier, which students took which vocational classes was seen as the result of a democratic "first come, first served" process about choice and responsibility. As demonstrated earlier, however, place of residence, social class, and favoritism were very much at work in that process. In spite of these contributing elements, the system was seen as fair. In fact, students were being taught to accept their lot in life.

VOCATIONAL EDUCATION AT SRHS

Profesora Aracely taught her vocational students that job satisfaction was key and that they ought to pursue whatever occupation they liked best, regardless of what their parents wanted them to do or what their remuneration might be. Other aspects of vocational classes, however, sent a different message. The very existence of vocational education had significant implications. Rural schools were most likely to have vocational programs, whereas schools in the city were more likely to be strictly academic. Thus, the curricula offered in rural and urban schools, respectively, already spoke to the expected futures of children from different regions of the country. This program was well-intentioned; its purpose was to train individuals from rural areas to work in fields at home and thus avoid urban migration. Father Sánchez's plan in creating the school was that it would allow students to learn theory and techniques to apply to their parents' farms to make them more productive. "Thus," Profesora Rosaura explained, "it had a very close relation to actual life."

Schools used to be categorized by the type of vocational specialty offered (industrial, agricultural, or mechanical). By 1999, in theory, each individual school's administration could decide which specialties to offer. The legacy of each school having been set up for one particular type of vocational study was still evident, however. Although a school administration may have wanted to replace unpopular vocational workshops with different ones, the acquisition of new equipment and new staff for these workshops would likely have proved prohibitively expensive. It would also have required replacing existing personnel, which in a small town, where staff members were not just employees and co-workers but neighbors, would have been exceedingly difficult.

Although many teachers thought several of the vocational workshops offered at SRHS were obsolete, irrelevant to students' lives, or ineffective, others felt the vocational program was of great usefulness to traveler students. Of the teachers initially interviewed on this topic, the majority listed the vocational program as a high point of the high school. Profesora Delia, a guidance counselor, explained that the vocational program was beneficial to traveler students from poor families, given that these students were unlikely to attend universities. Therefore, for these students the vocational program would offer "a first step toward opening themselves up to a particular profession of their choice." She further noted, "Many students are inclined to [participate in] the vocational program specifically, since their economic means do not allow them to pursue another program." She clarified that the vocational program was intended particularly for the traveler students, given that many students from Santa Rita would have the opportunity to pursue higher education because of their economic means.

I found Profesora Delia's explanation problematic for a variety of reasons. Although the vocational program was meant to provide training for traveler students, Riteño students had first pick of the workshops. The vocational program was also intended to aid students who would remain in the region and dedicate themselves to agricultural work. This would only be relevant, however, for students who owned farmland on which to carry out the practices they had learned. Those who owned farmland were mostly from Santa Rita. Therefore, those in the vocational program tended to be those who would move away and pursue university educations in careers not related to their vocational specialties. Computer courses would be relevant to their futures, but the rest of the vocational courses offered—including those from which they could choose their specializations—would not. Finally, given that Nambueseño students had repeatedly been removed from the workshops of their choice and placed in less desirable courses, I question Profesora Delia's contextualization of this discussion in the language of "choice" and "inclination." Who, then, did the vocational program serve? This question was reiterated throughout my conversations with students.

Jaime, the Riteño seventh grader referred to in previous chapters, was the focus of the classes he attended in that his presence was acknowledged by both teachers and students almost every time I observed his classes. His frequent participation and questioning made him the center of attention. As a Riteño, Jaime had his choice of workshops. He told me in 1999 that he planned to leave SRHS and attend a strictly academic high school in Majapiñao and later go to a scientific magnet school in Liberia. Following this, he would attend the University of Costa Rica and study law. Since he disliked the idea of defending people who did bad things, he planned to become a judge as soon as possible. Adrián, the Riteño who dreamed of becoming an astronaut, left SRHS to attend a scientific school in the city and eventually went on to study physics and astronomy at the country's most prestigious university. The overwhelming majority of eleventh graders I interviewed (most of whom were Riteños, as was the majority of the eleventh-grade class) planned to attend a university after high school. Their preferred areas of study included tourism, computers, anthropology, archaeology, journalism, business administration, dentistry, preschool education, and secretarial skills. Most of these careers would require them to live somewhere other than Santa Rita because of a lack of employment opportunities there. Thus, the professed goal of vocational workshops—to allow students to remain in their communities of origin—did not apply to the students who reaped the most benefits from (or had the most choices within) the system.

Teachers were divided on the issue of the (f)utility of vocational education. Some thought workshops like those offered in a nearby high school (which trained students to be mechanics, electricians, and secretaries) were more useful than those offered at SRHS. Twelve teachers (of twenty-six who addressed the issue) thought the vocational courses offered at SRHS were not helpful to students. Profesora Genofeva, a traveler teacher of academic courses, noted, "I don't know if learning to kill a pig or make sausages will help them later." Profesora Natalia, a "pillar" teacher of vocational courses, considered that students could learn more from their parents about these topics than they did at school. She also complained that the market was saturated for the specialties students learned at SRHS. Profesora Remedios, another "pillar" (who taught academic courses), thought one would have to change the community and the workshops offered to provide profitable options for students. In particular, she suggested courses oriented toward the tourist market, such as souvenir production. Profesora Alba, a younger traveler teacher of academic courses, noted that for the vocational track to be useful, students would have to pursue the topics of some vocational courses to the point of becoming agricultural engineers. Profesor Arturo, a young Riteño academic teacher, noted that too few people owned farms for these classes to be productive. Profesor Adán, another young Riteño academic teacher, explained that the vocational system as manifested at SRHS was "disconnected from the reality of the country." He added that, having been a student at SRHS himself, "I was a victim of this system. I didn't learn anything, it didn't do anything for me."

Others thought the system was fine but that the course offerings should be altered. One traveler vocational teacher thought workshops should be geared toward specialties likely to result in greater financial gain than those currently offered. Profesor Simón, a traveler vocational teacher, suggested adding coffee production, which was apt to the region, to the agricultural courses offered. Still others thought the system should have been able to fulfill its goals with the classes it did offer but noted that it had not done so. A member of the school board explained that students were supposed to graduate with the skills to start their own businesses, but they failed to do so. She added, "Tailors do not come out of [the high school], nor do pastry shop owners, which supposedly they are learning about there, nor do people prepared to start pig farms." Profesora Rosaura held a similar opinion. She thought the training given in the high school ought to be sufficient for graduates to begin businesses. She noted that dairy farmers sold milk to big businesses rather than starting their own businesses in which to produce ice cream, cheese, and other dairy products students learned to produce in school. In spite of this, however, she concluded that she still believed in the vocational school system.

Post–High School Employment: Estimations and Opportunities

Profesora Remedios, a traveler "pillar" and supporter of the vocational system, acknowledged that few students ended up working in their vocational specialties. She blamed this on students having had the choice to leave high school after the fifth year (upon receiving the academic diploma) rather than being required to attend the sixth year to receive a vocational certificate. She lamented that students only wanted to be doctors, lawyers, nurses, architects, and engineers. She added, "The country needs vocational specialists. That would be a big help for the country." She considered that the vocational workshops offered were appropriate but blamed students for not aspiring to those career goals. A student in ninth grade not planning to attend the optional sixth year of vocational classes noted that to take the sixth year was "to waste a year."

Profesor Teodoro, a vocational "pillar" teacher, disagreed. He noted that only 2 to 5 percent of students would go to the university, and the rest would work in agriculture. Others disagreed with his estimates. Most thought the percentage of students who would end up working in their vocational fields was low. Profesora Anatolia, also a veteran traveler (and "pillar") vocational teacher, noted that of thirteen graduating students from her class in a previous year, ten went to the university. Those who did not ended up working at home, and one was in the capital city. (Interestingly, this last student was a Nambueseña preparing to study at the university. She had not been informed of the admissions process, as her classmates were, and thus was not admitted at the same time they were.) Although preparing students to work at home was purportedly a goal of vocational education, many teachers referred to such students as "doing nothing" with their education. Of another class of Profesora Anatolia's students, only two of fifteen ended up working in a field related to their area of study.

The vice principal estimated that perhaps 20 to 30 percent of students would work in their vocational fields. The superintendent suggested that 40 percent of students would go on to study in universities and that the rest would work in factories or in their homes. Profesora Natalia, a veteran (and "pillar") vocational teacher residing in Santa Rita, suggested that 50 percent of students in her sewing class would end up working in the textile industry. She specified that many of her former students worked in factories. Profesora Greis, a young traveler academic teacher, estimated that up to 95 percent of students might continue to study at the university and do nothing with their vocational training.

I studied records of students who had been in the eleventh grade the previous year. Of a total of forty-eight students, twenty-two (46 percent) were studying in a university. Five had enrolled in the high school's optional sixth year to obtain their vocational title, but none had completed the process. Three of the students were working (although it was not generally known in what field), and one was also pursuing the equivalent of a general equivalency diploma (GED). Five students were living in their parents' homes and thus were discussed by peers and teachers as "doing nothing." Thirteen had not graduated and were trying to get the equivalent of a GED.

Of the sixteen students who graduated with their vocational certificate the year prior to my study (1998) as a result of taking the optional sixth year of vocational classes, three were working in fields related to the vocational areas they had studied. One of these was working in a factory. Of the twenty-two students who finished the vocational track in 1997, one was working in the dairy industry for his family. Teachers referred to this student as "doing nothing." Three of the students who had never received their academic diploma were reported as "working." One of those who had not completed the academic diploma was studying computers privately. Of the thirty-eight students in the vocational program the two years prior to my study, twenty-four (63 percent) were studying in universities. Given these figures, I must question the utility of the vocational program. It appears that the success stories—those who had put their vocational education to use—were working either in factories or on their parents' farms. Both options would likely have been open to students without a six-year education.

Indeed, factory labor was one of the avenues of work most sought by Nambueseños who never attended high school, along with domestic service and plantation labor. It appears these are the fields vocational courses trained them for as well. This struck me early on as I entered the sewing room, which had numerous factory-style industrial sewing machines arranged in rows. For two teachers' vocational classes, students toured assorted factories in the country, as well as the melon fields worked by numerous unschooled Nambueseño laborers. Thus, students' employment goals did seem to reflect the opportunities they could expect to have.[50]

I talked to a group of six eighth-grade boys, two of whom were from Nambué, and asked them what they planned to do in the future. Three students from Santa Rita answered first, noting that if they had the opportunity to study at the university, they would do so. A Nambueseño responded that he would also like to do that. None knew what they wanted to study. Juan Pablo, another Nambueseño, added that he wanted to be a soccer player. When I asked where (or for what team), he said he would play soccer in Nambué. He noted that he planned to go to school only through ninth grade and then look for work. When asked why he would drop out then, he said school was expensive. His brother, who only finished ninth grade, got a job in a factory, and he planned to do the same. Juan Pablo was correct in assuming that his job opportunities were likely to be the same regardless of whether he finished high school.

Lest readers doubt that the school's social reproductive agenda is so blatant as to deliberately produce factory workers, recall the sewing teacher, Profesora Natalia, calling her graduates who were working in factories successes. Furthermore, this blatancy was evident in a textbook used in the class Principles of Agroindustry called *Anthology of Occupational Health*. The title page revealed that this was specifically a textbook for vocational education. The book cover depicted construction workers, machine operators, housecleaners, and woodworkers. It warned of lead exposure, diseases provoked by working long hours in unacceptable work conditions, and problems caused by chemicals and heavy lifting. The text also discussed the effects on posture of jobs involving extensive sitting (examples given were of clothing manu-facture and transportation workers), standing (construction), lying down (mine work, automotive work), and kneeling (agricultural work or cleaning). Although the book did not specifically mention plantation labor, it did explain machete maintenance and warned of chemical exposure—two lessons appropriate to banana plantation workers. Jay MacLeod considers that the purported tie between school success and later professional success is one of the biggest myths of schooling.[51] This class's cur-riculum, however, did not appear to promote the myth. To the contrary, it seemed fairly explicit about where students could expect to end up.

Nowhere was the reproduction of the status quo and its relation to place more evident than in the dairy production class, where I saw students making, selling, and eating ice cream, yogurt, and cheese made from milk provided by Nambueseños and other unfortunate students in the cow milking class. Likewise, predominantly Riteño students in certain food preparation courses made pickled vegetables (for sale and for their own consumption) from vegetables harvested by section 7-5 and others in the horticulture class.

The issues noted here—students aspiring to factory work and being explicitly taught to accept that goal—all tie into what John Ogbu calls the perceived job ceiling explanation. This refers to students' awareness that a diploma may make no difference in their job opportunities.[52] Various scholars note that the job ceiling is even more apparent for girls.[53] This was certainly the case when vocational work-shops seen as "feminine" focused on sewing and, to a lesser extent, cooking. Further-more, as noted earlier, some academic teachers took it upon themselves to teach girls about their futures as mothers. Indeed, female students spoke of their futures in this respect. Some saw their future "jobs" as cleaning their houses.

SOCIAL REPRODUCTION THEORY REVISITED: TRUTHS AND DEPARTURES FOR NAMBUESEÑO GRADUATES

Still, although the school's messages—conveyed through tracking—were powerful, they did not entirely strip students of their goals. Among students from the reservation, one seventh-grade boy wanted to work as an electrician and hoped to transfer to another high school to pursue that goal. Another Nambueseño planned to study tourism or computers. A seventh-grade girl wanted to study at the university if possible, and if not, she would work—she did not know in what field. A seventh-grade boy wanted to study mechanics or work in an office. He added that he would like to study computers the following year. A ninth-grade boy from the reservation planned to study English and become a tour guide. Another ninth grader planned to switch schools the following year so he could study mechanics or become an electrician. A third ninth-grade boy hoped to become an architect. He was aware that he would have to move away to work. Several more students hoped to study after high school.

David, the student who questioned what the curriculum would do for him in the banana plantation, hoped to study after high school. I asked if he did not, in fact, plan to go to work on the banana plantations. He responded, "I hope not. I hope to God not." He was repeating the tenth grade and received failing marks again during the year of my study, which could have prohibited him from repeating the tenth grade again.[54] Thus, his university plans would have to wait, at least until he obtained the equivalent of a GED. His neighbor and friend informed me that David's parents were unlikely to allow him to continue studying and had explained, "It's time for him to work."

These career goals do seem to differ generally from those of the Riteño students discussed earlier in this chapter. Some of the Nambueseños' aspirations reflected goals that might be served by vocational training, but not by that offered at SRHS. Some students planned to attend another school. Those who planned to study computers would likely face obstacles, given the history of SRHS's removal of Nambueseños from computer classes. Thus, although not all of the Nambueseños' goals reflected awareness of a job ceiling, it remains to be seen if the jobs they aspired to will be attainable by Nambueseños.

It is legitimate to ask, ultimately, to what extent high school was beneficial for students from the reservation. To this end, I examined what both Nambueseño graduates of SRHS and nongraduates were doing. A young man of the age to be in high school but who did not have the opportunity to attend was working making furniture. The carpentry workshop was listed by teachers as one of the most applicable to life and among the most useful vocational degrees offered, yet this Nambueseño was employed in that field without having taken the class. A recent graduate's mother reported that her son was working in the city "at some little job"—she did not know what, but she did not consider it a career. A graduate from ten years earlier came to town for a visit during my research. He was working in the banana plantations, alternating between administrative work and physical labor. This is what many graduates hoped to avoid through secondary education. This man's high school diploma and years of service on the plantation earned him a reprieve only in alternate weeks.

Another young man of the age to be in high school but who did not attend worked as a mall security guard. One graduate was working in a casino to pay for her studies in criminology. When she completed her studies, she hoped to work for the Costa Rican equivalent of the FBI. Carlos, a recent high school graduate, had just gotten a job with this same agency; the job announcement listed requirements for eligibility as having a high school diploma, having a driver's license, being over eighteen years of age, and passing a series of tests given by the agency. Carlos had attended university classes for a time with the goal of becoming a math teacher. His former math teacher and mentor explained to me that it was fortunate he had not seen that line of study through: "there would not have been a job for him here anyway."[55] Another graduate was preparing to apply for work in a factory. She explained that she hoped her vocational certificate in the textile industry would prove helpful in getting the job. Various other graduates were housewives or worked in the melon fields or banana plantations. From these examples, it remains doubtful that a high school education (or higher education) leads to better employment opportunities than those obtained by individuals with less formal education.

The reservation does have success stories. Invariably, though, the telling of these stories by their protagonists involved accounts of not having been treated equally or of having to work harder to get recognition. A man who was studying to become a teacher told of waving his university admissions documents in the face of a former SRHS teacher who had been reluctant to let him pass a class. Two men working for government agencies told me they were proud of the fact that they had launched their careers on their own, without help from anyone and without letters of recommendation from and political connections to Father Sánchez. An elementary school-teacher mentioned the same thing—she was told she would never get a job without political connections, but ultimately she did.

Finally, the success story of Sara merits particular attention. Sara, who graduated from SRHS approximately three years prior to my study, was the best student in her class for several consecutive years. She recalled that each year the school made a point of recognizing the top student in the ninth-grade class. (I observed this at the graduation ceremony the year of my study.) She noted that there was public recognition of the best student each year, as well as a gift given by the school. When she was in ninth grade she was the top student in her class, but she received neither a gift nor special recognition. She attributed this to her being from Nambué.

In ninth grade, students were given the opportunity to take an entrance exam for a science magnet school located in the city of Liberia. Profesora Alodia (whose daughter attended the school) explained to me that any student who wished could take the entrance exam, and only thirty of all applicants throughout the province were chosen to attend. In my year of study at the high school I saw teachers encourage particular students to take the test. Amanda, a student who was not specifically encouraged to do so but who I knew was interested in studying science after high school, felt it was not her place to take the exam. When I repeated to her that anyone who wanted to was allowed to take the exam, she did and was one of the students selected. Thus, I saw firsthand that although in theory any student could take the exam, particular students were encouraged to do so, and others were indirectly discouraged from doing so.

Sara explained that when she was in high school "they always made a list [of] the people to take the entrance exam for the Technological High School of Liberia." They had not informed her that she was on the list, however, until the exam date had passed. The same fate befell one of the other four people on the list. She added politely, "I don't know if this had anything to do with it, but the two [who were informed of the test date] were daughters of teachers." Both were also Riteñas. Another student had heard that teachers assumed Sara's family would be too poor to send her to school in Liberia and thus did not inform her of her eligibility to take the exam. This is one more way schools can decide the outcomes for given students based on social class.

Sara was not discouraged in the long run, however. Although she did not get to attend the special school, she continued to excel at SRHS and earned a college scholarship. She went on to study psychology, for which she assumed she would have to work in another part of the country. Sara fantasized about a reunion with her classmates in which they might realize how far she had come and see that she became a professional while many of them had not.[56]

These examples of professional success among Nambueseño students in spite of the discrimination they confronted in school are relevant to the major criticisms of the social reproduction approach to education. As these examples demonstrate, some students "succeeded" (both in school and in the professional realm) in surpassing the limits the school had placed on them. Other students, although still trapped within them to some degree, protested these constraints or drew attention to their existence and injustice. In Chapter 7 I will examine the strategies students used to resist the school's efforts to channel them into particular fields or ways of being.

NOTES

1. "What good is this going to do me in the banana plantation?"

2. See Luttrell 1996 with regard to how schooling teaches students to foreground some aspects of identity more than others. Yon 2000: 32 writes of school as integral to the production of identity. See also Levinson, Foley, and Holland 1996; Luykx 1999: 125 with regard to the role of schools in shaping individuals vis-à-vis society.

3. For definitions of and fundamental writings about this concept, see Gearing and Epstein 1982: 243; Spindler 1982: 237; Wexler 1989: 99; Wilcox 1982: 274.

4. Bourdieu 1984: 172. See also Bourdieu 1995: 80, 82–83, 85, 164.

5. Bourdieu 1995: 78. See also MacLeod 1987: 13 for a discussion of habitus with regard to schooling.

6. As Luykx 1999: 196 notes, schools often assume student identities from the outset. I assert, as does Luykx, that students do not always come to school with an identity firmly entrenched but rather that the school's identification of the student and the student's school experiences are key to how that student comes to view himself or herself.

7. See Davidson 1996: 23; Olsen 1987: 80; Wexler 1989: 101.

8. Donna Deyhle 1995: 412 describes a similar situation confronting Navajo students in the United States. See also Rist 1978: 7.

9. See Dirks, Eley, and Ortner 1994: 7 for more on the shifting nature of power. McCarthy and Crichlow 1993 also address the complexity of power as it is tied to knowledge and culture.

10. Although his reputation did not help teachers' estimation of him, Jacobo might have enjoyed more status among his peers as a "bad kid" than as a student merely labeled "Indian."

11. Foley 1990: 89; MacLeod 1987: 106; Rist 1970: 413; Romo and Falbo 1996: 36.

12. Recall that this took place in 1999, when the year 2000 denoted a new millennium (thus indicating "future" rather than "one year from now").

13. Bourdieu 1995: 79. See also Sleeter 1993: 160 for further discussion of blindness to white privilege.

14. See also Deyhle 1995: 419.

15. Morales Cordero and Mora Chinchilla 1996: 35; translation mine.

16. Holland and Eisenhart 1990: 7 make this claim for the embedded nature of gender bias in schools.

17. Ibid.: 54.

18. For the final project in this class, students had to make skirts for themselves. When the one boy in the class inquired what his final project would be, the teacher told him to make a skirt for his mother. This seemed to reaffirm the idea that the course (and all its potential products) was for females.

19. See Holland and Eisenhart 1990: 3; Luykx 1999: 159–160; McLaren 1982: 24; McRobbie 1978: 102; Olsen 1987: 149. Arnove 1986: 88, 94 provides a good discussion of the role of vocational education in promoting traditional careers with regard to gender, as well as problems with attempts to remedy such gendered tracking in Nicaragua. He describes an instance in which a school tried to implement a lottery system to place students in vocational classes, after which parents complained about their sons being placed in classes such as sewing and cooking.

20. Luykx 1999: 164–165 notes that the Bolivian normal school she studied taught female students that the primary roles offered to them were those of "wife/mother and beauty queen." These options were made exceedingly clear to girls at SRHS as well.

21. Ibid.: 147 also implies a conflation of whiteness and attractiveness.

22. Holland and Eisenhart 1990: 222.

23. McLaren 1986: 128.

24. See Pinar 1993 for a thorough discussion of all curricula as racialized. According to Pinar 1993: 67, "In [the curriculum's] representations of race, difference, and identity, the school communicates images of who we are as individuals and civic creatures." Likewise, Luykx 1999: 128 notes that "schools transmit a selective and purposeful image of the individual's relation to society."

25. See Holland and Eisenhart 1990: 20.

26. Sibley 1995: 24.

27. See Luykx 1999: 81 on school control of student relationships.

28. See Holland and Eisenhart 1990: 47.

29. See McLaren 1982: 22 for an account of girls' double bind with regard to sexuality.

30. Foucault 1978: 27.

31. See Stoler 1995: 35 for a similar situation, albeit in a different era and place.

32. See Luykx 1999: 265; Yon 2000: 119 for more on the policing of identities in school.

33. See Yon 2000: 115 for a discussion of the "racializing and gendering of sexual identities."

34. In the case of Sereno, we see two standards of judgment at work. Whereas several teachers thought of Sereno as a dangerous town, negatively influenced by tourist culture, students had a different view. What made students from Sereno dangerous in the eyes of select teachers gave them status in the eyes of students. Thus, although particular teachers looked down on what they saw as interracial relationships between Riteños and Serenos, girls from Santa Rita and elsewhere considered boys from Sereno among the most desirable partners. This may be tied to what Dolby 2001: 69 sees as a tie between surfing culture and whiteness. It is also possible to look at this phenomenon similarly to the way Daniel Yon 2000: 109–114 views it. In Yon's work, students spoke both for and against interracial dating. This coexistence of two standards may reflect a generational difference (between the teachers' generation and the students' generation) with regard to race and interracial relationships. Given that some Riteña girls involved with boys from Sereno still discouraged relationships between white students and those from the reservation, however, it is likely that teachers and students had different views of Sereno and possibly of the perceived race of its inhabitants. See also Dolby 2001: 104 on the role of teachers in policing peer groups on the basis of race. Here Yon's comment (2000: 114) with regard to the concept of "interracial" dating only makes sense in a realm in which race is viewed as unchanging and static. Indeed, that is how the concept of race was often used at SRHS.

35. See Bourdieu and Passeron 1977; Ferguson 2000; McLaren 1986; McRobbie 1978; Wilcox 1982: 303; Willis 1977. See also Aronowitz and Giroux 1993: 75–76; Jacob and Jordan 1993: 7.

36. Aronowitz and Giroux 1993: 79–80.

37. Hubbard 1999: 365.

38. Aronowitz and Giroux 1993: 79–80; Erickson 1993: 35.

39. Jacob and Jordan 1993: 7; Levinson, Foley, and Holland 1996: 7.

40. Levinson, Foley, and Holland 1996: 3.

41. Ferguson 2000: 21–22 acknowledges that both human agency and structure are powerful influences on school experiences, but she admits to leaning toward "structural determinants." Levinson 2001 also contributes to this newer literature, as well as providing a thorough review of other scholars who do the same. Apple 1993: 24; Aronowitz and Giroux 1993: 67; Luykx 1999: 290, 317; and MacLeod 1987: 19 are others who acknowledge the role of student resistance and agency while still falling within a social reproduction framework. Arnove 1986: 10 offers an example of a school that produced revolutionary ideology, consciously contrary to social reproduction theory. Luykx 1999: 129 provides an example of a school that promoted middle-class values.

42. See MacLeod 1987: 152–153.

43. Ibid. See also Holland and Eisenhart 1990: 6; Luykx 1999: 139; Willis 1977: 127.

44. MacLeod 1987: 143.

45. Mora Chinchilla and Trejos Trejos 1996: 52.

46. Biesanz, Biesanz, and Biesanz 1999: 214.

47. I do not use the term *structure* as connoting social class, as do Levinson and Holland 1996: 3. Rather, I include in the school structure its system, bureaucracy, and often unquestioned manner of working. I also follow Yon 2000: 126 in viewing structures as "the materiality of the ideas and belief systems." These are also linked to structures of domination (Scott 1990: xi) if one sees schools as institutions for instilling dominant beliefs. As López, Assáel, and Neumann note, these are all "conditions internal to the school that could be contributing to school failure" (1984: 360; translation mine).

48. See Moll 1994: 388.

49. See Aronowitz and Giroux 1993: 74; Deyhle 1995: 430 for more on tracking.

50. See Deyhle 1995: 430 for more on student goals coming to approximate the vocational expectations set for students in schools and evidenced through tracking. See also Clarke et al. 1975: 49 for a discussion of the nexus between social class and future options.

51. MacLeod 1987: 97.

52. Ogbu 1978: 4. See also Erickson 1993: 32; Fine 1986: 399; Foley 1990: 136; Levinson 2001: 172; McCarthy 1993: 293; Romo and Falbo 1996: 38.

53. MacLeod 1987: 143–144; McRobbie 1978: 99. See also Arnove 1986: 88.

54. In fact, some students did get a third chance, but most assumed that two years was the maximum number of years any student could spend in any one grade.

55. Recall Profesora Rosaura's hope to replace the traveler math teacher with a Riteña. In such a context, almost certainly there would have been no job for a Nambueseño.

56. Although I do not wish to belittle Sara's efforts, it may be important to note that she is white with green eyes. This may have had an impact on her being allowed to succeed at SRHS.

7

"Para no dar a torcer el brazo"[1]

STRATEGIES OF STUDENT RESISTANCE

THROUGHOUT MY FIELDWORK I WITNESSED STUDENT ACTS THAT IN SOME WAY countered school policy, curriculum, teaching style, and the like. Although I might interpret as resistance acts such as deliberately sporting a nonuniform sock color in a school where frequent sock checks affected grades, tucking in shirts sensually, and student clowning and witty retorts, resistance theorists require the categorization of such acts as resistance to rest on more certain evidence. Toward the end of my year of fieldwork at Santa Rita High School (SRHS), I told Jacobo I planned to write a chapter on resistance and asked if wearing an "improper" sock color and escaping from classes counted as resistance in his opinion. He said they did and added that so did tucking in one's shirt slowly, wearing different shoes, or wearing nonuniform pants. He went on to say that when the vice principal told him, under threat of punishment, to change a hairstyle she deemed "vulgar," he waited a day to do so *"para no dar a torcer el brazo"*—literally, not to let them twist your arm, and figuratively, not to let them get the upper hand. In this chapter I will examine resistance theory, what constitutes resistance and how resistance strategies may vary in the long and short run, what was resisted at SRHS, and various examples of resistance.

Recent theorists in education and anthropology and proponents of resistance theory seek to address the shortcomings of early social reproduction theory, as noted in Chapter 6. Thus, whereas earlier social reproduction theorists saw the structures of schooling as all-powerful, resistance theorists examine student agency and the actions taken by students to counter, protest, or draw attention to the structures of power.

Still, resistance theory, too, has its shortcomings. One principal weakness is its general failure to address gender and race and its near-exclusive attention to the experience of males and to class-related issues.[2] Furthermore, critics of this stance (albeit critical supporters) consider that further research must address what constitutes resistance.[3] In this chapter I intend to address both gendered and racial resistance (as, indeed, much of the resistance I witnessed at SRHS was race-related). Furthermore, by linking the concepts of resistance theory with anthropological theorizing on resistance and noting more recent contributions to resistance theory, I will provide a thorough discussion of what constitutes resistance and how it was visible in the school context.

Although the school might have been powerful in teaching students their respective lots in life, ascribing their identities, and urging them to accept the relative values placed on their identities, students were not powerless in the face of such teachings. What James C. Scott refers to as the "thick version" of hegemony, which leads to an almost complete ideological incorporation of the dominant mode of thinking, was not in effect.[4] Indeed, as Aurolyn Luykx points out, "Students are social agents as well as social subjects."[5] As poststructuralist anthropology notes, "[w]here there is power, there is resistance."[6] Although schools are sites of power, they are also sites of contestation.[7] We may agree, then, that resistance is ubiquitous in contexts of power and domination, but much disagreement exists regarding just what constitutes resistance.[8] It is unclear whether it must be conscious or if it can be inadvertent; if it must be an overt, large-scale, formal act or if it can be an everyday activity. Little agreement exists on whether, to merit such a label, resistance must be successful at ending a given practice or be recognized as such by those perpetuating the protested actions. Various anthropological theorists contend that less visible, everyday acts of resistance must be given credence as such.[9] Whereas some warn that "resistance" ought not to become too broadly conceptualized,[10] others are more inclined to include under this umbrella all that remotely contests, protests, or calls attention to the constraints placed on students.[11]

Some suggest that analysts ought to respect local understandings of particular actions as resistant or not.[12] Taking this into account, I asked students about their sock color choices, their reasons for skipping class, and the criticisms behind comments such as "¿A qué me va a servir esto en la bananera?" (What good is this going to do me in the banana plantation?) to ascertain whether these behaviors did indeed count as resistance.

I found that not only were all these acts considered resistant by students but also each aspect of schooling discussed thus far—the ascription of stigmatized identities, preferential treatment in teaching and favoritism, teaching style, the teaching of gendered and racial identities and the relative values of these identities, and tracking—met with student resistance in one form or another. As always, resistance and accommodation were nearly inseparable.[13] Some of the forms resistance took were perhaps detrimental to students' interests in the long run, although they were effective in the immediate setting. I contend that resistance need not be completely overt or indisputably "successful" to merit its label. Rather, it can appear as a tug-of-war with the powers that be, at times resulting in positive effects and at other times not. Although I will address the effectiveness of student resistance in particular cases, my point at present is to prove that people played with the boundaries of power at every turn.

NAMBUESEÑO RESISTANCE STRATEGIES
RESISTANCE TO PLACE-BASED DISCRIMINATION

Exactly what students were resisting was wide in scope and was related to all previous chapters of this book. Whereas students from various communities resisted some aspects of schooling, other aspects were more specific to Nambueseños. What I have termed *placism*—discrimination against Nambueseños based on place of residence (although often discussed in terms of race)—was something only students from the reservation had to resist. I begin my discussion of resistance there.

As discussed in earlier chapters, Nambueseños were targeted most by their peers as a result of residing in the reservation. Nambueseño students responded to place-based discriminatory treatment by their peers (and sometimes their teachers) in a variety of ways. Upon my arrival at SRHS, particular teachers talked among themselves about my research. One reported to me that a "pillar" teacher had explained that I was studying the way being in Santa Rita affected Nambueseño identity. Profesora Rosaura asked, rhetorically, how Santa Rita could possibly influence Nambué if Nambueseños did not go there. On the one hand, this reaction was odd, given that she saw Nambueseños in high school in Santa Rita every day. On the other hand, she had a valid point. When given the choice, Nambueseños did their banking, shopping, and other errands in Majapiñao rather than Santa Rita to avoid prejudicial treatment.

Similarly, Nambueseño students tended to be part of school peer groups not dominated by Riteños. Numerous teachers considered this a result of Nambueseños isolating or marginalizing themselves. Various students, however, saw the phenomenon as a result of Riteño exclusion. For all practical purposes, to isolate oneself is the same as being marginalized by others, in that a sense of being unwelcome by the dominant group is at the root of both actions. Nambueseño students viewed this strategy along both extremes as well, and at times the precise locus of exclusion (as a result of one's own decision or of the decision of others) was ambiguous.

Although many Nambueseño students complained of being removed from the vocational workshop of their choice and placed in a less desirable one, one Nambueseño student used this as a tactic to escape from his racist, predominantly Riteño classmates from the previous year. Having withstood a year filled with discrimination and insult, Martín purposely chose the vocational workshop geared toward horticulture, knowing the Riteño students would not sign up for such a dirt-ridden, labor-intensive class. Happily, he described his classmates (in horticulture class) as poor and "humble" like himself. Martín sought relief through association with students from his own social class.[14] Paula, a Nambueseña girl, had a similar plan for the year following my research. I asked if she would try to stay with the same classmates she had in 1999. Paula responded, "With luck, I withstood them for a year." She planned to choose a workshop that would place her in a different homeroom class than her peers from that year. Yet these students' process of self-tracking was problematic as well in its accommodation.

Other students took less complicated routes. One student's response to peer discrimination was to "go around alone." He added that he only hung out with one other student, also from Nambué. A 1994 graduate commented on her exclusively Nambueseña peer group in high school by asking, rhetorically, "Could it be that one separates oneself?" A student who graduated the following year also felt that "it's oneself [who promotes exclusion]." She said she felt uncomfortable her first year in high school when students joked about Nambué, but she implied that her feeling bad about this was her own fault. Nelson, a student who left SRHS to attend night school, affirmed that in Santa Rita classmates teased him for being from Nambué "all the time" but that he did not give this behavior any importance. He explained, with regard to those who consider such chiding discriminatory, "it's that people from here have complexes."

On the other hand, a Nambueseño student explained that one manifestation of discrimination was that in choosing groups to work with in class, "they set one apart [from them]." This same student noted that his response to discrimination by his peers was "to separate myself from them," thus elucidating the link between feeling excluded from one's peers and excluding oneself.

An interracial couple in Nambué, both SRHS graduates from many years ago, viewed the Nambueseño (Indian, by his own identification) man's treatment in high school in different ways. The man saw his rebelliousness and tendency to fight as a result of his poor treatment and exclusion, whereas his white (but also Nambueseña) wife saw his exclusion as a result of his character and propensity to fight. (Along the same lines, she considered her school success to have resulted from her good grades and the sympathy of her peers rather than from her whiteness—although in my experience at SRHS, these were not mutually exclusive.) Two of the man's brothers also considered that they were not discriminated against in high school because they did not let themselves be discriminated against. Because of their earned reputation for violence, they were left alone.

Another Nambueseño justified his grabbing a classmate by the neck after hearing him call his cousin an Indian by explaining, "sometimes one has to impose respect." He added proudly that the issue never came up again. A girl who dropped out in her first year of high school, 1995, also said she did not let students bother her; she hit anyone who tried to do so. An eighth-grade boy had the same strategy. This type of defense, however, was a double-edged sword, as evidenced by the fact that the aforementioned self-defending girl was called to the office repeatedly because of her behavior. Recall that one of the stereotypes of Nambueseños was a propensity for violence (although another stereotype was passivity). Although several non-Nambueseños noted violence as a characteristic of inhabitants of the reservation, they did not recognize it as a strategy of self-defense. Thus, in the long run it may have been a strategy that only served to mark Nambueseños further and affirm this stereotype about them.

Between these extremes of quiet isolation (self-imposed or otherwise) and violent reaction were numerous other strategies for dealing with place-based discrimination and its corresponding ascribed, stigmatized identity. One Nambueseño, Chico, teased a non-Nambueseña who rode the bus from Nambué (as she lived on the outskirts of Santa Rita, near Nambué), saying he would not let her on the bus since she had made comments about Nambueseños pulling feathers out of birds for ceremonies and had made the stereotypical war cry. Chico said loudly to his busmates, "Let's not let those who call us Indians on the bus." He then looked at the girl who had made the comments and said in a joking voice, "I'm angry at you."

On the flip side of manifesting anger, two students explained that in the face of discrimination, teasing, and the infamous stereotypical war cry at the slightest mention of Nambué or students yelling out "Indian reservation" when the truckload of Nambueseños arrived at school, they did "nothing." Another said, "I kept quiet." A different student said peers made comments about Nambué as a joke, "and one doesn't have to pay attention. We just ignore it." Indeed, ignoring comments and "staying calm" were common reactions. For some, though, keeping quiet denoted not defiance but internalization.

A few Nambueseño students—mainly girls—came to believe that they were "stupid," "slow," or "mediocre" and revealed as much to me. Various scholars have reported internalization as a principal result of discrimination.[15] This appeared to be the case for various students from the reservation. One Nambueseña dropout explained that some students were so "traumatized by what they [classmates] say that they can't study well." Samuel's grandmother confronted the guidance counselor, Profesora Delia, who seemed to hold a grudge against her son, and added at the end of her defense, "Those who say [Nambueseños are Indians] are more Indian than we are"—thus invoking the seemingly internalized meaning of Indian as uneducated.

Others may not have internalized the discriminatory messages they received but knew that the remarks did not merit their consideration. A seventh-grade girl from Nambué, in the first month of school, reported, "It doesn't bother me." Perhaps this was not completely accurate, however, since later in the year, after dropping out, she recalled, "I got mad." Another girl, who had dropped out after seventh grade the previous year (because of discrimination), said that when students yelled "Indians" or asked where their spears were, she "just looked down. What can one do?" Later she added, "I just don't pay attention." In other parts of my interviews with her, however, she listed kicking a boy in the chin, calling kids by equally rude nicknames, skipping classes taught by racist teachers, making fun of the ignorance evident in racist students' stereotypes of Nambué, and crying as tactics she employed to counter or cope with discrimination. In a visit to the high school a year after dropping out, as students began to shout "Sexy Indian Girl" (her nickname from the previous year), she ignored them, pretending not to recognize the nickname as hers.

Rather than merely not paying attention, some students drew attention to the comments made about Nambué. When classmates asked him if he didn't feel a need to confront his being from Nambué, Federico asked, "Why would I need to confront being from that place?" When Nambueseño students finally got a bus instead of the truck of the type used for transporting cattle they had ridden to that point, other students made fun of them. Some told Nambueseños, "The little Indians are getting civilized!" Sofía, one Nambueseña student, responded, "So that you see that we can. We don't come to school in any old clunker like you." Likewise, when students made comments about them now being "civilized," Sofía asked, "Then what were we before?"

Alberto recalled that he used to do nothing in the face of discrimination and that he later spoke to a teacher about her son's discriminatory behavior (to no avail). In subsequent years, he relied on his own answers to student comments. At the beginning of the year, when teachers asked students to say where they were from, Alberto's response was met with laughter. He later recalled, "I stood up to them. I told them being from the reservation isn't any big deal." Alberto said his classmates had not teased him since.

Others viewed what I considered discrimination (exclusion, name-calling, and stereotypical comments about Indians) as mere joking. Carmen, in tenth grade, talked about fellow students making fun of "Indian" speech, but she was only offended when a teacher did so. She explained that the teacher abused the trust that existed among classmates, and that offended her. She was unsure whether students who made such comments were "bothering [implying cruel intentions] or joking." A seventh grader said students had bothered him for being from Nambué but added that it was just a joke. He said, "It doesn't have anything to do with me." Later, however, he commented that joking like this was all right, but one should not cross the line. He suggested that because he got along with his peers, they did not cross the line with him.

Some students responded with jokes of their own. When a Riteño found himself in Nambué at the house of a classmate[16] who was cooking dinner, he asked if it was armadillo meat she was cooking. Carmen replied, "Why yes, I just hunted it."[17] She explained her rationale behind this strategy as follows: "I try to be friendly so they see that we aren't so bad." For other students, this joking took the form of responding to racist nicknames with an equally offensive nickname or one that evoked whiteness. Juan Pablo, a Nambueseño, meowed at a blue-eyed Riteño classmate, thus alluding to the feline nicknames commonly applied to blue- or green-eyed people. Chico, when met with comments on Indianness from Jaime and one other heavyset Riteño, shouted back "Cellulite" and "Lard" at them.[18]

Some Nambueseños replaced their stigmatized Indian identity with an equally strong, nonracialized one. The identities powerful enough to take precedence over an Indian one included class clown, "bad kid," and athlete. In the case of "bad kid," we have already seen how a reputation for violence may have only entrenched racial stereotypes more deeply.[19] Unfortunately, this response often resulted in lowered conduct grades and even expulsion. Thus, in the long run it was less effective in countering discrimination.

In Chapter 5 I discussed Federico's clowning in social studies classes when the curriculum addressed indigenous history. Although this was not as detrimental to a student's reputation as being a "bad kid," it still had negative consequences on conduct grades and other grades. In this case, the social studies teacher seemed to respond to two Nambueseño students' clowning with empathy. Profesor Sergio remarked, "I, too, would prefer to be somewhere else," but he threatened to punish the next inappropriate comment all the same.[20]

David, the student who questioned aloud what good particular items of the curriculum might do for him on the banana plantation, was also engaging in a form of clowning—albeit perhaps a less playful, more critical one. This student, indeed, was labeled a "bad kid." Often, however, that is not the case. Rather, the clown's comments may be taken lightly in the classroom.[21]

The tie between clowning and a perceived job ceiling is significant.[22] Although at times clowning at SRHS may have been playful, at others it was wrought with criticism. The student who questioned the relevance of teachers' lessons to his future in the banana plantations not only temporarily seized control of the classroom situation but questioned that situation as well.[23] Another student from Nambué also provided an example of clowning that invoked the concept of a job ceiling. Lisandro, stuck against his will in a vocational workshop that centered on milking cows, slacked off in class. When the teacher questioned his lack of participation, the student (from a poor family that owned no cattle) declared, "I'm never going to have a dairy."[24]

Given that those chosen to participate in extracurricular activities were mostly Riteños, it was rare that a Nambueseño could successfully replace his or her "Indian" label with that of "athlete." Only one Nambueseño student, Juan Pablo, achieved this, and he did so through sheer talent that allowed him to compete at the national level. It is doubtful that anything less would have sufficed.

Another identity taken on with varying success was simply that of a person who rejected Indian identity.[25] Particular teachers, who agreed that Nambué was not a "legitimate" reservation since its inhabitants were no longer "pure" Indians, supported students in this endeavor. This rejection of Indian identity (and consequent school success) was the strategy used by Carlos, a student who graduated several years prior to my study at the high school and whose strategy and resulting success were integral to shaping this study. Carlos adhered to the view of many Costa Rican social scientists that Nambueseños were "no longer" Indian, given their failure to exemplify an indigenous identity according to stereotypical expectations. He simply considered—and explained as much to his discriminatory peers—that their comments did not apply to him, as he was not indigenous.[26]

What is unclear (given that I was not conducting research in the high school at the time Carlos was enrolled there) is why his non-Nambueseño peers allowed him to shed his stigmatized identity. Many Nambueseño community members criticized Carlos for pretending to be someone he was not. Some scholars view "acting white" as delegitimizing to the actor's ascribed ethnic or racial group.[27] Alan Peshkin, in contrast, effectively describes the complexity of the dilemma Carlos may have faced: "If you act white, you are not acting Indian. If you can't act white, then what is school good for? If you don't act Indian, then who are you? If you act both white and Indian, you invite both personal and communal strain and discomfort."[28]

This may have been less of a dilemma for Nambueseños than it might be for some indigenous peoples, in that to act Indian or white was not, for Nambueseños, about choosing between distinct cultures. For Nambueseños, it was about being humble or putting on airs, the latter of which could also be detrimental to one's community belonging. In Jay MacLeod's study, a student of a lower socioeconomic class succeeding in school might be tantamount to betraying one's peers.[29] Indeed, some Nambueseños resented Carlos's rejection of Indian identity and interpreted it as evidence of a superiority complex.

Other students maintained their ethnic identity but simply bided their time in high school. Martín revealed that he was just waiting to turn eighteen so he could leave Nambué. Graduates from earlier years who waited out their high school existence have since gone on to wave their university admissions papers in the faces of teachers who belittled them. Sara, as mentioned in Chapter 6, dreamed of flaunting her subsequent academic success in the faces of those who made her high school years difficult.

Still other Nambueseños turned their frustration toward those from their own community whom they deemed below them. In one homeroom class dominated by Nambueseños, the predominantly Nambueseño student body gave its peer (also from Nambué) a nickname that suggested he was homosexual and thus placed him even lower in the social ranks. The same happened to a heavyset Nambueseño boy in a Nambueseño-dominated homeroom section.

Given that the discrimination was largely place-based, so were some of the strategies used to confront it. A teacher mentioned to me that some of his Nambueseño students pretended to be from other towns. Particular students also admitted that they did this. Samuel, a seventh grader, recalled that at the beginning of the year, people frequently asked where students were from. He only responded when teachers (rather than students) asked this question, and then he raised his hand quickly, then put it down again. Otherwise, he reported, students would say he was an Indian and ask if his dad was the cacique. On another occasion, Samuel explained that he avoided problems by "hardly ever pronouncing where I'm from." He was the student who, by the end of the year, correctly recognized that his "crime [was] being from here." Martín explained, "It is embarrassing to say you're from Nambué." A seventh-grade girl from Nambué asked me, in front of her peers, if it was not true that she was from the United States.

Alberto, a ninth-grade boy, rebuked classmates who denied being from the reservation, stating, "They don't have any reason to deny it." He said that in his first years at the high school, it was a terrifying experience to say anything at all in class, but saying where he was from was no worse than saying anything else. Other Nambueseños seemed to agree that school in general had certain traumatic elements but that such traumas were bound to happen, be they place-based or otherwise. A ninth grader commented that although his classmates had given him a nickname of which he was not fond, they did this to everyone. A seventh grader noted that his classmates replaced his name with the name of his hometown but that this was not an issue that caused him grief.

Some went so far as to express not only tolerance of these comments but pride in their focus. Federico noted that comments directed toward him about living on the reservation did not bother him. "What would bother me is not having a place to live," he responded. "I'm proud to live in an indigenous reservation because one is living in a place that has history." Sofía, who was white enough to pass as non-Nambueseña and whose Nambueseño peers thought she considered herself "Spanish" rather than mestiza or Indian (although this was not the case), shrugged off discriminatory or racist comments. She explained, "We are all equal before God. I don't have any reason to feel [I am] worth less than any other person. What's more, I'm proud to be from here." The originally Riteña mother of Carmen, a Nambueseña girl discriminated against by teachers and students alike, told her daughter to respond "and proud of it" to comments on her being Indian. In all three cases, however, it was people who could pass as non-Indian—who did not receive the same treatment as their nonwhite peers or who held a somewhat higher status than the majority of Nambueseños—who took this attitude.

It is interesting that ethnic pride was not more common as a response to discrimination, as it was in other regions of the country. Various scholars suggest that embracing and emphasizing ethnic identity is one common strategy of ethnic minorities faced with discrimination.[30] Yet this is not a response I saw in Nambué generally or in the school setting specifically. This may be a result of the disagreement regarding ethnic identity within the reservation, the relatively small size of the Nambueseño population attending high school (not enough to afford these individuals safety in numbers), or the relative isolation of the reservation. In the southeastern area of the country where reservations are nearer to one another, perhaps indigenous people have the benefit of pan-indigenous support. This is unavailable to Nambueseños, given their questionable (or at least questioned) status within the larger indigenous community of Costa Rica, as discussed in earlier chapters.

Ethnic pride is not the only strategy that was not accessible to all students from the reservation. Gender also appeared to be a consideration in responses to discrimination.[31] The wife of the man who considered his rebelliousness a response to exclusion while she saw it as the reverse noted that what saved her husband in the long run was his self-esteem. This may be more possible for men in a strongly patriarchal society that privileges boys over girls. It may also explain why internalization was more common in girls than among boys.

THE ROLE OF GENDER IN RESISTANCE

In Chapter 4 I speculated that girls might be less able to deny Indianness (and, indeed, this was a response I saw enacted only by boys) because of a common conflation of ethnic stereotypes with traditional gender roles or a view of women as the bearers of culture.[32] Although this may be the case, it may also be true that girls responded differently because race was not always the focus of insults against them. Rather, their gender was often the subject of attacks against them. A group of seventh-grade girls who entered the high school in 1995 received the homogenizing, sarcastic nickname "the Babes of Nambué"—a term inherently offensive, given that Nambué implied Indianness and Indianness connoted ugliness in Riteño society. The "Sexy Indian Girl" nickname again mixed race and gender in ways that suggest an inappropriate school identity.[33] Cameron McCarthy and Warren Crichlow provide another explanation for this. They suggest that "minority women and girls have radically different experiences of racial inequality than do their male counterparts, because of the issue of gender."[34] Similarly, Aurolyn Luykx contends that

> girls' education is *not* the same as that of boys, even when both share the same classroom. Though exposed to the same curriculum, male and female students are differently positioned with regard to that curriculum, and thus experience it in different ways. Female students are likely to have difficulty reconciling the school's gendered atmosphere to their professional aspirations, whereas boys do not.[35]

These may be reasons Nambueseñas and their male counterparts differed with regard to strategies for dealing with discrimination. Nambueseño boys tended to stick together during free time, regardless of what grade or homeroom they were in. In contrast, during the year of my study, girls from Nambué tended to have few friends in their homeroom classes, but they stuck with them rather than seek Nambueseño support outside their classroom, across grade levels. I saw no Nambueseñas clowning or taking on alternative identities, although these were tactics employed by boys from the reservation. One avenue of resistance open to girls was to take on a sexualized feminine identity. This strategy, however, was not a reaction to the school's categorization of Nambueseños as Indians and was by no means unique to Nambueseña girls. I will address this strategy in greater detail later, along with more generalized student resistance.

PARENTAL INVOLVEMENT AND RESPONSES TO DISCRIMINATION

The students from Nambué whose parents or older siblings had attended the high school were more apt to use the formal system for placing complaints. The grandmother of Samuel, the student who understood that his crime was simply being from the reservation, confronted the guidance counselor who had repeatedly accused her grandson of rule infractions and had asked her to pull her grandson out of school. At first, according to the student's grandmother, the counselor threatened to expel the boy. The grandmother drew upon her knowledge as the mother of an elementary schoolteacher and recognized that expulsion was an illegal response to Samuel's minor breach of conduct. She talked about the national school guidelines and defended her grandson's rights. She informed Profesora Delia that the latter had picked the wrong person to talk to as she had.

She confronted Profesora Delia's apparent (mis)perception of her ignorance by telling the counselor that all of her children had high school diplomas and that she herself "got [her] good six years [of elementary school]." Furthermore, she let the counselor know that she knew various teachers personally and named two "pillars" and me, the visiting anthropologist. The counselor acknowledged, "Karen is a very good person." The grandmother, a longtime friend of mine, answered, "So you see, we have good things in Nambué."

Other parents also got involved in their children's resistance efforts. Federico's mother, originally from a Riteño family, filed a formal complaint with the Ministry of Education regarding the school's failure to comply with its obligation to provide services for her son's learning disability. A student whose mother had graduated from the high school asserted that she would do the same. Federico, however, feared that if the complaint was not taken seriously at the higher levels, he would suffer the consequences, and his resistance would make matters worse.

Some of these parents became jaded throughout the course of the year and shared the above-mentioned students' fears. Samuel's grandmother considered that he was the target of false accusations because his grandfather had visited the school early on to protest the boy's removal from computer class and placement in the agriculture class. A mother explained that she did not complain to administrators about the poor treatment of her children because if she did, they would be more likely to hold a grudge against her children. Thus, various parents, like their children, came to believe that resistance was not only futile but damning as well. A graduate of the high school who was related to other students there explained student inaction by noting "they're already accustomed" to the treatment they receive.

Other parents had still different ways of interpreting discrimination against their children. Some dismissed it as something other than discrimination. The mother of a student who dropped out early in seventh grade—who was labeled with a variety of racist nicknames from the start (including "Cocorí" and "Mono jamaiquino") and whose classmates included the infamous Jaime—insisted that although she knew discrimination was a problem in the school, her son's decision to drop out was unrelated to that issue. She insisted that it was not a matter of differential treatment by teachers or peers: "It's him. The problem is with him." Another mother disagreed with blaming students from the reservation for the way they were treated and turned the blame on herself and fellow parents. She insisted that discrimination occurred "because we, the parents, are passive. We come to the meetings sometimes, and we only listen—maybe out of shyness or maybe because of shame, I don't know, but I think that it is because of that, we make ourselves marginalized in that environment."

Thus, this parent blamed the exclusion of Nambueseño students on parents' self-imposed alienation. A third mother did not go so far as to blame Nambueseño parents, but she did believe the solution was in their hands. "We have to learn to value ourselves" and to teach that value to the children in Nambué, she told her fellow Nambueseño parents. This was the best solution in the eyes of one of Nambué's elementary schoolteachers as well. One of them told graduating sixth-grade students to know they were worth no less than any of their classmates in the high school.

In the case of students from section 7-5—Nambueseño students and other social misfits placed in a class that was the target of gossip, ridicule, and self-fulfilling prophecies of school failure—parental involvement did not occur. Those students joined forces, however, to write a letter of complaint to the high school administration about one of their teachers who only taught to Wilmer, the white student in the class who had no visible social problems or reason to be placed in the misfit category. Whereas many students would be afraid of taking such direct action, these students perhaps had nothing to lose. One interesting result of Nambueseños' being set apart in a sort of group isolation was that three students who reported never having been teased by classmates for being from Nambué were from this Nambueseño-dominant section. Two other students who reported never having been teased had gone to elementary school in Santa Rita and thus had learned to deal with Riteño peers prior to their secondary education.

DISENGAGEMENT AS RESISTANCE

Samuel, a student in section 7-5, early on stopped doing his homework and participating in class. Samuel had been the best student in his sixth-grade class, and during the first week of school at SRHS he had told me how much he liked it and looked forward to going each day. It did not take long for him to cease participating, though, when his participation was not recognized or valued. His aunt remarked on this change in her nephew. She commented on his having been the best student in his class and having loved school. In contrast, this year she brought him supplies to do a homework assignment, and he simply did not do it. It was an assignment that required him to report on the reservation.

The strategy of resistance used by Samuel was that which scholars refer to as "refusing to learn."[36] There are, however, other explanations for this behavior as a resistant act of refusal to learn. Some see it as something between internalization and "self-alienation," leading to an eventual silencing.[37] Sofía, who was frequently teased for her manner of speech, explained that she stopped speaking in class to avoid being teased.[38] She learned silence as a way to avoid being marked ethnically. In the long run, refusal to learn may be considered less resistant (or less effective ultimately) in that it fulfills stereotypes of students from the reservation and does little to open doors for such students in the future. Yet, as noted in Chapter 6, it is questionable just how useful high school is in this regard anyway.

Refusing to learn is akin to (and perhaps a precursor to) a strategy employed by many others: dropping out. This was the solution for the student called "Sexy Indian Girl" who was falsely accused of rule infractions by the guidance counselor, punished for removing racist propaganda around campus, and teased for her Indianness by teachers and peers alike. This former student perceived—perhaps rightly so— that the result of high school for her would not be a positive one.

It may seem surprising that such a wide variety of interpretations of discriminatory treatment in the high school existed among Nambueseños. Other researchers in different contexts have questioned why members of a single ethnic group fare so differently in the same school context. This may have to do with various subgroups' acceptance or rejection of the achievement ideology. Nubuo Shimahara, discussing the Burakumin in Japan, explains that some do not elect to challenge discrimination.[39] This scholar's thoughts on the matter seem to resonate with the experiences of Nambueseño students and parents who feared that resistance would jeopardize them further in the long run. Perhaps students from 7-5 were so steeped in differential treatment as a group that the discrepancy between their treatment and that of students in other classrooms was less visible. Certainly, other issues, such as individual students' abilities to "pass" and gendered access to particular strategies of resistance, affected student perceptions of their specific situations.

INTERPRETATIONS OF DISCRIMINATION
INTRAGROUP VARIATION AMONG NAMBUESEÑOS

As noted earlier, resistance theory was initially criticized for failing to adequately address intragroup variation and gender.[40] Anthropological musings on these topics shed light on the intricacies of student reactions to and perceptions of discrimination and render intragroup variation less surprising. Micaela di Leonardo examines different interpretations of discrimination against the Italian Americans with whom she worked in terms of "framing/feeling rules"—the ways her informants conceptualized discrimination and how it affected them.[41] The frames used to describe discrimination by those who were targets of it are applicable to the case of Nambueseño students at SRHS as well. Some Nambueseño students felt discriminated against and reacted to that directly through feeling unjustly singled out, whereas others felt discrimination but did nothing. Others felt racial comments were jokes and ought to be dealt with as such. Still others changed their identity to avoid being the target of discrimination aimed at "Indian" students. Some did not have the option to "pass," as their appearance more closely corresponded to that of stereotypical Indian students and thus reinforced their ascribed identities as Indians.

Thus, students were bound to view discrimination in various ways because they were not homogeneously affected by it.[42] Donna Deyhle suggests that students who confront discrimination in the school setting but whose families are supportive and encouraging of maintaining indigenous identity are likely to fare better in high school than those whose ethnic identity is not supported in the family setting.[43] Thus, the disagreement on what constitutes ethnic identity within the reservation may have affected students' school experiences as well. Gender also had a fundamental influence in how girls from Nambué were attacked and how they confronted it.

Whereas di Leonardo found that many of her respondents explained their discrimination in terms of religious difference, this was not so for Nambueseños.[44] The minority religion followed by a few Nambueseños was Evangelical Christianity (as opposed to the dominant Catholicism). Although I expected that students from Nambué who were Evangelical might feel discriminated against in a predominantly Catholic high school, no Evangelical Nambueseños considered that religious difference affected their schooling. All students in this category merely said that while Catholic prayers were said in class, they worshipped in their own manner and felt no discomfort at doing so. This may be explained through Deyhle's view of the support such a minority community receives at home, as the Evangelical community in Nambué was close-knit and its members were supportive of one another.[45] They may also have been accustomed to a religious minority status in Nambué. It may be significant that there were no Nambueseño Jehovah's Witnesses at SRHS, given that this was the religious minority that faced the most negative consequences in the high school.

In sum, students and parents alike had different ways of framing and interpreting what I saw as discriminatory behavior against them. Thus, it makes sense that intragroup variation would exist. Just as we cannot expect that all Nambueseño students were alike and would agree on any one topic, we cannot expect that they would view or react to discrimination in the same way. The very axes along which Nambueseños were set apart from larger Riteño society—race, ethnicity, and class, combined with gender—divided Nambué as well.

TEACHERS' INTERPRETATIONS OF DISCRIMINATORY BEHAVIOR

Micaela di Leonardo's insights with regard to framing discrimination can be applied to the teachers' varying views of discrimination in school as well. Generally speaking, the variety of teachers' explanations of discrimination matched that of Nambueseño students. Twenty-nine of thirty-six teachers and administrators responded directly to questions about the existence of discrimination at SRHS. Some gave contradictory answers or answers that fit into more than one of the framing categories I will discuss. Eleven teachers (38 percent of those who addressed this issue) insisted there was no racism there (although two of these—Natalia and Anatolia, both "pillars"—had already explained that Riteños were racist, and two others—Ramiro and Antonio, both young teachers, one Riteño and one traveler—gave examples of behavior that in my opinion constituted discrimination, such as preferential treatment or labeling students as "Little Indians"). Eight people, 28 percent (including the two "pillars" just mentioned), asserted that Riteños, generally speaking, were racist; and eight others (not among the eight just mentioned) insisted that there was discrimination at SRHS.

Four teachers (14 percent of those who addressed the issue) considered that discrimination was the incorrect term to describe the effects of mere cultural "difference."[46] Five people (17 percent), including four "pillars" (one of whom also said Riteños were racist and that there was no discrimination at the high school), considered that the issue at hand was that Nambueseños marginalized or isolated themselves but that they were not marginalized or alienated by others. One of these teachers also considered that this sort of thing happened to everyone, thus implying that it was not an issue that merited any action or excessive consideration. Four individuals (14 percent, not among those who said there was discrimination in the high school and also all "pillars") were of the opinion that there might have been discrimination in the school, but they asserted that it was up to the Nambueseño students to overcome it.

Other than the groups consisting entirely of "pillars," the teacher respondents were of varying social groups (older, younger, traveler, Riteño, *moreno*, white, vocational, and academic teachers). The superintendent was of the opinion that such behavior was common anywhere and thus expressed little concern for the situation. When I discussed possible ways to address this situation, he expressed a "boys will be boys" attitude that implied that this was not an issue to be dealt with at his level. The main lines of division seemed to be whether discrimination was evident in the high school and, if so, where the blame lay—with those who discriminated or those who were the targets of discrimination. To elaborate on these distinctions, it is useful to provide some examples of teachers' comments.

Of the teachers who considered that discrimination was a problem to be dealt with by those discriminated against, one commented, "Some [students who confront discrimination] are courageous and stand it. Others don't." The second teacher who espoused this belief had told Nambueseño students who complained to her of discriminatory treatment at the hands of her student son, "You have to rise above this. It's not OK that your peers do it, but you have to rise above it."

Another explained, "The problem with those Nambueseño kids is that they don't want to accept that they are from Nambué. . . . This shouldn't be [the case]." On a different occasion, this same teacher expressed the opinion that "there exists [among Nambueseño students] a subestimation of themselves. They don't like for one to tell them they are from a reservation or that they are Indians." The fourth teacher who offered this sort of response also pointed out that Nambueseños "don't like it if one tells them they are from there. They confront their own identity." It is interesting in the last two comments that these teachers explained Nambueseños' reactions as rooted in a dislike for their Nambueseño origin rather than in resentment toward being treated differently as a result of being from Nambué.

The various opinions of the existence, manifestations, and seriousness of discrimination at the high school made it an even more elusive topic, one that could not be easily pinpointed and thus not easily eradicated. Once again, it appeared that habitus was at work in not allowing some teachers to view particular behaviors as anything other than the norm, "what kids do," or something that happened everywhere and thus not in need of curtailment. Another issue that made the discrimination against Nambueseño students less obviously visible perhaps was that discrimination was not always limited to them (since it rested not only on race and place but on class as well). Furthermore, the same strategies of resistance employed by Nambueseños to counter the results of their ascribed, inferior identity were also used by other students to resist all of the aspects of schooling criticized thus far in this book.

GENERAL RESISTANCE STRATEGIES
ALTERNATIVE DISCOURSES

Aside from place-based, imposed, stigmatized identity, other forms of discrimination targeted students from various places and perhaps were geared more toward class, gender, and other issues. Preferential treatment in school, favoritism and (conversely) the disproportionate surveillance of particular students, teaching style and questionable grading techniques, the cost of education, the enforcement of absurdly strict uniform guidelines, tracking, and the recognition of a job ceiling were among the issues protested or resisted by many students, not only those from Nambué.

Nambueseños were not the only students to seek solidarity with others within their same category. Although some Nambueseños socialized mainly with other Nambueseños to avoid problems, some non-Nambueseño students who were set apart or treated differently did the same. Riteño "bad kids" hung out together and talked about being "organized." Teachers referred to this group as a "gang." Jacobo belonged to a smaller group of friends that referred to itself by combining the first initial of each of the four friends' names. These four letters were scratched into desks along with statements such as "the community IGLJ. We are unique and original." Thus, these students, self-defined as the members of a community, asserted their uniqueness—what others might criticize as their failure to fit in—as a positive attribute.[47] During one conversation with Jacobo, he explained that he and his three buddies were discriminated against precisely because "we separate ourselves." Thus, his isolation was not a result of discrimination but the reverse.

This is not the only example in which resistant sentiments toward the school's policies of preference and exclusion were expressed through vandalism. In Chapter 4 I demonstrated how Riteño students from affluent families were the recipients of favoritism in school, to the extent that they were sometimes seen as "good kids" in spite of their actions. The scrawled messages on desks sometimes provided alternative views of those students. One desktop listed two homeroom classes, both predominantly Riteño, and followed the section numbers with the phrase *putas todas* (all whores), thus presenting a different opinion of these girls than was usually expressed in the school. The same desktop declared that the girls in a section dominated by travelers—not usually upheld as epitomes of beauty—were "gorgeous." On a similar note of providing different views of the "good kids," a notorious "bad kid" tattled on favorite Riteño students who had party plans for the weekend to see if they would be punished the same way his peer group was.

USING THE ANTHROPOLOGIST (AND OTHER "SPIES")

The opposite extreme to receiving preferential treatment was that of being under watch and frequently accused of rule infractions. Federico explained that his strategy to counter disproportionate surveillance and suspicion of traveler students was lying: "I put on the expression of a good kid and lie." Given that a white student may have been more likely to have a face considered that of a "good kid," this option was not open to all. This same student also listed among his strategies for resistance (which he described in just those terms) learning who the school's spies were and being wary of what he told them.

Another way to counter being on the losing end of preferential treatment was to use the anthropologist, who might be more sympathetic to the concerns of less privileged students. This occurred in a variety of ways and was not without precedence.[48] One of these methods refers to the anthropologist serving intentionally as a mediator between cultures.[49] My own actions as a mediator, in the examples that follow, were mostly inadvertent on my part. When students in a given class were required to type their final projects on a computer, Carmen, a student from Nambué who had not had the privilege of taking computer class, had me type her project on the school's office computer. Joaquín, the student who relied on my status as a native English speaker and my opportune presence as an observer in the class to have his English test graded more fairly, also used me in his resistance. In another class that I observed, Irene was disgruntled at her test grade. She turned to me and requested, "Teacher, scold the [other] teacher."

Finally, another way in which I was used in student resistance strategies had to do with my role as an English teacher. As usual in my fieldwork experiences in Costa Rica, various individuals requested that I teach English classes in Nambué. My students tended to be teenagers who may have had a greater interest in a sanctioned, coed evening activity than in the English language, and classes usually drew upon students' favorite pop and rock songs in English as principal texts. Students provided me with their favorite cassettes to translate, discuss, and practice using vocabulary from lyrics in different contexts. Although it was not my intent that one such "different context" would be high school resistance, that turned out to be the case.

For one lesson, the chosen song was a favorite song of students, frequently requested at dances (also as an act of resistance, according to my students): Pink Floyd's "Another Brick in the Wall—Part II." The day after the lesson in which we discussed the song's lyrics, one Nambueseña student got off the bus at school singing the song. Later in the day, as I headed to observe a "pillar's" class, a Nambueseño student from the previous night's English class, Alberto, alerted me to "look at the blackboard." On the blackboard it said, "We're [sic] don't need not [sic] education. Hey Teacher! Leave those kids alone!"[50] I felt the odd combination of the pride of someone who roots for the underdog and the guilt of the anthropologist who may have crossed the line.

Another focal point of student resistance was teaching style. Cheating was common in SRHS, and students employed a variety of techniques that they shared with me. Some of their more elaborate cheating strategies required far more thought than the memorization that would have been necessary to study for their tests in particular classes. Sometimes, though, cheating tactics were more mundane, such as switching papers with a classmate in the middle of a test. In this strategy, one student, more adept at a given subject, would write an essay answer for a friend. It was not necessary to change the wording much, since many answers required memorizing an exact wording from a textbook or lecture. Thus, cheating might reflect a strategy that, inadvertently or not, resisted a teaching style based on rote learning and memorization.[51]

Boredom in classes was often addressed through student negotiation for extra recess, less dictation, early dismissal, or the cancellation of class. Often, students were successful in their negotiations. Sometimes these negotiations included criticisms of teaching style or course content. Other times they appeared to be mere distracting games.[52] I observed one class in which Juan Pablo, a Nambueseño student, suggested to the teacher that she explain more and dictate less. The teacher later commented to me that this student was displaying rebellion with the comment and that he did so that day because he felt shielded by my presence in the class. I also saw Juan Pablo negotiate for additional explanation and clarification but then chat with a friend when the explanation was given, suggesting that his request was what I might consider a distracting game and what the teacher thought of as "rebellion."

Other distracting games (which students admitted to me were such) included asking Profesor Agustín, an avid sports fan, about the results of a soccer game the night before and asking Profesor Sergio to elaborate on the teachings of the *Chilam Balam*,[53] a favorite tangent of his. As Luykx notes, such a strategy is fairly safe, in that it appears to constitute interest or "compliance."[54] Many of the distracting games I observed were related to dictation as the teaching method of choice for many practitioners in SRHS. It was common for students to repeat the last word of dictation they had taken to let the teacher know where to begin repeating a phrase. This was not always a distracting game. For many students it was a valid technique to ensure they had copied down all the material provided. For others, though, this established learning technique provided the framework for a distracting game.

I watched one student employ this technique and pretend to write, although his pen never touched the paper. He grinned at me as he did this, so I asked if he did this only to distract the teacher. He nodded and smiled. I saw another, in a different class, ask for repetition, although he was not even pretending to write. In yet a different class, a third student used the same technique. His pen did touch the paper but formed only squiggles rather than letters as he requested repetition. I saw another student feign misunderstanding of the last word dictated—*"discernimiento"* (discernment)—and repeat it as *"estreñimiento"* (constipation) as a way of "acting" that mimicked typical student responses to dictation. In a class in which I never saw the teacher employ any technique other than dictation, a student asked, "Why don't we just photocopy it [the material]?" In a physical education (PE) class in which students were taking dictation on the benefits of practicing sports, a student questioned, "Why did I change [into my PE uniform] to sit here?" The student may have been resisting both the uniform requirements for PE and the fact that PE class involved learning "theory."

Some students (including Nambueseños) directly contested not only teaching style but also evaluation. I saw a Nambueseño seek out a teacher off campus to negotiate his grade. He informed the teacher that he would fight for even one point. Recall that one point has caused school failure for some Nambueseños. In another case, Sofia's mother went to the school to check official records to contest the number of absences her daughter had, which was affecting her grade.

Protests of Uniformity and Conformity

Excessively strict uniform requirements were also the target of student resistance.[55] Given that several teachers' pet peeve was untucked shirts, many students' resistance tactics stemmed from that dislike. In response to common cries of "Tuck in that shirt!" male and female students alike stopped in their tracks, unzipped their pants, opened the front placket widely, and slowly tucked in all sides of their shirttail—smoothing it down against their bodies, sometimes in a deliberately sensual display.

A member of the school's "gang" recalled that years ago they had spray painted the road to school, writing "Welcome to the National Penitentiary." In the year of my study, a similar phenomenon occurred. A few weeks prior to the end of the school year, I rode the Nambueseño students' bus to school as usual. As the bus approached the school, Arelys, a girl from the outskirts of Santa Rita seated near me, read aloud the words that had been spray painted in green capital letters on the cement wall surrounding the school: "Alcatras [sic] 20 mts" approximately twenty meters from the guarded metal gates that locked students into the school. Arelys commented, "It's true. It *is* like prison." To clear up any doubt that the artist indeed was making a comparison to prison,[56] the next segment of the wall was labeled "The Rock" in English, likely inspired by the Hollywood film by that name. Another such comparison appeared in white liquid correction fluid that designated a select few classrooms as "Cell #13." Thus, critical vandalism was not limited to desktops. It also appeared written on walls, blackboards, homemade posters, and in bathrooms. In addition to providing alternative opinions of the school's "favorite" students (as noted earlier), desktop vandalism also had other messages.

Many desktops featured students' signatures, which people spent a great deal of time developing and practicing. Although the creation of a unique signature was common outside the high school as well, at SRHS it may have served as a brand of individuality in a school that promoted conformity. Desks, blackboards, and, once, a student's shoes appeared with swastikas drawn on them. On a blackboard, a swastika was drawn on a flag whose form and flagpole appeared to be an exact copy of that drawn on the program for Civic Week. I asked Jacobo, who had formed swastikas out of masking tape on his shoes, if he knew what the swastika symbolized, as he was not a white Riteño with racist tendencies. He explained that he did not know what it meant other than that it got Profesor Agustín, his social studies teacher, up in arms without fail. When I explained what the swastika stood for, Jacobo replied, "We're ignorant, but we use it." In effect, this student, himself a target of Riteño white supremacist attitudes and actions, used the symbol as a countersymbol.

Another countersymbol may have been the drawing of Bob Marley, smoking a joint, on a desk with the accompanying label "Black Christ." On another desk, a student drew an Indian with a headdress, below which was written *Cuatro plumas* (Four feathers)—the phrase commonly used to refer to a nationally distilled brand of liquor whose label depicted this same figure. Below the drawing it repeated the advertising slogan *"El sabor de mi tierra"* (The flavor of my land [implying nation]). It is unclear if this was a different view of national pride than that promoted in school or if it was merely a drawing incorporating forbidden subject matter that might incite teachers' anger.

A student artist showed me drawings he had made to put up around campus to protest the conduct grade and marching practice. One drawing depicted a teacher (resembling a teacher from the high school) with a joint in his hand and a bottle of vodka tied to his belt heading for the school's horticultural zone (a sign indicated his destination and a suggestion of what might be planted there in the form of a marijuana leaf). The drawing was accompanied by the phrase *"Así de apretado estamos en el cole este año"* (This is how strict we are in high school this year). The student told me this was a protest of the conduct grade and implied that those who graded them were not in a position to pass moral judgment on their students.

A second drawing was titled *"Marcha Ruta Mortal"* (Fatal Marching Route) and depicted three students marching in single file, in uniform, with Death—in the form of a skeletal figure with flowing long hair (and bearing a striking resemblance to Profesora Delia)—brandishing a machete and pointing a finger behind them. A third drawing had a similar theme. It bore the words *"Todos en Silencio Entanto Vamos Al Hueco de la Estupidez"* (Meanwhile, We All Go Silently Toward the Pit of Stupidity). It depicted Death, this time specifically identified by the student artist as symbolizing the guidance counselor ("but drawn with a better body, to be nice") behind three marchers, holding a whip and a branding iron that said "MARCH." This one protested the cancellation of classes throughout a three-week period so students could practice marching for the Independence Day parade that would last no longer than one and a half hours and cover the distance of 500 meters. One must view absenteeism from marching practice as resistance as well.

The practice of marking students absent for a variety of rule infractions unrelated to attendance was also protested. One student used his "absent" status to deny accusations of his other behavioral problems. Profesora Rosa María announced at the beginning of a class period one month into the school year, "If you are wearing patch-style back pockets [not condoned by the strict uniform guidelines], you will be [marked] absent." In the ensuing uniform inspection, she found two boys with illegal back pockets and marked them absent. One of these boys, Yeison, did a considerable amount of clowning throughout the class. Toward the end, as her frustration level rose, the teacher announced that this student was disturbing the rest of the class. I thought Yeison had a good point when he asked aloud, "How can I be disturbing the class? I'm absent." Another student protested this disciplinary practice as well. I saw this Nambueseño off campus and inquired if he was free. He explained that he had been marked absent in PE for not participating fully, so he decided that if he was absent anyway, he might as well leave.

Both the artist mentioned earlier and a friend of his, while suspended for failing to march in the Independence Day parade, came to school in full uniform. Although one of these students often violated uniform rules to resist school control by his own account, he also engaged in uniform-related accommodation. He had removed his earring to be allowed to attend high school—a fact he lamented when he was kicked out of school anyway. I have already addressed the ways students used exaggerated sensuality in tucking in their shirts to conform to demands that they have their shirts tucked in without submitting entirely to teachers' expectations.

Another (related) way to maintain individuality in spite of uniform use was employed by girls. A skirt was required according to specifications. Many girls, however, wore short, tight skirts, knowing that some teachers among the strict uniform enforcers believed girls should promote their femininity. Girls may have taken this a bit farther, however, and projected a sexualized image of femininity that was questionable. Girls wore makeup (in spite of guidelines against doing so) and short skirts and tended to get away with it. Many of those who did this were Riteñas from prominent families, making it less likely that disciplinary action would be taken against them.[57] Teachings of "appropriate" femininity might have been the focus of this resistance. These girls may have been responding to the underlying assumption that academic affairs were ultimately for boys, as girls were expected to dedicate themselves to the home. Thus, by stretching the limits of uniform rules, girls may have been drawing attention to themselves in the school setting, which otherwise may not have considered them central to its goals (although I do not rule out that for some, it might also have been done in an effort to look attractive and not as resistance).

Student Reactions to the State of the School

In Chapter 5 I addressed the ways the state of the school affected students' learning. I described students clowning about lab equipment and missing air conditioning as indicative of the fact that they noticed these lacks. Students protested the condition of the school in other ways as well. On any given day, the campus reeked of urine as a result of the poor maintenance of the bathrooms. Students frequently broke bathroom doors and wrote on the walls. It was in the bathrooms that students hung a racist poster the year prior to my study, removed by Nambueseñas who resented its message. Thus, for some the bathrooms provided a teacher-free space in which to send messages to peers. (The teachers' bathroom was only slightly better, also with no toilet seat and a bring-your-own-toilet-paper policy but with no vandalism). On a day in which students from another high school visited SRHS, an administrative assistant reported to teachers in the lounge that a girl had stuck a used sanitary napkin to the bathroom door. Teachers in the lounge considered that this was the result of an appalling lack of manners. It seemed to me, though, that the act might have called attention to the bathroom's filth and lack of privacy (given non-functional doors) on any given day.

In the lesson (described in Chapter 6) in which students were taught about occupational hazards and were "prepared" to confront common effects of menial labor, a student brought up the heat and uncomfortable chairs in the classrooms as a hindrance to their job as students. Jacobo mentioned "mental stress" resulting from classmates' actions. Much to her credit, Profesora Aracely welcomed these comments and the application of the concept of occupational hazards to the school setting as valid criticism. In another case (reported to me by the student involved), a teacher's behavior and lack of credentials were the focal point of classroom criticism. In this case, a teacher who was still in training (common for teachers at SRHS) was rude to students. Federico pointed out to the teacher that his lack of experience showed in his poor human relations skills, and he expressed thankfulness that the teacher might still learn these things in his continued studies. Thus, the state of the school and preparedness of its teachers were also contested by students in informal ways.

Dropping Out as Resistance and Accommodation

Finally, a tactic of resistance many students employed is one that perhaps contests many of the categories already discussed. A high proportion of students dropped out of school—to pursue the equivalent of a general equivalency diploma (GED), to go elsewhere for schooling, or to end their formal education definitively. When I asked a Nambueseño dropout what he disliked about school, he explained, "I didn't like anything [about it]." One Nambueseña attributed her dropping out as a direct response to discrimination in school. She explained, "If they're going to treat me badly, I'm better off not going back." She suggested that many students found out that students in the high school would treat them badly and decided not to attend in the first place. She assumed that these students thought, "I'm better off staying home to learn my parents' trades." She—and they—may have been right. For other students, the reason was less easy to pinpoint.

For some, dropping out was an act of giving up. A student who was kicked out of school for unjust reasons gave up his fight. Three students were excused by their parents for not marching in the Independence Day parade because of their religion, which prohibits such behavior. The three students were Jehovah's Witnesses, and their religion prohibited paying homage to the nation in ways owed only to God. The school's administrators, however, who were fervently patriotic, did not accept the excuse (although, ironically, the Independence Day parade and its surrounding rhetoric celebrated not only national independence but a revised constitution that guaranteed, among other things, freedom of religion). These students were told to march or pay the consequences. They did not march, and the consequences varied. Two were suspended (although one of these students did not return to high school, thus making her suspension more akin to expulsion). For the third, the situation was much worse.

Jacobo already had several discipline problems in his guidance counselor's folder on him for the year, and his punishment, given the counseling office's familiarity with his presence, was more severe. Jacobo himself noted the irony of the fact that to remedy his having skipped one day of school, he was mandated to miss fifteen days. Not only would he be suspended, he was informed, but he would also fail his conduct grade. The difference between failing conduct and failing any other subject was that if one was failing an academic or a vocational subject at the end of the school year, she or he could take a test in an effort to pass. Unfortunately for Jacobo, there was no makeup exam for conduct. If a student failed conduct, he or she failed the year. There was a chance for leniency, but if a student was failing three or more subjects, he or she was not eligible for the "Olympic trials," as the academic makeup exams were popularly known. If a student was failing two subjects plus conduct, he or she would have to repeat the year.

Given his track record, Jacobo doubted his chances of being shown lenience in the conduct grade by the end of the year (although the guidance counselor revealed too late that she had been bluffing about his receiving a failing grade). He was convinced he would fail. He summarized, "Let them win." Yet he did not give up on himself entirely. He planned to get the equivalent of a GED and assured his teachers and me that his failing in school was "not for lack of intelligence." This was the student (alluded to in the Introduction) who explained that although he was giving up this particular battle, he would not be defeated in the long run. Jacobo declared, "I won't stay Indian. I'll keep studying."

For others, dropping out may have been an act of resistance, albeit in a way that was less productive in the long run and involved a great deal of accommodation. For the two girls from Nambué who dropped out in seventh grade, by their own account as a direct reaction to discrimination in the high school, such action can be viewed as both resistance and learning.[58] As Michelle Fine points out, there is a certain danger in looking at dropping out as an individual choice,[59] which ignores the existing structural constraints and blames the victim. Dropping out was a reaction to a variety of issues, many of which are related to those discussed throughout this book.

First, it is useful to distinguish between what Douglas Foley terms "dropouts" and "pushouts."[60] I have described students who were encouraged to drop out, who were forced out (directly, through suspension, or indirectly, by being discouraged to return after suspension), or whose parents were asked to remove them from the school. Samuel, the student from Nambué who was frequently falsely accused and whose grandmother reported having been asked to remove him, eventually did drop out. Although his grandmother knew it was illegal for the counselor to suggest that she take Samuel out of school and Samuel knew it was his right to be there, the counselor's illegal request was ultimately effective.

Several students who were suspended never returned and were not encouraged to do so. Their punishment gave the impression of temporality, in that it was suspension rather than expulsion, but the words were often used interchangeably—suggesting that, for all practical purposes, they were one and the same. Yet their peers also used the language of choice in explaining their dropping out. In the case of the two seventh-grade students, peers (addressing each individual case) said, "She didn't want to come back."

Certain teachers suggested fairly openly (with students within earshot) that particular students ought to drop out. Profesora Eugenia said to another teacher that a named seventh-grade student did not come to her class consistently: "He's doing nothing by coming to high school. I don't know why they don't send him home already." She made it clear to me that she felt certain students were "better off at home." During a staff meeting, she laughed as she recounted how a student who had complained of being in homeroom section 7-5 dropped out soon after switching homerooms and finding it too difficult to adjust to a new one. Profesora Natalia complained of a notorious "bad kid" in a staff meeting and asked, "Why don't they tell the mother to take him out already?" Profesora Alodia, one of her "pillar" colleagues, explained that the boy's home situation would be even worse for him: "With those people [his family], we would do worse damage by throwing him in the street [throwing him out of school]." The same teacher who came to this boy's defense reported a student having dropped out as a result of being erroneously labeled a "bad kid" and falsely accused of rule infractions. Thus, he was allowed to drop out for reasons that could have been explained away.

A lack of encouragement to return to school came not only from the school but also from parents. In the case of a Nambueseño who dropped out early on after being the target of rampant name-calling, his mother told him he had to study but reported to me that "he didn't do it," thus indicating that ultimately this was not a matter of parental control. She explained, "I can't obligate him to do it." Another Nambueseña gave similar reasons for her son's dropping out: "He was failing and said he wouldn't go back." Another Nambueseño who dropped out prior to my fieldwork perhaps did not intend to drop out, but, as his mother explained, he merely did not go back after a lengthy teachers' strike. There were exceptions, however. A Nambueseña girl faced with repeating the year wanted to drop out and expressed concern over wasting her parents' money by continuing to go to school. Her mother, however, convinced her to go back. Again, we see the language of "choice" implied by teachers who talked about Nambueseño and other marginalized students as "isolating themselves," as if this were a choice independent of other dynamics in the school setting. Many students who dropped out of SRHS were those on the periphery who teachers considered were "alienating themselves."

Another reason for dropping out was related to kinship duties. Profesora Rosaura listed parents needing their children's labor as a reason they took their kids out of school. At times, kinship duties were related not to students' direct economic contributions to the household but to taking care of "women's" work in the house when a mother was employed outside the home. Other students dropped out as a result of pregnancy. A seventh grader who was suspended for not marching and never returned and whose attrition Profesora Marta Iris attributed to her "strange religion" (she was a Jehovah's Witness) revealed to me (prior to her suspension) that she wanted to drop out. She explained that her sister had moved out of the house, meaning her mother was left alone there while her father was at work during the day: "I feel bad for my mother [being alone]."

For some girls school was never an option, if there were both sons and daughters in a family and insufficient resources for every child to obtain an education. In other cases, girls had to leave school to help their mothers with housework. I know of one girl in Nambué who left elementary school to attend to kinship duties. She explained that both her sister and her mother found employment in a nearby town, leaving the house empty all day. She insisted that she had decided as a third grader to remain home to take care of the house and livestock instead of attending school.[61]

I am told that in the past it was more common for students who got pregnant to be kicked out of school or encouraged to leave. This was less often the case during the year of my study, when there were at least two teenage mothers and one pregnant student in school. One teacher talked about encouraging the pregnant student to continue her studies even after giving birth. Profesora Anatolia explained that she "made [the student] see the responsibility she had as a future mother" and that this necessitated her continuing her schooling. According to a peer, however, the student did not intend to continue her schooling after the birth of her child. Her friend explained to me that the school would only allow her two weeks off after giving birth, and the mother-to-be worried that this would negatively affect her health.

Perhaps related to kinship duties, especially those of girls, is the issue of gender roles. A girl told me that if she had a boyfriend she would never tell her parents because they would likely take her out of school. In the teachers' lounge one day, a teacher reported that a parent had taken two children out of school. Profesor Agustín speculated that the girl had a boyfriend in school, and the parents found this out in spite of the girl's brother having covered for her. In this case the teacher suggested, out of concern for their education, that he and others write a letter to the parents to persuade them to allow their children to return to school, as they were good students. Federico's mother explained that her husband always insisted that "either marriage or schooling," but not both, was the choice for his daughters. Girls in school also expressed that either having a boyfriend or going to school was the choice presented to them. The underlying assumption was that an education might be wasted on a girl who pursued marriage rather than a career (as these were seen by many as opposing goals). At other times, this decision may have come not from parents but from a girl's boyfriend. This was the case for a seventh-grade girl with whom I spoke.

Rebeca, a traveler student, revealed to me that she was thinking of dropping out. When I asked why, she said that if she broke up with her boyfriend she would not drop out. He had heard unfounded gossip about her being unfaithful to him at the high school and demanded that she quit school. I tried to convince her not to drop out (rather than sit back, watch it happen, and document it as data). She eventually decided to stay (and to break up with the boyfriend). She concluded, "If he's going to get mad, let him. I'm better off going to high school."

The issue of the job ceiling was another factor contributing to the dropout rate, which may have been related to family economic needs. Many students realized (correctly) that getting their diploma might not lead to a better professional future.[62] Teachers and students provided a variety of other reasons for dropping out. The director, in a staff meeting, reported that the national newspaper *Al Día* listed the two main reasons for students' dropping out as economic crisis at home and student boredom. These reasons appeared among those listed by teachers in interviews also. The reasons teachers listed (in order of most to least frequent) were economic reasons (listed by nineteen teachers or administrators), poor academic standing (eight), poor preparation or a difficult transition from elementary school to high school (eight), family situations (either unspecified or related to kinship; six), lack of interest on the part of teachers (four), poor treatment by teachers or peers (four), parental disinterest or lack of encouragement by parents (three), student lack of interest (two), being the target of false accusations (two), lack of goals or motivation (two), laziness (two), diminished motivation as a result of poor grades (two), illiteracy (one), low self-esteem (one), dislike of school (one), preference for dropping out rather than repeating a year (one), high school not meeting students' expectations (one), removal by parents because of students' immaturity (one), rejection by students and teachers (one), behavior problems (one), transfer (one), and a dislike of getting up early (one). Most of these reasons placed the blame outside of the school.[63]

Generally, teachers agreed that traveler students were more prone to drop out than those from Santa Rita. This was rooted in structural issues, given the institutionalized barriers to travelers' education (discussed in earlier chapters). Students in seventh grade dropped out at much higher rates than did their peers in higher grades (15 percent of students enrolled in seventh grade at the beginning of the year dropped out, as opposed to between 2 percent and 7 percent for most other grades), giving credence to teachers' explanations about poor preparation in elementary school or an inability to become accustomed to the change from grade school to high school. Another possible explanation is that students were more likely to "stick it out" as they got closer to graduation.

Students explained their peers' reasons for dropping out as follows (in order of most cited to least cited): poor academic standing/bad grades, boredom, suspension, pregnancy, poor treatment by a teacher and unwillingness to comply with demands to change one's appearance, employment, kinship duties, and behavior resulting in parents removing the student from school. Note that student analyses of reasons for dropping out neither blamed students for their lack of motivation or laziness nor blamed teachers as much as teachers themselves did.

The reasons contributing to poor academic standing, according to a guidance counselor who analyzed the situation, were as follows:

- The student does not know how to interpret what he/she reads
- Students do not master the four basic operations [addition, subtraction, division, multiplication]
- Students do not know their multiplication tables
- Students lack study habits
- Students lack discipline
- General indiscipline [in the school environment, perhaps]
- Lack of interest in studying
- Little interest in reading
- Students lack established goals
- Absenteeism
- They don't study
- Problems at home
- Lack of motivation

It is perhaps significant that several of these factors (such as lack of study habits, discipline, interest, goals, or motivation) are related to the hidden curriculum I discussed in Chapter 4. A prominent Riteña citizen explained students' dropping out as a result of being "spoiled." Students who dropped out described their reasons in ways I have already mentioned (such as not liking anything about school or because of discrimination) or as a result of receiving failing grades in more than one subject. This was the case for two students. Jacobo, practically forced out, explained that he was "resigned to failing."

Doing poorly in school was a common reason for dropping out, according to both teachers and students. One boy explained that if he failed, he would not repeat the year because of the embarrassment caused by doing so. A Nambueseña mother told me her daughter also refused to go back to school if she failed. She preferred to drop out rather than bear the shame of repeating a grade. In this situation, dropping out may not have been the worst possible reaction. Recall a student, described in Chapter 4, who committed suicide prior to my study. Profesor Ramiro implied that his desperation was related to his isolation: "He was a *morenito* who didn't accept who he was. He didn't accept that his family was poor. He wanted to dress fashionably. . . . He had problems. . . . He didn't have much help, much self-esteem." The words of another teacher seem apt to this situation as well, although she was not addressing this tragedy but was speaking of the greater tendency of traveler students to drop out. Profesora Rosaura commented that traveler students often dropped out because they did poorly: "They do poorly not because they didn't learn but because they don't share the same way of being [as Riteños]."

Yet the case was not so hopeless for most students. Some students who dropped out returned later. Others earned the equivalent of a GED. By the end of 1999, a Nambueseño seventh grader who had dropped out early in the year revealed that he was "thinking about going back" the following year. Others—the target of false accusations, threats of expulsion, requests that their parents remove them from school, and "failure"—ended up graduating. Thus, the structural barriers that may have led students to drop out were not all-determining for all students. Many of those who resisted in the ways discussed in this chapter have since graduated or passed the grade they were in at the time of my study. Others have pursued the equivalent of a GED. Strategies of resistance, then, have served some purpose, even when they involved a great deal of accommodation.

This chapter has shown that student agency was active in contesting the school's messages. I have also demonstrated the complicated ways students perceived what was to be resisted, how to do so, and how those strategies may or may not have been effective in the long run. It is precisely because of the convoluted nature of these issues that they are difficult to pinpoint, making "discrimination" hard to identify as such and therefore difficult to eradicate. I have discussed accommodation as an element of resistance that in some ways conforms to expectations of students or gives in to certain demands. One scholar, though, has a different interpretation of the term. John van Willigan defines accommodation as mediation by the anthropologist.[64] In the conclusion of this book, I will examine the effects of an applied anthropological study on the situation at hand, with regard to the ways it may or may not alleviate a situation wrought with complex, often hidden, but frequently resisted forms of discrimination in school.

NOTES

1. "Not to let them get the upper hand."

2. Aronowitz and Giroux 1993: 96. Here, too, more recent scholars have addressed gender more thoroughly. See, for example, Ferguson 2000; Luykx 1999.

3. Aronowitz and Giroux 1993: 98.

4. Scott 1990: 73.

5. Luykx 1999: 295.

6. Foucault 1978: 95. See also Aronowitz and Giroux 1993: 99; Dirks, Eley, and Ortner 1994: 19; Pérez 1993: 269; Scott 1990: 45, 293.

7. McCarthy 1993: 293.

8. For varying perspectives on this debate, both in general terms and with regard to education specifically, see Comaroff and Comaroff 1991: 31, 33; Luykx 1999: 219; McLaren 1986: 147.

9. Dirks, Eley, and Ortner 1994: 19; Kondo 1990: 259; Luykx 1999: 218–219. Scott 1990: 19 terms this concept "infrapolitics" and describes it as "low-profile forms of resistance."

10. Aronowitz and Giroux 1993: 100–101.

11. McLaren 1986: 146; Wade 1997: 108.

12. MacLeod 1987: 19–20; Wade 1997: 109.

13. Kondo 1990: 221. See also Luykx 1999: 281; Scott 1990: 34–36.

14. See Willis 1977: 59 on resistance through class culture.

15. Freire 1995: 45; Jenkins 1997: 60; McLaren 1982: 23; Nagengast and Kearney 1990: 65; Oboler 1995: xvii; Rist 1970: 428.

16. This was a very rare occurrence, given that many Riteños thought Nambué was a dangerous place. This student's father had business with the local general store owner that night, and the Riteño student visited his classmate next door as his father conducted his business transaction.

17. This is tied to Scott's 1990: 117 discussion of the "hidden transcript" and its ability to "answer daily insults to dignity."

18. Hatcher and Troyna 1993: 116 examine racist nicknames and question whether their use necessarily reflects racist attitudes on the part of children. For at least one student in their study, "[R]acist name-calling was a legitimate part of her interactional repertoire, functionally no different from the non-racist forms of name-calling that were a crucial interactional resource in the conflictual world of children." These authors suggest that racist nicknames were no more severe than any other cruel nicknames. Although it is true that in SRHS nearly all students had offensive nicknames of one form or another, the fact that Nambueseños had racialized nicknames, coupled with overt comments made by students about their negative stereotypes of the reservation and its inhabitants, suggests that at least some students did have racist attitudes in labeling Nambueseños in this manner. Others likely repeated racist nicknames without thinking through their racist implications.

19. For another discussion of replacing stigmatized academic identities with "bad kid" labels, see Ferguson 2000: 193–194. Ferguson analyzes the use of physical power by particular African American elementary school students (deemed "troublemakers") as a way of gaining status among peers. See also Willis 1977.

20. Whereas some scholars (Luykx 1999: 219; Scott 1990: 137, 142) see gossip as a resistance strategy, at SRHS it tended to be perpetrated most by the powerful as an offensive strategy. Several "pillars" used it so frequently against new traveler teachers that the latter often requested transfers within one year of arriving at SRHS. Students also picked up on staff gossip and contributed to its spread. That might constitute resistance against teachers' power over them. Conversations with Profesor Sergio suggest that gossip was a main reason for his preference to be somewhere else.

21. McLaren 1986: 164. See also Scott 1990: 137–138 on forms of resistance that are "disguised, muted, and veiled for safety's sake." Clowning might fit this category. Levinson 2001: 142–143 discusses "echando relajo" as a way to "lighten the school experience." Luykx 1999: 222 compares students' "dawdling and delaying" strategies to factory slowdowns.

22. See Davidson 1996: 2 for another analysis of this link.

23. See D'Amato 1993: 183.

24. Whereas Ogbu's perceived labor market theory was largely an unconscious phenomenon for students, those at SRHS appeared to be fully conscious of the limitations they might face in employment.

25. See Levinson 2001: 307 for further comments on masking identity to fit into school culture.

26. See Barth 1969: 30; Comaroff 1985: 314 for more discussion of the revision of ethnic labels or categories as resistance.

27. Fordham 1999: 283.

28. Peshkin 1997: 114.

29. MacLeod 1987: 120.

30. Barth 1969: 33; Gruzinski 1988: 42.

31. Other scholars have also found gendered differences in resistance in schools. Levinson 2001: 141 found that boys engaged more in "goofing off" than did girls. Luykx 1999: 223 found that silence was a strategy used by girls more than boys and that girls more commonly resorted to cheating. Although my findings support the first two contentions, I found that both boys and girls used cheating.

32. See de la Cadena 1995.

33. See McRobbie 1978: 108 for another account of femininity as both constraining and liberating in the school setting. See Yon 2000: 106 for additional accounts of combined objectification and sexualization of students.

34. McCarthy and Crichlow 1993: xix.

35. Luykx 1999: 165, emphasis in the original.

36. Erickson 1993: 36, 43; McLaren 1986: 159. See also Fordham 1999: 281.

37. Deyhle 1995: 404; Foley 1995: 64–65; Luykx 1999: 222; McLaren 1982: 23.

38. See Luykx 1999: 223 for further discussion of class participation involving risks for students.

39. Shimahara 1971: 30.

40. More recent scholars (such as those represented in the volume edited by Levinson, Foley, and Holland 1996; Ferguson 2000; Luykx 1999; Yon 2000) do problematize these issues to a greater degree.

41. di Leonardo 1984: 164–165.

42. Nadine Dolby 2001: 40–41 likewise found that not all students at the school she studied in South Africa interpreted what many of us would call discrimination as such. Aurolyn Luykx 1999: 108 also found that students responded to contentions of discrimination in a variety of ways. Daniel Yon 2000: 103 asserts, "[Y]outh are racialized subjects, but they situate themselves in the discourses of race in complex and contradictory ways."

43. Deyhle 1995: 420.

44. di Leonardo 1984: 166.

45. Deyhle 1995: 420.

46. Dolby 2001: 53, 55 found that individuals at the school in which she conducted her study were also quick to label racial and racist issues as attributable to "culture" instead.

47. Luykx 1999: 217–218 suggests that U.S. conceptualizations of student resistance— such as the formation of subcultures—might be ill suited to schools in Latin America and elsewhere. Both Luykx and Bradley Levinson 2001: 306 found that no subcultures or countercultures, respectively, were present in the schools they studied. Although I agree that scholars should be wary of the easy application of concepts appropriate to one region to situations in another geographic and cultural context, in this case I did find at least one example of student counterculture in IGLJ.

48. Kondo 1990: 201; van Willigan 1981: 161. See also Luykx 1999: xxv for an account of how students used the anthropologist to "air grievances."

49. van Willigan 1981: 161.

50. Waters 1977.

51. Luykx 1999: 237 arrives at a similar conclusion in her study of a normal school in Bolivia.

52. What I term "distracting games" are similar to what Foley 1990: 112–114 calls "making out games."

53. The *Chilam Balam* is a Mayan text written in the colonial era that sheds light on colonial Yucatán and describes Mayan culture and religion prior to and after contact.

54. Luykx 1999: 219.

55. Dolby 2001: 70 contends that students in a South African high school where she conducted research used diversion from the uniform guidelines to assert racial identity. In SRHS, in contrast, students from all racial and social groups used various forms of uniform resistance. Thus, resistance to strict uniform rules seemed to be a strategy common to students at SRHS.

56. See Ferguson 2000: 232–233; Foucault 1979: 293–296 for more on the comparison between schools and prisons.

57. See McLaren 1982: 22; McRobbie 1978: 104; Willis 1977: 18 for additional accounts of use of dress as resistance. Likewise, Hebdidge 1979: 101 provides an analysis of style as resistance, as do Clarke et al. 1975: 52–56.

58. For other authors who allude to dropping out as resistance, see Aronowitz and Giroux 1993: 17; Thomas and Wahrhaftig 1971: 247; Willis 1977.

59. Fine 1986: 407.

60. Foley 1995: 67. See also ibid.: 403–405.

61. This girl did, however, attend evening literacy courses offered by one of the elementary schoolteachers in Nambué.

62. See also Fine 1986: 399, 405; MacLeod 1987: 107.

63. See López, Assáel, and Neumann 1984: 294, 362 for similar reasoning by teachers in Chile for student failure.

64. van Willigan 1981: 163.

8

"Cuesta escribir algo de que nadie puede decir nada"[1]

CONCLUSIONS, APPLICATIONS, IMPLICATIONS, AND THE ETHICAL DILEMMAS OF APPLIED ANTHROPOLOGY

INCREASINGLY, APPLIED ANTHROPOLOGY[2] REQUIRES A CERTAIN SENSITIVITY TO MULtiple audiences.[3] In the case of my research, these audiences were of not only various realms but opposing ones. As I mentioned early in this book, I was well aware of my professional duty of being accountable to those who made my research possible. To which community—Riteño or Nambueseño—however, was I primarily committed? Both communities contributed to my research in innumerable ways. Yet to support one was to betray the other. What, then, does advocacy look like in a research population that is divided on the fundamental issue the anthropologist addresses?

Toward the end of my year of fieldwork at Santa Rita High School (SRHS), having garnered the support of many traveler teachers and students and having angered several "pillar" teachers, I talked to Profesor Isidro, an older Riteño but *moreno* (and non-"pillar") teacher. Likely commenting indirectly on the fact that various veteran Riteño teachers were angry with me (as a result of a report of my findings that I will describe shortly), he announced that he would not distrust my work or my conclusions. Profesor Isidro commented that I had worked hard and well that year, in his opinion, and not just to "*salir del paso*" (get it over and done with). He added, "I'm very rarely wrong about people" and predicted that my work would be sought by other academics. He compared my manuscript to a project about mango cultivation he had coauthored with students years ago, based on research conducted at SRHS: "You have to write, erase, and start over. It's hard to write something that nobody can say anything about" (i.e., that nobody can contest).

As I neared the end of this arduous process of writing, erasing, and starting over, that very issue weighed heavily on me. I eventually rejected as impractical my original plan of sending my dissertation back, chapter by chapter, for review and comments by the communities involved in favor of turning over the finished product (translated, in dissertation form) for commentary to be added to a later, published version.[4] Thus, I have been and continue to be faced with questions surrounding reactions to my work and my conclusions and with ethical dilemmas about to whom ultimately I am most accountable. These questions—along with the implications of my research for educational policy, its theoretical contributions, and the ethical dilemmas faced by an applied anthropologist along the way—are of concern in this concluding chapter of the book.

ETHICAL DILEMMAS AND THE TIMING OF ADVOCACY

Although I was committed to advocacy from the start and felt my findings merited such a stance, taking on the role of an advocate was not so simple. Must one really wait until after the research has been conducted to take on such a role? One question raised for anthropologists who take on an advocacy role is at what stage to become an advocate. I grappled with numerous situations that made me wonder at what point one has enough data to start speaking out against the social condition addressed by the research. How many incidents of discrimination did I have to witness before I could contest them as unjust?

When Jaime began to express racist opinions at the start of my study, should I have nodded, smiled, and taken notes or made my opinion known? When students confided in me that they wanted to drop out, was I to maintain their confidentiality and watch them do so, collecting it as data, or do something about it—either on my own or by enlisting the help of particular teachers? When students' suspensions were unconstitutional, was I to silently document that fact or speak up? When students confided in me that they knew which individuals were responsible for the rape of a student, was I to take that gossip at face value, and, if so, was I to hold the information as privileged or report it to authorities? Were my responsibilities more clear if the students damaged by discriminatory behavior were my own (affinal) kin? The advantage of the "detached observer" stance would be not to feel responsible for dealing with such issues. That, however, has never been my position.

Although I responded to each of these cases after thinking through the unique circumstances and consequences of each (and eventually deciding to address some and leave others alone), in the end it was an attack on my sister-in-law that moved me to action on a larger scale. Throughout this book I have mentioned a teacher teasing Carmen, a Nambueseña girl, for the way she spoke and later lowering her grade on a group project to 74 percent while her peers received a 98 percent mark for the same work. Profesor Teodoro, the teacher involved, threatened to fail her at the end of the year. This was not a result of her work or of her intelligence—it was a direct result of my being related to Carmen and the teacher taking his anger toward me (and my questioning of his discriminatory tactics) out on my sister-in-law. These actions served as the last straw, on top of so many others throughout the year, and led me to schedule a meeting with all teachers and staff to present my findings.

REACTIONS TO THE RESEARCH FINDINGS

Teachers from all factions, at one point or another, had requested that I hold such a meeting. I was the one who dreaded it—in part because it meant I would be required to take on the role I had so strenuously avoided: that of the invading outsider who imposes her ideals on others and tells people what to do. At the risk of becoming *la prepotente dama del norte* (the supreme lady of the north), I agreed to report my findings—findings I knew would sound like betrayal to the "pillars" and would anger teachers implicated in discriminatory practices. I considered, however, that one of the best ways to make my knowledge of this school situation applicable, in my particular circumstances, was to report my findings to the practitioners directly involved in that knowledge.

I recalled that at the first staff meeting of the year I had introduced myself as an anthropologist who had worked with the community of Nambué for several years and found that school was important in the way students from the reservation came to identify themselves. I had made it clear (both through interview questions and informal conversation) that I was concerned with discrimination in the school. Profesor Ramiro and Profesor Teodoro, during the first month of school, had specifically asked me to give them "constructive criticism." Profesor Teodoro perhaps came to regret that request. By the end of the year, 100 percent of the teachers in the school had agreed (individually) to allow me to observe their classes and interview them. In conversing with Profesor Isidro, I once noted that I would translate my manuscript so teachers and students could tell me what I had gotten wrong (a request I reiterated at the meeting).[5] Profesor Isidro commented, "No, no. You have to just write the truth." Thus, it seemed they should have been both prepared for my results and willing to hear them.

This sort of study, however, places teachers in a precarious position of both wanting to be helpful and being rightfully wary of the outcome of the research and the representation of themselves within it. Although they had the option to deny my request for interviews or permission to observe their classes, doing so might have made them appear as if they had something to hide.[6] Perhaps teachers held power over the research in terms of the way they presented themselves in the classes I observed (although some students told me how their teachers' behavior differed when I was not observing). Once I stood before them to reveal the findings of my study, that power was out of their hands. The power inherent in writing and representing a culture became evident in the field—for me—as I presented my findings to the high school staff.[7]

At the staff meeting, held nine months into my school-based observations, I began by listing examples of discrimination I had seen in the high school. I made sure to obscure people's identities the best I could, and I was careful to edit out examples whose protagonists would be easily identified. I outlined possible ways to overcome stereotypes, which included visits to the various communities so teachers might understand their realities. (It was unlikely that such a plan could happen, however, given that the school had no funds for it.) I suggested that teachers think individually about who they called on and which students they did not know by name to see if they may have been participating in the dynamics I discussed. I made it clear that such actions were usually unconscious so as not to accuse teachers of racism directly.

I discussed students' embarrassment at having to say publicly that they were from Nambué (given their peers' reactions) and noted that this information could be gathered in writing at the beginning of each year rather than having students speak it, only to be placed immediately into a stigmatized category. My purpose in doing this was to draw attention to the issue of ascribed identity on the basis of place and its repercussions in the high school. I promoted awareness of the fact that the perception of racism may have been stronger than the intent. Teachers who made comments perceived by Nambueseños as discriminatory or as furthering stereotypes may have been, in reality, well-intentioned, but the outcome may have been offensive.

I talked about the effects of teachers' preferential treatment of particular students. In sum, I addressed the issues that have been elucidated in detail throughout this book. Finally, I urged teachers who disagreed with my opinions and findings to take them up with me rather than taking them out on students. My greatest fear was that my attempt at advocacy anthropology would backfire and make matters worse for students from the reservation. (My fears were not unfounded, given one teacher's treatment of Carmen, my sister-in-law.) I explained that another reason for requesting feedback was so I might incorporate alternative views of the events I described into this published version.

At the request of teachers from all social factions in the school, I also addressed staff relations and the effects of rivalries and gossip within that sphere. Although at first this seemed less relevant to my larger goal of exposing discrimination in the high school, it was in fact tied in. Traveler teachers, for all practical purposes, were being driven out of the high school after a year or two of teaching there because of gossip and their treatment and exclusion by "pillars." Given the Roger Harker effect, in which teachers tend to direct their lessons to students most like themselves, it is vital that the teacher population be as varied as that of the students.[8] For SRHS, it was important that both traveler and *moreno* teachers, as well as those from different class backgrounds, be employed at the high school so the staff would be more likely to reach students of varying backgrounds. In 1999 there were no Nambueseño teachers at SRHS, but hiring Nambueseño staff could prove effective at reaching students from the reservation.[9] Thus, the issue of staff relations was also significant to my advocacy-related goals.

Teachers' Reactions

Reactions to my presentation were varied. The principal, who had endorsed my study from the initial staff meeting of the year, was the first to speak after my presentation. He addressed all the teachers, counselors, and administrators present at the staff meeting and expressed his concern about my findings that the school staff promoted racism, albeit unconsciously. He relied on a favorite trope of teachers to get his point across when he commented, "I want to remind you that we are formers of people." He warned that by forming students with racist ideals, "We are creating who knows what kind of person." He alluded to the incident at Columbine High School, which I had mentioned at the beginning of my presentation (noting that school violence was escalating elsewhere and could erupt at SRHS as well) and which was prominent in the news in Costa Rica that year. Again, he endorsed my study by insisting, "As I said at the beginning, Karen's vision is very important because she is seeing us as an outsider. Let's say [she sees] things that we ourselves do not. And I think it is important that each one of us analyze ourselves." He thanked me for having "painted them" as I had. Other staff members were somewhat less appreciative.

Profesor Teodoro—one of the teachers who had requested my constructive criticism on more than one occasion—felt I was asking teachers to baby students from the reservation. His equation of not discriminating against Nambueseños with "babying" them or with a request for showing favoritism toward them provided further evidence of the problem at hand.

I made a concerted effort in the presentation to point out that what I was suggesting was not a reversal of the targets of favoritism and discrimination but basic decency in the treatment of all students, an end to discriminatory treatment of Nambueseños, and an increased awareness of the more subtle forms of discrimination that existed at SRHS. As discussed in Chapter 7, however, not everyone viewed the treatment of Nambueseños as discriminatory. Profesor Teodoro said he had no reason to hide from Carmen the fact that she was from the reservation. He suggested that the answer was "consciousness raising" among the Nambueseño students so they would stop coming to school ashamed of being from Nambué. The principal supported my response that students did not come to school ashamed of their place of residence but rather that such shame was learned in school.

Most teachers' reactions to my presentation became apparent in the days following the event. It appeared that teachers were on one of two sides: either they felt outrage and anger toward me, or they believed I had been insufficiently aggressive. The outrage of certain teachers was evident to all. After the mud pit incident following my presentation, a few teachers thought I had gotten into a brawl because of my results. Certainly, particular teachers were angry enough to have warranted that suspicion.

Although I made a considerable effort not to single anyone out, to give everyone the opportunity to save face by not having to own up to any particular example, and to point out that these acts were often unconscious, the teachers implicated in my assertions made their identities clear through their comments and actions in the days following the presentation. Teachers of a faction opposing the "pillars" reported that Profesora Eugenia, a key "pillar" (who in fact had coined that label), had said that everything I reported was *"pura paja"* (something akin to "pure crap") and that *"me resbala"* (it slides right off me)—a phrase indicating that she felt my report was intended for her but that she was not willing to be affected by it.

Some days later this "pillar" and other uniformed teachers (uniform both in dress and in their opinions of me at that point) were gathered in the teachers' lounge, and I got the distinct impression that I was the topic of their discussion. I heard from others that this group was questioning whether I had permission to do such a study (although each of them had expressly given me permission every time I entered their classroom or conducted an interview with them). Profesora Delia reported this to me and suggested that I carry my letter of permission from the principal (solicited before the year began). I did so, but no one from the "pillar" group ever asked me directly who had given me permission, nor did they take me up on my request to point out any errors in my data or conclusions. Given that they had conceded permission for me to study their classrooms and allowed me to interview them, given their requests for my report, and given their prior knowledge of the focus of my study, I wondered why they were so surprised by my findings. Several possible explanations occurred to me.

Various teachers, in interviews and conversations, lamented teachers' loss of authority over students as a result of recent legislation on student rights. Teachers were well aware of students' right to sue them for behavior not condoned in the guidelines for school conduct, by which both students and teachers were bound. Yet this group of teachers had maintained a certain unquestioned power—until, that is, I questioned it at the staff meeting. Their reaction may also be related to the double bind faced by teachers who are in some ways compelled to participate in such a study.[10] Although they granted me permission to interview and observe them, it is likely that they felt some pressure to do so. Finally, their sense of betrayal might have been related to the question of racial privilege. As I discussed in Chapter 1, there seemed to be some expectation on the part of white teachers and Riteños generally that I would agree with their positions or feel loyalty to their community on the basis of *my* race. Thus, my presentation to teachers and staff, like my marriage to a man from the reservation, may have been viewed as one more act of treason against my race.

In light of these extreme reactions, I feared my presentation might only exacerbate the unjust treatment of Nambueseños. I also wondered if perhaps I should have taken less care to make the perpetrators of such acts anonymous, given that those I had protected most were those most angry with me anyway. Several "pillars" (Profesores Teodoro, Natalia, Anatolia, and Rosa María) manifested their discontent by ceasing to greet me (an overt snub in a place where appearances of politeness were upheld).

Profesora Rosaura only greeted me when the "pillar" teachers were not present. Two "pillars" (Profesoras Natalia and Eugenia) declined to participate in any meetings or functions at which I might be present. I suppose this, too, points to an advantage of the hypothetical detached observer. I might have felt less compelled to be diplomatic and less wary of outing particular racists were I not so tied to the communities involved. Had I taken less care to guard the anonymity of racist individuals, the guilty teachers' reactions would likely have been the same, although my arguments could have been better supported by a greater number of examples and been more convincing. I was not the only one who wondered if I ought to have been less tactful.

The teachers who generally agreed with my assessment (who were, for the most part, traveler teachers and younger teachers) thought my presentation was too passive. One disappointed traveler teacher, Profesora Alicia, revealed that she had hoped I would be more aggressive and name those responsible for discrimination. The vice principal regretted that I had not named the chief "pillar" and pointed out her defects. Profesora Alba commented that I needed to be "stronger" in implicating people (although she had benefited from my censure of examples too easily identified). Profesor Sergio asked why I had been so "complacent." Still, he commented that in spite of this complacency, I had come off as *la prepotente dama del norte.* He had watched his "pillar" colleagues' expressions as they mouthed comments suggesting that what I reported was *pura paja,* not an issue or not of concern. Profesor Sergio asked if I would do it the same way if I had the presentation to do over again. I imagine I would, even though the two extremes of teacher reactions were disappointing to me and both sides were unsatisfied. Given that I seemingly offended half of the population and left the rest wanting more pointed accusations, however, I must have reached some sort of middle ground.

Some teachers who were not implicated in my indirect accusations felt disappointed as well. Profesor Ramiro said he had hoped my presentation would point out the high school's failings in a "more realist panorama, although it wouldn't be to my benefit." He thought my comments on discrimination were not useful because he already agreed that students should be treated equally. He felt I was preaching to the choir and regretted that I had pointed out no wrongdoings on his part, from which he could learn. The librarian (and friend of the "pillars") was disappointed that I had not discussed the traveler teachers' "low morality." Profesor Efraín, a young traveler teacher who did not agree that my findings revealed problems in the high school, also thought I was too passive in my report. "Even so," he added, "you made some people jump."

Confused about the overall reactions to my presentation, on the following day I went to talk to the principal and ask for his opinion. He responded succinctly, "I liked it." Hoping for more than a comforting, fatherly word from the principal to the dejected gringa anthropologist, I asked if he thought what I had talked about was an issue at SRHS. He agreed that "it is that way" at the high school and added that teachers had already complained to him about the presentation. He informed those teachers that this was only the beginning of "a change that will occur in the high school." He assured them and me that they would continue to talk about these issues. In sum, he said, "You helped me." He explained that nobody likes to get "painted" (represented in that manner), and I would receive the reaction I was getting anywhere I carried out such a study.

Indeed, I might have helped him. From the beginning, he did not seem overly threatened by my research. It had been within his power to deny me permission to conduct this research when I wrote him to request as much before I went to Costa Rica in 1999. Early on, he admitted to me that racism and discrimination were problems at SRHS. He was both *moreno* and a traveler, however. He did not enjoy the respect of the "pillars"—as they were quick to point out—and they would be unlikely to abide by his suggestions on the matter. He may have been aware of the status my race and nationality may have accorded me in conducting such a study. White teachers might have been more likely to allow me, a white researcher, to discuss such things as racism and discrimination and listen to my comments on them. This brought up a whole new ethical dilemma for me: Was it acceptable to take advantage of the racial hierarchy that was at the very heart of the issue I studied, even if my intent in doing so was to subvert that hierarchy? Did the ends justify the means? The answer is still unclear, and recognizing myself in this position of power is uncomfortable for me, but the ends remain to be seen. Before I examine the possible effects and implications of this study, it is necessary to discuss the reactions of individuals other than the teachers.

STUDENT RESPONSES

On the day following my presentation to the high school staff, Jaime, the seventh grader, passed me in Santa Rita. Although he usually chatted with me anytime he saw me, this time he merely opened his eyes wide and raised his eyebrows. Jaime—a favorite among "pillar" teachers—was often privy to their opinions about the school, its staff, its students, and in this case it seemed, its anthropologist. Another possibility also existed. Jaime had asked to read my dissertation when it was finished. I was clear about my opinions of his racism and had asked what he would think if he found himself quoted throughout my written analysis and dominating particular sections of it. He thought for a moment and then commented that it would be fine, given that "it is good to dominate." At this juncture, he may have been rethinking that agreement and my potential portrayal of him in written work. If this were the case, though, he made no direct comment on the matter.

Underdog Riteño and traveler students who heard about the presentation let me know that they applauded me and were proud of my actions. Most Nambueseños did as well—although not all. I have mentioned the plight of my sister-in-law, Carmen, who suffered the most as a result of my research. She considered Profesor Teodoro's attempt to fail her because of his resentment toward me to be the worst experience she had ever had in high school. Consequently, I examined the possibilities for dealing with this situation. It was clear to me that her suffering because of my advocacy was unjust and that it went against all ethical guidelines for an anthropologist. One of the representatives of the token Department of Indigenous Education within the Ministry of Education had suggested that I report racist teachers to her and her fellow representative and have them removed from the school. Following their suggestion, I could have turned Profesor Teodoro in.

I was well aware that this option was strongly opposed to the ethics of my discipline. I was also aware of various situations in which Riteño favoritism had taken precedence over the school system's rules in the past and was convinced that teachers whose power at SRHS was such that they could behave in the ways they did would simply not leave. Political connections with prominent Riteño community members were likely to save them from the ministry's demands. Although I rejected this option, generally for the reasons outlined earlier, I must admit I considered it in the case of this teacher.

POWER DYNAMICS IN FIELDWORK REVISITED

The ethical guidelines of the American Anthropological Association assert that an anthropological study must not jeopardize the researcher's respondents. As discussed in Chapter 1, however, what should an anthropologist do when those respondents are at odds with one another? Whose rights should I have privileged? I decided that the spirit of the guideline is to protect those disadvantaged by power and that my responsibility lay more with a relatively powerless student unjustly affected by my study than with a fairly powerful teacher crossing his own profession's ethical guidelines.

I went to school with Carmen on the day she was to respond to her failing status. I was prepared to defend her against Profesor Teodoro and perhaps turn him in to the Ministry of Education. Fortunately for my professional conscience and for me, between the time he listed Carmen as failing and the time we went to contest that action, Profesor Teodoro had removed her name from the list of failing students. He had also made it known that he would not return to teach at SRHS the following year. Thus, the standoff came to a standstill, and I was not forced to make a choice. I still grapple, however, with the fact that my sister-in-law (although she has since graduated from the high school) was the one who suffered most for my well-intentioned advocacy and my career. At the beginning of the year, when I explained to her that I would be studying the effects of schooling on identity and vice versa, she commented, "how nice, because sometimes they marginalize you for being Indian." By the end of the year, she had every right to express disdain for my study. If Carmen did feel resentment toward my work and me, she did not reveal it.

Nambueseño Responses and Potential Solutions

Other Nambueseños were overwhelmingly supportive of my work. I held a meeting for Nambueseño students and parents in which I presented the same material I had laid out at the teachers' meeting, as well as further options for dealing with the situation. Twenty-one people (including nine students) attended the meeting, which took place in Nambué. At the meeting, I outlined examples of discrimination in the high school and explained the laws that made such discrimination illegal, with regard to both students and inhabitants of Costa Rica's reservations (as outlined in the nation's constitution, as well as in the International Labor Organization's Treaty 169: Convention Concerning Indigenous and Tribal Peoples in Independent Countries, 1989). Furthermore, I suggested various options for action and entertained comments and questions by Nambueseño parents and students.

I revealed to parents several teachers' unspoken expectation that they were to go to the school to check up on their children,[11] as well as the fact that almost all Nambueseño students were discriminated against. Formerly, many parents had declined to discuss what were seen as their children's "behavior problems" (sometimes false accusations) with other parents, as this was a source of shame. Thus, parents who were not already aware of the discriminatory dynamic within the high school, including the tendency of Nambueseño students to be falsely accused of rule infractions, now were aware. I discussed various items of the hidden curriculum, such as the option of asking for scholarships (to which Riteño parents were clued in but others were not) to defray the costs of education. I reiterated the importance of signing up for vocational workshops on the first day of registration and noted with whom they should speak if their children were removed from their workshops of choice and placed in others.

In response to parents' questions about whom to complain to in cases of discrimination, I provided information on the school's procedure for handling complaints. In addition to providing information about the school system and hidden curriculum, I presented more drastic options I had been made aware of by students, parents, and representatives from the Department of Indigenous Education. Although it was against my code of professional ethics to report teachers, parents and students could do so. I provided the names of individuals in the regional office of the Ministry of Education as well as those in the Department of Indigenous Education to whom parents could complain. Although I never named problematic teachers, parents at the meeting did so.

I also discussed the even more extreme option of moving students from SRHS to one of the high schools in the nearby towns of Majapiñao or Aserradero. I had discussed this option with students from Nambué and with representatives from the Department of Indigenous Education. The latter had informed me that this was a viable option, should parents agree to it. One representative discouraged this solution, arguing that moving the students would "take away their right" to attend the high school in their own township and would perpetuate racism and stereotypes rather than confront them. I had given a great deal of thought to this issue. It is my opinion that since the high school's inception in the 1970s, the more than twenty-five-year experiment to see if discrimination would diminish with time has not produced positive results. Still, it is not up to me to make this decision. For this reason, I presented the option to parents and promised my support for whatever solution they chose. In keeping with another suggestion proposed by Nambueseño community members, I explained that if conditions in the local government and local clinic were as discriminatory as they were in the high school (as various community members had reported them to be), the community might consider removing itself from the township of Santa Rita and returning to Majapiñao.

Numerous students supported the idea of switching to a different high school. Several already had tentative plans to change schools so they could take vocational workshops more in keeping with their future goals. The students who were against this idea, although they would have preferred another high school, thought the alternative schools (although relatively close) were too far away to allow them to walk home when teachers failed to come to class or when classes were unexpectedly canceled. In fact, the school in Majapiñao might be too far for students living on one end of the reservation. For others, it might be closer than SRHS. The school in Aserradero is only one kilometer (km) farther from the social center of Nambué (ten km) than SRHS (which is nine km away), so it might indeed be an option.

Some parents shared the opinion of the representative of the Department of Indigenous Education with regard to moving students to another school. One mother opined, "I think we shouldn't leave the community of Santa Rita. No. We have to confront the problem. We live in a free country." On that note, various Nambueseño parents discussed ways they might organize to confront discrimination against their children in the high school.

One mother led an effort to organize parents to rent a vehicle to take them to register their children early for vocational workshops. She added that if, subsequently, school officials removed their children from the classes of their choice, parents ought to support one another in their complaints. Another emphasized the need to eradicate discriminatory attitudes within the reservation as a starting point for dealing with discrimination elsewhere. Another suggested that they demand that the Ministry of Education—based on the guarantees in the laws I outlined at the meeting—raise the standard of education in Nambué's elementary school so students might enter high school on a more equal footing with Riteño students. Thus, the desire for empowerment was evident.

My guilt surrounding the potential negative effects of my research on students from the reservation was also assuaged to a certain extent as parents began to thank me individually for the study I had carried out, which they deemed to be of help. Various community members affirmed their support of my study on numerous occasions, and this was most evident when the sixth graders graduating from Nambué's elementary school dedicated their graduation ceremony to me (an honor usually reserved for a community member).

IMPLICATIONS AND APPLICATIONS

The implications and applications of this study may be more far-reaching still than the empowerment of particular Nambueseño students and parents. As the principal of the high school noted, he took my work as the starting point for change. It remains to be seen if that will come to pass, but early signs suggested it might. Shortly after my presentation, a Riteña "pillar" approached the vice principal to inform her that Riteño parents had selected the teachers they wanted to teach classes to their fifth-year students the following year. The vice principal reported that she told this teacher that those parents "are very much mistaken" and must realize that there is a principal who makes that decision. Thus, at least momentarily, Riteño control over school matters was curbed.

We must consider, however, that the superintendent had overturned the principal's administrative decisions in the past as a result of Riteño parental pressure and that it could happen again. Given the superintendent's opinion of racism in the school as so common that it did not merit further consideration, the outlook for change may not be optimistic. In my interview with the superintendent, I asked whether it would be possible to address stereotypes at the elementary school level in Santa Rita in particular. He answered hesitantly that yes, they could discuss culture in elementary school, but then noted that they already did so. He added, "But you know how kids are; when they're small they'll even confront their own mothers." With this "boys will be boys" attitude so prevalent within the school system, change may not be forthcoming.

On a higher level, though, the Department of Indigenous Education requested a copy of my translated dissertation to support the department's as-yet-unheeded claim that a multicultural curriculum is needed in Costa Rican schools. According to the representatives of the department, higher-ups in the Ministry of Education have not seen a need to implement a new (and thus costly) curriculum. Much for the same reasons white Riteños might be more receptive to criticism from a white North American visitor than from the *moreno* traveler high school principal, the higher authorities in the Ministry of Education might be more receptive to arguments made in a North American doctoral dissertation. Again, the question of whether buying into such a hierarchy is ethical crosses my mind. Although I agree that the anthropologist is not always the most appropriate individual to apply findings to policy[12] (nor do I wish to be a meddling outsider or *la prepotente dama del norte*), the existing racial hierarchy may contribute to the power of these findings if reported as mine rather than if they are presented by someone with a lesser status in the ministry hierarchy.

Even if my work proves influential in promoting a multicultural curriculum, numerous scholars have noted that multicultural curricula are not necessarily antiracist.[13] To effect real change in this matter, the alternative curriculum proposed must have the express goal of countering racism in schools. Thus, a different curriculum alone may not help. In SRHS, racism served as a frame for interactions both between teachers and students and among students. This racism, though, was not easily categorized as such. Rather than being confined to a particular group, place, social class, or racial category, it was about how these categories intersected to produce inequality. As I have demonstrated throughout this book, the precise nature of the discrimination that occurred at SRHS was elusive and difficult to locate in only one race, one place, or one social class. Rather, these traits overlapped in any given student's situation to produce their rank within the school's hierarchy. At times, one of these aspects may have predominated, and at other times another would take precedence.

THE NATURE (OR CULTURE) OF DISCRIMINATION AT SRHS

In the case of SRHS, although discrimination hinged more on place, race, and class, marginalization may sometimes have been even greater for Riteño *morenos* who were excluded from both Riteño cliques and other unified groups like Nambueseño boys' cliques. Gender was also at play. Like *moreno* or poor students from Santa Rita, Nambueseña girls also found themselves excluded from many cliques and lacked the visible support of girls from their own community.

Thus, whereas discrimination may only be recognized as such when it is visible along racial lines, "race" itself is not such a simple category. And although the dynamics of discrimination—when acknowledged—may be discussed in terms of race, clearly they are about much more than that. "Race," as constructed in SRHS and the surrounding area, had to do not only with skin color but also with socioeconomic class and place of residence. This study has aimed to demonstrate the ways discrimination—occurring along the intermingling lines of race, place, class, and gender—was institutionalized at SRHS. In demonstrating the institutionalization of discriminatory practices, I hope to shed light on the school's social reproductive agenda (although it might not have been a conscious one for most members of the teaching and administrative staffs). I seek not only to expose the variety of discriminatory practices that existed in the high school setting but also to illustrate the complex nature of their perpetuation.

I have intended to paint an intricate portrait of racist practice to show that racism does not always come from expected sources. None of the teachers I portray here were consistently racist or always complicit in the school's social reproductive agenda. Not all teachers who were prejudiced were white. Not all of them were Riteños. Not all the white or Riteño teachers upheld the dominant ideology of Santa Rita. Not all *moreno* teachers were free of discriminatory behavior. Those individuals whom I found to be most racist and whom I tended to dislike as a result still had good things to offer. For example, Profesora Eugenia's treatment of gender in the classroom was commendable in a largely patriarchal society. Similarly, those I considered innovative in pedagogical techniques and felt were overall good teachers with regard to racial equity, and with whom I formed friendships as a result, still had flaws. Profesor Sergio's objectification of some female students and Profesora Aracely's comments on physical disability disappointed me, as the former was a friend and the latter struck me as overwhelmingly fair and admirable most of the time. Certainly, none of us, as educators, can be at our best all the time. Most important, the majority of teachers at SRHS were dedicated, skilled teachers. It only took a few (among them Riteños, travelers, younger teachers, veteran teachers, white teachers, and *moreno* teachers) to create and perpetuate a largely racist environment.

CONTRIBUTIONS TO THEORY AND PRACTICE

Critics of earlier studies in the fields of anthropology and education have noted their shortcomings with regard to addressing gender, intragroup variation, and other issues. This and other research responds to the call for more scholars to address the ways gender affects students and how gendered messages are internalized.[14] My attention to the variety of ways in which both teachers and students viewed what I consider to be discriminatory acts also addresses criticisms of studies that have failed to account for why individual members of any particular ethnic group might be affected in different ways. With regard to this issue, I have attempted to address the formation of identity in such a way as to demonstrate how any particular resident of the reservation may or may not have adhered to the identity ascribed to her or him. I have done this by discussing the various discourses that have affected questions of indigenous identity in Costa Rica generally and Nambué specifically, as well as through showing how perceived race, class, and gender were also important to this equation for any given individual.

My focus on the ways race was constructed in this setting, as well as the ways racial and gendered identities were taught in school, may further research in this area.[15] I have also intended to elaborate on current literature regarding race and ethnicity by outlining a context in which race was largely defined through place, as mixed with social class, gender, family situation, and other elements of status. In doing so, I hope to point to the socially constructed nature of these concepts, as they are often rendered more visible to local readers through unfamiliar and distant contexts.

Furthermore, through this book I seek to contribute to the growing body of literature on schooling in Latin America and to the existing ethnographic work on schooling in such a way as to combine a social reproductionist stance with one that acknowledges agency. Although several studies of anthropology and education set out to unveil discriminatory practices in high schools—a goal of my research as well—this study elaborates on that process. Rather than taking the existence of discrimination as the conclusion, my research seeks to demonstrate the ways the constraints present in the school system are contested—directly and indirectly—by the very students these limiting elements seek to control, define, and channel into particular paths.

It is this last contribution of my work—the knowledge that students, indeed, do resist discrimination in school—that led me to reject the local proverb "*¿Para qué cerrar el portón si la cerca está en el suelo?*" (Why shut the gate if the fence is on the ground—a proverb that alludes to a situation beyond hope) as the title I had previously chosen for this chapter in favor of a less pessimistic one that acknowledges the often problematic role of the anthropologist in this entire project. Here, at the end of this lengthy process of writing, erasing, and starting over, I must agree that, indeed, it is hard to write something that nobody can contest. In fact, I believe it is impossible, and I reject it as a goal.

My work has sought to question a situation few people were openly critiquing and in which fewer still were giving those select voices merit. This research project has sought to call attention to the variety of ways traveler students generally and Nambueseño students specifically were affected by intersecting axes of prejudice and discrimination and the ways in which that system was resisted at every turn. Had teachers and community members been comfortable with my findings, my research might have been useless. By inciting contention, however, this project has brought the dynamics of discrimination in this rural Costa Rican high school and their effects on students' identity out from under the veil of hegemonic acceptance and the silence of habitus into a realm where they are more visible.

A return visit to Santa Rita and Nambué in July 2001 confirmed the general findings reported here. Headed for Santa Rita, translated dissertation in hand, I began to wonder if perhaps I had been too harsh in my assessment. Precisely at that moment of doubt I ran into Erick, the "best" student from the graduating class of 1999—a white Riteño rumored to be the illegitimate son of a powerful community member. My subsequent conversation with him was the first of a series of interactions that ultimately left me assured of my conclusions. Erick, the focus of any classroom he sat in, spoke of his present difficulties as a university student and his feeling that his high school experience had left him ill prepared for that level of study. This supported my assertion that even those who reaped all the benefits available to select students in Santa Rita may not have received an adequate education. At the high school, I heard new reports of teachers prophesying students' failures and holding grudges, to the detriment of their pupils. Students complained of learning trivial facts for the national exams instead of anything that might be useful outside of that context. The teacher who threatened to fail my sister-in-law was allegedly embroiled in an ethical nightmare far more severe than that I described here, thus confirming my negative portrayal of him.

I was pleased to find that Rebeca, the girl whose boyfriend wanted her to drop out, was still in school and that the outspoken David was not working in the banana plantations. I was unable to find Martín, and his brother explained that he was probably in sewing class, thus proving that he was still choosing less desirable vocational courses so he could enjoy more favorable peer groups. Adrián, the student who aspired to become an astronaut, was at the University of Costa Rica in San José studying physics (although in Santa Rita rumors abounded that this successful young man was actually in a mental institution). Jacobo was preparing to take the last exam for the equivalent of a GED before starting his studies at the university. Although he admitted that he sometimes wished he had gotten his diploma in Santa Rita, he asserted that he was better off than his fellow "bad kids" who had graduated but who stayed in Santa Rita with no job possibilities. Both Adrián and Jacobo (independently) were writing books.

During my visit, the high school's administrative assistants read two-thirds of my manuscript and managed to decipher all the pseudonyms (although I did not confirm their accuracy). Nobody seemed overtly offended. In fact, just as I was about to leave the high school, "Jaime" passed by me on his bicycle. He shouted out (proudly, it seemed), "*Profe, ¡Ya conocí a Jaime!*" (Teacher, I just met Jaime!). He had reported to a friend of mine that he was an "important figure" in my analysis. My friend interpreted Jaime's comment as revealing pride in being the "villain."

Although the priest and the superintendent were not available to meet with me, the principal, various teachers, the Riteña president of the Board of Education, and representatives from the Department of Indigenous Education of the Ministry of Education all used terms such as *valuable* and *important* to describe my work. The president of the Board of Education requested authorization to present my work to the minister of education, and I received a call from Nambué's current representative to the National Commission on Indigenous Affairs requesting permission to give a copy of my work to the First Lady of the nation, with whom he had spoken about the situation at the high school and who had expressed an interest in reading my analysis.

Whereas the more lasting effects of this project remain to be seen, the project has met its short-term goals. On a theoretical level, I have built upon the foundation laid by earlier literature regarding anthropology and education and responded to its calls for further research in gendered and intragroup variation. On a substantive level, I have written a document that students, administrators, parents, and officials from various camps considered "valuable" and a potential "seed for change." In response to my initial questions about the apparent exclusivity of Indianness and school success in Santa Rita, it is now clear that the two extreme effects of schooling on identity noted at the beginning of the book—school success accompanied by a rejection of indigenous identity, on the one hand, and school failure and maintenance of Indian identity on the other—are only two poles marking a broad range of reactions to a situation wrought with discrimination based on place, race, and class. The seemingly pessimistic nature of these two extreme reactions is mitigated by the fact that in the face of such discrimination, such a variety of resistant strategies do indeed exist, countering the all-too-common message that indigenous identity and school success are incompatible.

NOTES

1. "It's hard to write something that nobody can say anything about."

2. A variety of interpretations of "applied anthropology" exist. I consider that applied work, in the context of education, includes research that is not geared toward the academy alone but that deliberately seeks to inform educational policy, make contributions to the community of study in keeping with the needs its members express, and empower respondents. This view is in keeping with active discussions within the Council of Anthropology and Education (CAE). One such discussion took place over the CAE listserv in March and April 2004. Among examples of applied anthropology cited in this

discussion were various ethnographic projects that intended to promote change by influencing policy. The painstaking process of translating my analysis to return it to the communities involved was not required for academic purposes. It is a project I undertook as one part of the applied focus of this work. This project was applied on various levels. It impacted Nambueseño students, other underdog students at SRHS, teachers, parents, and the Ministry of Education.

3. Agar 1987:433.

4. As of 2005, and four years after my delivery of the translated manuscript to the communities involved, I have received only one such written response. It came from Jaime, who recognized himself in my work, confirmed my analysis, and signed his message with his pseudonym, followed by the phrase "Racist and Elitist in 1999 and forever." Contrary to when he first recognized himself in the work and seemed proud, during my return visit to SRHS in 2001 he seemed annoyed and offended, although he acknowledged that my descriptions of him were accurate. In his response, Jaime also updated me on his future plans. He no longer planned to go to the scientific magnet school in Liberia or to the academic high school in Majapiñao. He had decided to stay at SRHS and told me he had been offered the opportunity to study law at the University of Salamanca, Spain, after graduation from high school. It seems to me that there might be poetic justice in this outcome. Should Jaime proclaim his identity to be "Spaniard," as he did in Santa Rita, he might be questioned, given his place of origin and his manner of speaking (in Costa Rican Spanish)—which would place him in a particular position in the racial, ethnic, and linguistic hierarchy of Salamanca. It remains to be seen whether such an experience will cause him to view Nambueseños with greater compassion.

5. See Warren and Jackson 2002: 3 for a call for more researchers to translate their analyses and return them to their communities of study.

6. See McLaren 1986: 65–66.

7. See D. Wolf 1996: 2.

8. Spindler and Spindler 1982. See also MacLeod 1987: 156.

9. See Sleeter 1993: 168 for one argument on how increasing the number of teachers of color is integral to antiracist education.

10. McLaren 1986: 65–66.

11. As discussed previously, several teachers told me that Nambueseño parents were disinterested in their children's education, as evident in the fact that they never came to check on their children's progress. In fact, school officials never informed parents that they ought to come to school periodically to do so, and since most Nambueseño parents had not attended high school, they had no other way of knowing about this unspoken expectation of them.

12. Jordan and Jacob 1993: 260.

13. See Chapter 4.

14. Holland and Eisenhart 1990: 30; McLaren 1982: 20.

15. See Foley 1990: 203–204 for a criticism of past research that essentializes ethnic categories.

Appendix 1

THE QUESTIONS HERE ARE ENGLISH TRANSLATIONS OF THOSE I ASKED EACH MEMBER of the teaching and administrative staff at Santa Rita High School (SRHS), in one form or another. My wording and, at times, the ordering of questions changed to fit each individual interview. In each case, I asked if I could record the interview prior to asking any questions, and I prefaced my interview with a brief description of my project.

1. What subject or subjects do you teach?
2. What is your title (what degrees do you hold)?
3. How many years have you been teaching?
4. How many years have you taught at SRHS?
5. How do you like teaching here?
6. What do you consider is your role as an educator?
7. In addition to your subject, are there other lessons you like to teach to students?
8. What is the level of this school? How does it compare to others in the area (with regard to resources, quality, and similar factors)? How does it compare with urban schools in Costa Rica?
9. How many students end up working in the vocation they studied at SRHS? What percentage of students continue their studies after high school? What do they end up doing with their degrees?

10. What do you think of vocational education here?
11. What do you like best about this school? What is the best part of it?
12. What do you like least? What is the most problematic aspect of this school?
13. Often, gossip was the answer to #12. If not, I brought it up and asked if the respondent thought it was a problem among teachers.
14. What do you think of the students, generally speaking?
15. Do you see differences between the students from Santa Rita and the traveler students?
16. Do you see differences between traveler teachers and those from Santa Rita? Are there rivalries or divisions among teachers? What is the basis of those divisions (academic vs. vocational, traveler vs. Riteño, older generation vs. younger generation)?
17. Do the best students tend to come from any particular place?
18. Do the worst students tend to come from any particular place?
19. How do the students from Nambué compare with others? What about the students from Puerto Sereno?
20. Are you familiar with Nambué? Have you been there? What do you think of it? or How do you imagine it to be?/What is your impression of it?
21. Generally, do you know which students in your classes are from Nambué?
22. Are you a homeroom teacher? What does that involve for you?
23. Have you heard complaints about discrimination here, or do you think there is discrimination in this school (against anyone)?
24. What are the main reasons students drop out of school? Are there tendencies in where students who drop out come from? What do you do if you know a student wants to drop out?
25. Is discipline part of your role? How do you discipline students?
26. Do you think there is equal access to vocational courses for all students?
27. What do you think of the uniform guidelines?
28. What do you think of *adecuación curricular* (the program for learning disabled students)? What forms of assistance do you use?
29. What do you think of the conduct grade?
30. Is there really free and obligatory education in Costa Rica? What is the cost of education/your vocational workshop/your course in terms of what materials students must bring or pay for?
31. Do you think students act differently when I observe your classes?
32. Where are you from? How do you identify yourself (Riteño, traveler, vocational, academic)?
33. May I observe your class?

With students from each homeroom section I asked the following questions, although not necessarily in this order. I also followed students' lead on topics of conversation, thus this list is not exhaustive.

1. Do teachers act differently when I observe your classes? How?
2. Who are the best teachers? Why?
3. Who are the worst teachers? Why?
4. What makes a teacher good or bad?

5. Do you see favoritism here?
6. What do you like best about high school?
7. What do you like least?
8. Is gossip a problem for students?
9. Have students from your homeroom section dropped out? Why?
10. What do you want to do after high school?
11. Do you plan to take the optional sixth year of vocational education? Why or why not?
12. What are the nicknames of students in your homeroom section? How did they get them? What do they mean? Which nicknames are the worst?
13. What are teachers' nicknames (including mine)?

I took this opportunity to answer questions students had about me as well.

In longer interviews with Nambueseño students in Nambué, I asked these questions after explaining the project. I noted that in past years of research in Nambué, I had heard about racism and discrimination in the school.

1. Do you think there is discrimination in the school? What is it based on? Can you give me examples of discrimination that you have seen or that have happened to you?
2. What do you do when you are discriminated against?
3. Do you like the fact that Nambué is a reservation? Why or why not?
4. Would you get rid of Nambué's reservation status if you could?
5. When people ask you where you are from, how do you respond?
6. How do you identify yourself?
7. What does it mean to be indigenous? What makes a person indigenous?
8. Who are the best teachers? What makes them so?
9. Who are the worst teachers? What makes them so?
10. Where are your closest friends in school from?
11. What would you like to do after high school?
12. Do you like school? Ten years from now, do you think you will look back on your high school experience with nostalgia?
13. What do you think of the idea of switching to another high school in the area?
14. How much does your education cost you?
15. How did you choose your vocational workshop?

I took this opportunity to answer their questions about me and to see if there was anything else I had not asked but should have.

Appendix 2

Teachers' Affiliations

Teacher	Field	Place of Residence	Level of Experience	Pillar
Adán	academic	SR	new	no
Agustín	academic	SR	new	accepted by pillars
Alba	academic	traveler	new	accepted by pillars and travelers
Alicia	vocational	traveler	midcareer	no
Alodia	vocational	SR	veteran	yes
Anatolia	vocational	traveler	veteran	yes
Antonio	academic	traveler	new	no
Aracely	vocational	SR	veteran	accepted by pillars
Arnoldo	academic	traveler	new	no
Arturo	academic	SR	new	no
Belisa	academic	traveler	new	no
Delia	counselor	traveler	new	no
Efraín	academic	traveler	new	no
Eugenia	academic	SR	veteran	yes
Genofeva	academic	foreign, but resided in SR	veteran	no
Greis	academic	traveler	new	no
Isidro	vocational	SR	veteran	no
Lidieth	vocational	SR	veteran	yes
Manuel	vocational	SR	midcareer	no
Marielos	counselor	traveler	new	no
Marta Iris	academic	SR	veteran	yes
Miguel	vocational	traveler	midcareer	no
Natalia	vocational	SR	veteran	yes
Ramiro	vocational	SR	midcareer	no
Raúl	vocational	traveler	new	no
Remedios	vocational	traveler	veteran	yes
Rosa María	vocational	traveler	veteran	yes
Rosaura	academic	SR	veteran	yes
Sergio	academic	traveler	new	no
Simón	vocational	traveler	veteran	no
Soledad	taxi[1]	traveler	veteran	no
Tadeo	academic	traveler	veteran	no
Teodoro	vocational	traveler	veteran	yes
Yolanda	academic	traveler	new	no

Note: 1. This term refers to teachers who taught at a variety of schools. This was the case only for the religion teacher at SRHS.

Bibliography

Abercrombie, Thomas
    1991   "To Be Indian, to Be Bolivian: 'Ethnic' and 'National' Discourses of Identity,"
        pp. 95–130 in Greg Urban and Joel Sherzer, eds., *Nation-States and Indians in Latin America*. Austin: University of Texas Press.

Abu-Lughod, Lila
    1991   "Writing Against Culture," pp. 137–162 in Richard Fox, ed., *Recapturing Anthropology: Working in the Present*. Santa Fe: School of American Research Press.
    1993   *Writing Women's Worlds*. Berkeley: University of California Press.

Adams, Richard N.
    1991   "Strategies of Ethnic Survival in Central America," pp. 181–206 in Greg Urban and Joel Sherzer, eds., *Nation-States and Indians in Latin America*. Austin: University of Texas Press.

Agar, Michael H.
    1987   "Whatever Happened to Cognitive Anthropology: A Partial Review," pp. 425–433 in Herbert Applebaum, ed., *Perspectives in Cultural Anthropology*. Albany: State University of New York Press.

Allport, Gordon
    1974   "Linguistic Factors in Prejudice," pp. 107–119 in Paul A. Eschholz et al., eds., *Language Awareness*. New York: St. Martin's.

Alonso, Ana María
  1992   "Gender, Power, and Historical Memory: Discourses of *Serrano* Resistance,"
          pp. 404–421 in Judith Butler and Joan W. Scott, eds., *Feminists Theorize the
          Political.* New York: Routledge.
  1994   "The Politics of Space, Time, and Substance: State Formation, Nationalism,
          and Ethnicity," *Annual Review of Anthropology* 23: 379–405.
Anderson, Benedict
  1983   *Imagined Communities: Reflections on the Origin and Spread of Nationalism.* Lon-
          don: Verso.
Anzaldúa, Gloria
  1987   *Borderlands/La Frontera: The New Mestiza.* San Francisco: Aunt Lute.
Apple, Michael W.
  1993   "Constructing the 'Other': Rightist Reconstructions of Common Sense,"
          pp. 24–39 in Cameron McCarthy and Warren Crichlow, eds., *Race, Identity,
          and Representation in Education.* New York: Routledge.
Arnove, Robert
  1986   *Education and Revolution in Nicaragua.* New York: Praeger.
Aronowitz, Stanley, and Henry A. Giroux
  1991   *Postmodern Education: Politics, Culture, and Social Criticism.* Minneapolis: Uni-
          versity of Minnesota Press.
  1993   *Education Still Under Siege.* Westport, Conn.: Bergin and Garvey.
Arroyo, Victor Manuel
  1972   *Lenguas indígenas costarricenses.* Costa Rica: Editorial Centroamericana, EDUCA.
Asamblea Legislativa de la República de Costa Rica
  1986   Expediente 10933. San José: Asamblea Legislativa.
  1997   "Consulta a la comunidad de Matambú, Nicoya, Guanacaste, 10 de agosto
          de 1997," Expediente 12032. San José: Asamblea Legislativa.
Bakhtin, Mikhail
  1984   *Rabelais and His Work.* Bloomington: Indiana University Press.
Banks, Marcus
  1996   *Ethnicity: Anthropological Constructions.* London: Routledge.
Barrientos, Guido, Carlos Borge, Patricia Gudiño, Carlos Soto, Guillermo Rodríguez, and
  Alejandro Swaby
  1982   "El caso de los Bribris, indígenas talamanqueños, Costa Rica," pp. 249–255 in
          Guillermo Bonfil et al., eds., *América Latina: etnodesarrollo y etnocidio.* San José:
          Ediciones FLACSO.
Barth, Fredrik
  1969   *Ethnic Groups and Boundaries: The Social Organization of Culture Difference.* Bos-
          ton: Little, Brown.
Bhabha, Homi K.
  1990   "DissemiNation: Time, Narrative, and the Margins of the Modern Nation,"
          pp. 291–322 in Homi K. Bhabha, ed., *Nation and Narration.* London: Routledge.
Biesanz, Mavis Hiltunen, Richard Biesanz, and Karen Zubris Biesanz
  1999   *The Ticos: Culture and Social Change in Costa Rica.* Boulder: Lynne Rienner.

Blu, Karen L.
    1996   "'Where Do You Stay At?': Home Place and Community Among the Lumbee,"
          pp. 197–227 in Steven Feld and Keith Basso, eds., *Senses of Place.* Santa Fe:
          School of American Research.

Bonfil Batalla, Guillermo
    1972   "El concepto del indio en América: Una categoría de la situación colonial,"
          Anales de Antropología 9: 105–124.
    1989   *México profundo: Una civilización negada.* México, D.F.: Grijalbo.
    1990   "Aculturación e indigenismo: La respuesta india," pp. 189–209 in José Alcina
          Franch, ed., *Indianismo e indigenismo en América.* Madrid: Alianza.

Bourdieu, Pierre
    1984   *Distinction: A Social Critique of the Judgment of Taste.* Trans. Richard Nice. Cam-
          bridge: Harvard University Press.
    1995   *Outline of a Theory of Practice.* Trans. Richard Nice. Cambridge: Cambridge
          University Press.

Bourdieu, Pierre, and Jean-Claude Passeron
    1977   *Reproduction in Education, Society, and Culture.* London: Sage.

Bourgois, Philippe I.
    1989   *Ethnicity at Work: Divided Labor on a Central American Banana Plantation.* Balti-
          more: Johns Hopkins University Press.

Bourricaud, François
    1975   "Indian, Mestizo, and Cholo as Symbols in the Peruvian System of Stratifica-
          tion," trans. Barbara Bray, pp. 350–387 in Nathan Glazer and Daniel P. Moynihan,
          eds., *Ethnicity: Theory and Experience.* Cambridge: Harvard University Press.

Bozzoli de Wille, María Eugenia
    1969   *Localidades indígenas costarricenses 1960–1968.* San José: Publicaciones de la
          Universidad de Costa Rica.
    1986   *El indígena costarricense y su ambiente natural.* San José: Editorial Porvenir.

Casey, Edward
    1987   *Getting Back Into Place: Toward Renewed Understanding of the Place-World.*
          Bloomington: Indiana University Press.
    1993   *Remembering: A Phenomenological Study.* Bloomington: Indiana University Press.

Castaneda, Diana
    1981   "Crisis y amenaza a la sociedad Guaymí," pp. 127–133 in Comité Patroncina-
          dor del Foro Sobre el Pueblo Guaymí y Su Futuro, *El pueblo Guaymí y su
          futuro.* Panama: Impretex, S.A.

Castegnaro de Foletti, Alessandra
    1992   "La alfarería tradicional de La Paz Centro," pp. 145–196 in Germán Romero
          Vargas, ed., *Persistencia indígena en Nicaragua.* Managua: CIDCA-UCA.

Castile, George Piere
    1981   "On the Tarascanness of the Tarascans and the Indianness of Indians," pp.
          171–191 in George Piere Castile and Gilbert Kushner, eds., *Persistent Peoples:
          Cultural Enclavement in Perspective.* Tucson: University of Arizona Press.

Cazden, Courtney, and Vera P. John
   1971   "Learning in American Indian Children," pp. 252–272 in Murray Wax, Stanley Diamond, and Fred O. Gearing, eds., *Anthropological Perspectives on Education.* New York: Basic.

Chapin, Mac
   1989   "The 500,000 Invisible Indians of El Salvador," *Cultural Survival Quarterly* 13(3): 11–16.

Clarke, John, Stuart Hall, Tony Jefferson, and Brian Roberts
   1975   "Subcultures, Cultures, and Class," pp. 9–74 in Stuart Hall and Tony Jefferson, eds., *Resistance Through Rituals: Youth Subcultures in Post-War Britain.* London: Hutchinson & Co.

Clifford, James
   1986   "Introduction: Partial Truths," pp. 1–26 in James Clifford and George E. Marcus, eds., *Writing Culture.* Berkeley: University of California Press.

Cohen, Abner
   1993   "Culture as Identity: An Anthropologist's View," *New Literary History* 24: 195–209.

Comaroff, John L.
   1985   "Of Totemism and Ethnicity: Consciousness, Practice, and the Signs of Inequality," *Ethnos* 52(3–4): 301–323.

Comaroff, Jean, and John Comaroff
   1991   *Of Revelation and Revolution: Christianity, Colonialism, and Consciousness in South Africa.* Chicago: University of Chicago Press.
   1992   *Ethnography and the Historial Imagination.* Boulder: Westview.

Cousins, Linwood H.
   1999   " 'Playing Between Classes': America's Trouble With Class, Race, and Gender in a Black High School and Community," *Anthropology and Education Quarterly* 30(3): 294–316.

Crumrine, N. Ross
   1981   "The Ritual of the Cultural Enclave Process: The Dramatization of Oppositions Among the Mayo Indians of Northwest Mexico," pp. 109–131 in George Piere Castile and Gilbert Kushner, eds., *Persistent Peoples: Cultural Enclavement in Perspective.* Tucson: University of Arizona Press.

D'Amato, John
   1987   "The Belly of the Beast: On Cultural Differences, Castelike Status, and the Politics of School," *Anthropology and Education Quarterly* 18(4): 357–360.
   1993   "Resistance and Compliance in Minority Classrooms," pp. 181–207 in Evelyn Jacob and Cathie Jordan, eds., *Minority Education: Anthropological Perspectives.* Norwood, N.J.: Ablex.

Davidson, Ann Locke
   1996   *Making and Molding Identity in Schools.* New York: State University of New York Press.

Davis, Shelton H.
   1988   "Agrarian Structure and Ethnic Resistance; The Indian in Guatemalan and Salvadoran National Politics," pp. 78–106 in Remo Guidieri et al., eds., *Ethnicities and Nations.* Austin: University of Texas Press.

de la Cadena, Marisol
   1995   " 'Women Are More Indian': Ethnicity and Gender in a Community Near
           Cuzco," pp. 329–438 in Brooke Larson, Olivia Harris, and Enrique Tandeter,
           eds., *Ethnicity, Markets, and Migration in the Andes.* Durham, N.C.: Duke Uni-
           versity Press.

Deloria, Vine, Jr.
   1988   *Custer Died for Your Sins: An Indian Manifesto.* Norman: University of Okla-
           homa Press.

Deyhle, Donna
   1995   "Navajo Youth and Anglo Racism: Cultural Integrity and Resistance," *Harvard
           Educational Review* 65(3): 403–444.

di Leonardo, Micaela
   1984   *The Varieties of Ethnic Experience.* Ithaca: Cornell University Press.
   1991   *Gender at the Crossroads of Knowledge: Feminist Anthropology in the Postmodern
           Era.* Berkeley: University of California Press.

Díaz Polanco, Héctor
   1997   *Indigenous Peoples in Latin America: The Quest for Self-Determination.* Trans. Lucía
           Rayas. Boulder: Westview.

Dirks, Nicholas B., Geoff Eley, and Sherry B. Ortner, eds.
   1994   *Culture/Power/History: A Reader in Contemporary Social Theory.* Princeton:
           Princeton University Press.

Dolby, Nadine
   2001   *Constructing Race: Youth, Identity, and Popular Culture in South Africa.* Albany:
           State University of New York Press.

Durán, Guido
   1990   "El desarrollo socio-económico de Hojancha," *Comunidades* 3(16): 6–17.

Edelman, Marc, and Joanne Kenen
   1989   "The Origins of Costa Rican Exceptionalism—Colonial Period and the
           Nineteenth Century," pp. 1–9 in Marc Edelman and Joanne Kenen, eds., *The
           Costa Rica Reader.* New York: Grove Weidenfeld.

Eidheim, Harold
   1969   "When Ethnic Identity Is a Social Stigma," pp. 39–57 in Fredrik Barth, ed.,
           Ethnic Groups and Boundaries: The Social Organization of Culture Difference. Bos-
           ton: Little, Brown.

Enslin, Elizabeth
   1994   "Beyond Writing: Feminist Practice and the Limitations of Ethnography,"
           Cultural Anthropology 9(4): 537–568.

Erickson, Frederick
   1993   "Transformation and School Success: The Politics and Culture of Educa-
           tional Achievement," pp. 27–51 in Evelyn Jacob and Cathie Jordan, eds.,
           Minority Education: Anthropological Perspectives. Norwood, N.J.: Ablex.

Eriksen, Thomas Hylland
   1993   *Ethnicity and Nationalism: Anthropological Perspectives.* London: Pluto.

Fallas, Carlos Luis
   1998   *Marcos Ramírez.* San José: Editorial Costa Rica.

Feld, Steven, and Keith Basso
    1996   *Senses of Place.* Santa Fe: School of American Research.
Ferguson, Ann Arnett
    2000   *Bad Boys: Public Schools in the Making of Black Masculinity.* Ann Arbor: University of Michigan Press.
Fernández de Oviedo y Valdés, Gonzalo
    1959   *Historia general y natural de las Indias. Edición y estudio preliminar de Juan Pérez de Tudela Bueso.* Madrid: Ediciones Atlas.
Field, Les W.
    1995   "Constructing Local Identities in a Revolutionary Nation: The Cultural Politics of the Artisan Class in Nicaragua, 1979–1990," *American Ethnologist* 22(4): 786–806.
    1998   "Post-Sandinista Ethnic Identities in Western Nicaragua," *American Anthropologist* 100(2): 431–443.
    1999   *The Grimace of Macho Ratón: Artisans, Identity, and Nation in Late Twentieth-Century Western Nicaragua.* Durham, N.C.: Duke University Press.
Fine, Michelle
    1986   "Why Urban Adolescents Drop Into and Out of Public High School," *Teachers College Record* 87(3): 393–409.
Fishman, Joshua
    1972   *The Sociology of Language.* Rowley, Mass.: Newbury House.
    1996   "Ethnicity as Being, Doing, and Knowing," pp. 63–69 in John Hutchinson and Anthony D. Smith, eds., *Ethnicity.* Oxford: Oxford University Press.
Foley, Douglas
    1990   *Learning Capitalist Culture Deep in the Heart of Tejas.* Philadelphia: University of Pennsylvania Press.
    1995   *The Heartland Chronicles.* Philadelphia: University of Pennsylvania Press.
Fordham, Signithia
    1999   "Dissin' 'the Standard': Ebonics as Guerrilla Warfare at Capital High," *Anthropology and Education Quarterly* 30(3): 272–293.
Foucault, Michel
    1978   *The History of Sexuality.* Trans. Robert Hurley. New York: Vintage.
    1979   *Discipline and Punish: The Birth of the Prison.* Trans. Alan Sheridan. New York: Vintage.
Frake, Charles O.
    1996   "Pleasant Places, Past Times, and Sheltered Identity in Rural East Anglia," pp. 229–257 in Steven Feld and Keith Basso, eds., *Senses of Place.* Santa Fe: School of American Research.
Franklin, Wayne, and Michael Steiner, eds.
    1992   *Mapping American Culture.* Iowa City: University of Iowa Press.
Freire, Paolo
    1995   *Pedagogy of the Oppressed.* Trans. Myra Bergman Ramos. New York: Continuum.
Friedlander, Judith
    1975   *Being Indian in Hueyapan: A Study of Forced Identity in Contemporary Mexico.* New York: St. Martin's.

Frye, David
  1996   *Indians Into Mexicans: History and Identity in a Mexican Town.* Austin: University
          of Texas Press.

Gagini, Carlos
  1917   *Los aborígenes de Costa Rica.* San José: Trejos Hermanos.

Gal, Susan
  1989   "Language and Political Economy," *Annual Review of Anthropology* 18: 345–
          367.

García Bresó, Javier
  1992   *Monimbó: Una comunidad india de Nicaragua.* Managua: Editorial Multiformas.

García Canclini, Néstor
  1990   *Culturas híbridas: Estrategias para entrar y salir de la modernidad.* México, D.F.:
          Grijalbo.

Gearing, Frederick, and Paul Epstein
  1982   "Learning to Wait: An Ethnographic Probe Into the Operations of an Item
          of Hidden Curriculum," pp. 240–267 in George Spindler, ed., *Doing the
          Ethnography of Schooling: Educational Anthropology in Action.* Prospect Heights,
          Ill.: Waveland.

Geertz, Clifford
  1973   *The Interpretation of Cultures.* New York: Basic.
  1995   *After the Fact.* Cambridge: Harvard University Press.

Giroux, Henry A.
  1989   "Schooling as a Form of Cultural Politics: Toward a Pedagogy of and for
          Difference," pp. 125–151 in Henry A. Giroux and Peter L. McLaren, eds.,
          Critical Pedagogy, the State, and Cultural Struggle. Albany: State University of
          New York Press.

Giroux, Henry A., and Peter L. McLaren, eds.
  1994   *Between Borders: Pedagogy and the Politics of Cultural Studies.* New York: Routledge.

González, Alex, and Fher González
  1997   "Chamán," *Sueños líquidos.* Recorded by Maná. Warner Music Mexico.

Gould, Jeffrey L.
  1990   " 'La Raza Rebelde': Las luchas de la comunidad indígena de Subtiava, Nica-
          ragua (1900–1960)," *Revista de Historia* 20–21: 69–117.
  1993   "¡Vana ilusión! The Highlands Indians and the Myth of Nicaragua Mestiza,
          1880–1925," *Hispanic American Historical Review* 73(3): 393–429.
  1998   *To Die in This Way: Nicaraguan Indians and the Myth of Mestizaje, 1880–1965.*
          Durham, N.C.: Duke University Press.

Graham, Laura
  2002   "How Should an Indian Speak? Amazonian Indians and the Symbolic Poli-
          tics of Language in the Global Public Sphere," pp. 181–228 in Kay B. Warren
          and Jean E. Jackson, eds., *Indigenous Movements, Self-Representation, and the State
          in Latin America.* Austin: University of Texas Press.

Green, Vera M.
  1981   "Blacks in the United States: The Creation of an Enduring People?" pp. 69–
          77 in George Piere Castile and Gilbert Kushner, eds., *Persistent Peoples: Cul-
          tural Enclavement in Perspective.* Tucson: University of Arizona Press.

Grosby, Steve
  1996   "The Inexpungeable Tie of Primordiality," pp. 51–56 in John Hutchinson
          and Anthony D. Smith, eds., *Ethnicity.* Oxford: Oxford University Press.
Gruzinski, Serge
  1988   "The Net Torn Apart: Ethnic Identities and Westernization in Colonial Mexico,
          Sixteenth–Nineteenth Century," pp. 39–56 in Remo Guidieri et al., eds.,
          Ethnicities and Nations. Austin: University of Texas Press.
Guerrero C., Julián N., and Lola Soriano de Guerrero
  1982   *Las 9 tribus aborígenes de Nicaragua.* Managua, Nicaragua: S.h.
Guevara Berger, Marcos
  1993   "Guaymí of Costa Rica," p. 226 in Marc S. Miller, ed., *State of the Peoples: A
          Global Human Rights Report on Societies in Danger.* Boston: Beacon.
Guevara Berger, Marcos, and Rubén Chacón
  1992   *Territorios indios en Costa Rica: Orígenes, situación actual y perspectivas.* San José:
          García Hermanos, S.A.
Gumperz, John
  1972   "The Speech Community," pp. 219–231 in Pier Paolo Giglioli, ed., *Language
          and Social Context.* Harmondsworth, England: Penguin.
Gutiérrez, Joaquín
  1918   *Cocorí.* 2nd ed. San José: Editorial Costa Rica.
Hall, Stuart, ed.
  1977   *Representation: Cultural Representation and Signifying Practices.* London: Sage.
Hall, Stuart, and Tony Jefferson, eds.
  1975   *Resistance Through Rituals: Youth Subcultures in Post-War Britain.* London:
          Hutchinson & Co.
Hartman, C.V.
  1914   (1st ed. 1907) "Archaeological Researches on the Pacific Coast of Costa
          Rica," pp. 1–188 in W. J. Holland, ed., *Memoirs of the Carnegie Museum,* vol. 3.
          Pittsburgh: Carnegie Institute.
Hatcher, Richard, and Barry Troyna
  1993   "Racialization and Children," pp. 109–125 in Cameron McCarthy and War-
          ren Crichlow, eds., *Race, Identity, and Representation in Education.* New York:
          Routledge.
Hebdidge, Dick
  1979   *Subculture: The Meaning of Style.* London: Methuen.
Hendrickson, Carol
  1991   "Images of the Indian in Guatemala: The Role of Indigenous Dress in In-
          dian and Ladino Construction," pp. 286–306 in Greg Urban and Joel Sherzer,
          eds., *Nation-States and Indians in Latin America.* Austin: University of Texas
          Press.
Hobsbawm, Eric, and Terence Ranger
  1983   *The Invention of Tradition.* Cambridge: Cambridge University Press.
Holland, Dorothy C., and Margaret A. Eisenhart
  1990   *Educated in Romance.* Chicago: University of Chicago Press.

Horowitz, Donald L.
  1975   "Ethnic Identity," pp. 111–140 in Nathan Glazer and Daniel P. Moynihan, eds., *Ethnicity: Theory and Experience*. Cambridge: Harvard University Press.

Hubbard, Lea
  1999   "College Aspirations Among Low-Income African American High School Students: Gendered Strategies for Success," *Anthropology and Education Quarterly* 30(3): 363–383.

Isaacs, Harold R.
  1975   "Basic Group Identity: The Idols of the Tribe," pp. 29–52 in Nathan Glazer and Daniel P. Moynihan, eds., *Ethnicity: Theory and Experience*. Cambridge: Harvard University Press.

Jackson, Jean E.
  2002   "Contested Discourses of Authority in Colombian National Indigenous Politics: The 1996 Summer Takeovers," pp. 81–122 in Kay B. Warren and Jean E. Jackson, eds., *Indigenous Movements, Self-Representation, and the State in Latin America*. Austin: University of Texas Press.

Jackson, John L., Jr.
  2004   "An Ethnographic *Film*flam: Giving Gifts, Doing Research, and Videotaping the Native Subject/Object," *American Anthropologist* 106(1): 32–42.

Jacob, Evelyn, and Cathie Jordan
  1993   *Minority Education: Anthropological Perspectives*. Norwood, N.J.: Ablex.

Jenkins, Richard
  1997   *Rethinking Ethnicity: Arguments and Explorations*. London: Sage.

Jordan, Cathie, and Evelyn Jacob
  1993   "Contexts of Education, Contexts of Application: Anthropological Perspectives and Educational Practice," pp. 253–271 in Evelyn Jacob and Cathie Jordan, eds., *Minority Education: Anthropological Perspectives*. Norwood, N.J.: Ablex.

Kahn, Miriam
  1996   "Your Place or Mine: Sharing Emotional Landscapes in Wamira, Papua New Guinea," pp. 167–196 in Steven Feld and Keith Basso, eds., *Senses of Place*. Santa Fe: School of American Research.

Knight, Alan
  1990   "Racism, Revolution, and *Indigenismo*: Mexico, 1910–1940," pp. 71–113 in Richard Graham, ed., *The Idea of Race in Latin America, 1870–1940*. Austin: University of Texas Press.

Kondo, Dorinne
  1990   *Crafting Selves: Power, Gender, and Discourses of Identity in a Japanese Workplace*. Chicago: University of Chicago Press.

Levinson, Bradley A.U.
  2001   *We Are All Equal: Student Cultures at a Mexican Secondary School, 1988–1998*. Durham, N.C.: Duke University Press.

Levinson, Bradley A.U., Douglas E. Foley, and Dorothy C. Holland
  1996   *The Cultural Production of the Educated Person: Critical Ethnographies of Schooling and Local Practice*. Albany: State University of New York Press.

Levinson, Bradley A.U., and Dorothy Holland
  1996   "The Cultural Production of the Educated Person: An Introduction," pp. 1–
          54 in Bradley A.U. Levinson, Douglas E. Foley, and Dorothy C. Holland,
          eds., *The Cultural Production of the Educated Person: Critical Ethnographies of
          Schooling and Local Practice*. Albany: State University of New York Press.
Lienhard, Martín
  1991   *La voz y su huella*. Hanover: Ediciones del Norte.
Limón, José E.
  1989   "*Carne, Carnales,* and the Carnivalesque: Bakhtinian *Batos,* Disorder, and Nar-
          rative Discourses," *American Ethnologist* 16(3): 471–486.
López, Gabriela, Jenny Assáel, and Elisa Neumann
  1984   *La cultura escolar ¿Responsable del Fracaso?: Estudio etnográfico en dos escuelas urbano-
          populares.* Santiago, Chile: Programa Interdisciplinario de Investigaciones en
          Educación.
Luttrell, Wendy
  1996   "Becoming Somebody in and Against School: Toward a Psychocultural Theory
          of Gender and Self-Making," pp. 93–117 in Bradley A.U. Levinson, Douglas
          E. Foley, and Dorothy C. Holland, eds., *The Cultural Production of the Educated
          Person: Critical Ethnographies of Schooling and Local Practice*. Albany: State Uni-
          versity of New York Press.
Luykx, Aurolyn
  1996   "From *Indios* to *Profesionales*: Stereotypes and Student Resistance in Bolivian
          Teacher Training," pp. 239–272 in Bradley A.U. Levinson, Douglas E. Foley,
          and Dorothy C. Holland, eds., *The Cultural Production of the Educated Person:
          Critical Ethnographies of Schooling and Local Practice*. Albany: State University of
          New York Press.
  1999   *The Citizen Factory: Schooling and Cultural Production in Bolivia*. Albany: State
          University of New York Press.
Macklem, Patrick
  1993   "Ethnonationalism, Aboriginal Identities, and the Law," pp. 9–28 in Michael
          D. Levin, ed., *Ethnicity and Aboriginality: Case Studies in Ethnonationalism*. Toronto:
          University of Toronto Press.
MacLeod, Jay
  1987   *Ain't No Makin' It: Leveled Aspirations in a Low-Income Neighborhood*. Boulder:
          Westview.
Mallon, Florencia E.
  1992   "Indian Communities, Political Cultures, and the State in Latin America,
          1780–1990," *Journal of Latin American Studies* Special Issue 24(3): 35–53.
  1996   "Indigenous Peoples and the State in Latin America," pp. 291–294 in John
          Hutchinson and Anthony D. Smith, eds., *Ethnicity*. Oxford: Oxford Univer-
          sity Press.
Marroquín, Alejandro D.
  1972   *Balance del indigenismo: Informe sobre la política indigenista en América*. Mexico
          City: Instituto Indigenista Interamericana.
  1975   "El problema indígena en El Salvador," *América Indígena* 35(4): 747–771.

Martínez Cobo, José R.
1987   *Study of the Problem of Discrimination Against Indigenous Populations.* New York: United Nations.

Matamoros Carvajal, Ananías
1990   *Acción indigenista en Costa Rica.* San José: CONAI (Comisión Nacional de Asuntos Indígenas).

McCarthy, Cameron
1993   "After the Canon: Knowledge and Ideological Representation in the Multicultural Discourse on Curriculum Reform," pp. 289–305 in Cameron McCarthy and Warren Crichlow, eds., *Race, Identity, and Representation in Education.* New York: Routledge.

McCarthy, Cameron, and Warren Crichlow
1993   "Introduction: Theories of Identity, Theories of Representation, Theories of Race," pp. xiii–xxix in Cameron McCarthy and Warren Crichlow, eds., *Race, Identity, and Representation in Education.* New York: Routledge.

McLaren, Peter
1982   "Bein' Tough: Rituals of Resistance in the Culture of Working-Class Schoolgirls," *Canadian Woman Studies* 4(1): 20–24.
1986   *Schooling as a Ritual Performance: Towards a Political Economy of Educational Symbols and Gestures.* London: Routledge.

McNamara Horvat, Erin, and Anthony Lising Antonio
1999   "'Hey, Those Shoes Are Out of Uniform': African American Girls in an Elite High School and the Importance of Habitus," *Anthropology and Education Quarterly* 30(3): 317–342.

McRobbie, Angela
1978   "Working Class Girls and the Culture of Femininity," pp. 96–108 in Women's Studies Group, *Women Take Issue: Aspects of Women's Subordination.* London: Hutchinson of London.

Membreño Idiáquez, Marcos
1992   "Persistencia étnica en Sutiava y Monimbó," pp. 105–144 in Germán Romero Vargas, ed., *Persistencia indígena en Nicaragua.* Managua: CIDCA-UCA.
1994   *La estructura de las comunidades étnicas.* Managua: Editorial Envío.

Moll, Luis C.
1994   "Mediating Knowledge Between Homes and Classrooms," pp. 385–410 in Deborah Keller-Cohen, ed., *Literacy: Interdisciplinary Conversations.* Cresskill, N.J.: Hampton.

Monge Alfaro, Carlos
1959   "Primeras manifestaciones del estado costarricense 1821–1835," *Revista de Ciencias Sociales (Universidad de Costa Rica)* 4: 81–121.
1960   *Historia de Costa Rica.* San José: Trejos.

Mora Chinchilla, Carolina, and Isabel Trejos Trejos
1996   *Cívica 7.* San José: Editorial Santillana.

Morales Cordero, Elsa María, and Carolina Mora Chinchilla
1996   *Cívica 7.* San José: Editorial Santillana.

n.a.
1990   *Comunidades* 3(16).

Nagata, Judith
  1974   "What Is a Malay? Situational Selection of Ethnic Identity in a Plural Soci-
          ety," *American Ethnologist* 1(2): 331–350.
  1981   "In Defense of Ethnic Boundaries: The Changing Myths and Charters of
          Malay Identity," pp. 88–116 in Charles F. Keyes, ed., *Ethnic Change.* Seattle:
          University of Washington Press.

Nagengast, Carole, and Michael Kearney
  1990   "Mixtec Ethnicity: Social Identity, Political Consciousness, and Political Ac-
          tivism," *Latin American Research Review* 25(2): 61–82.

Narayan, Kirin
  1993   "How Native Is a 'Native' Anthropologist?" *American Anthropologist* 94: 671–
          686.

Nash, Manning
  1996   "The Core Elements of Ethnicity," pp. 24–28 in John Hutchinson and An-
          thony D. Smith, eds., *Ethnicity.* Oxford: Oxford University Press.

Nederveen Pieterse, Jan
  1996   "Varieties of Ethnic Politics and Ethnicity Discourse," pp. 25–44 in Edwin
          N. Wilmsen and Patrick McAllister, eds., *The Politics of Difference: Ethnic Premises
          in a World of Power.* Chicago: University of Chicago Press.

Ng, Roxana
  1993   "Racism, Sexism, and Nation Building in Canada," pp. 50–59 in Cameron
          McCarthy and Warren Crichlow, eds., *Race, Identity, and Representation in Edu-
          cation.* New York: Routledge.

Oboler, Suzanne
  1995   *Ethnic Labels, Latino Lives: Identity and the Politics of Re(Presentation) in the United
          States.* Minneapolis: University of Minnesota Press.

Ogbu, John U.
  1978   *Minority Education and Caste: The American System in Cross-Cultural Perspective.*
          New York: Academic.

Olsen, Laurie
  1987   *Made in America: Immigrant Students in Our Public Schools.* New York: New
          Press.

Omi, Michael, and Howard Winant
  1986   *Racial Formation in the United States: From the 1960s to the 1980s.* New York:
          Routledge.

Organización Internacional del Trabajo (OIT)
  1989   *Convenio no. 169 sobre pueblos indígenas y tribales.* San José: OIT Oficina para
          América Central y Panamá.

Ortner, Sherry B.
  1996   *Making Gender: The Politics and Erotics of Culture.* Boston: Beacon.

Palmer, Paula, Juanita Sánchez, and Gloria Mayorga
  1993   *Taking Care of Sibö's Gifts: An Environmental Treatise From Costa Rica's Kéköldi
          Reserve.* San José: Asociación Integral de Desarrollo de la Reserva Indígena
          Cocles/KéköLdi.

Parsons, Talcott
    1975   "Some Theoretical Considerations on the Nature and Trends of Change of Ethnicity," pp. 53–83 in Nathan Glazer and Daniel P. Moynihan, eds., *Ethnicity: Theory and Experience*. Cambridge: Harvard University Press.

Peralta, M. Manuel de
    1893   *Etnología Centro-Americana: Catálogo razonado de los objetos arqueológicos de la República de Costa Rica*. Madrid: Hijos de M. Gines Hernández.

Pérez, Laura Elisa
    1993   "Opposition and the Education of Chicana/os," pp. 268–279 in Cameron McCarthy and Warren Crichlow, eds., *Race, Identity, and Representation in Education*. New York: Routledge.

Peshkin, Alan
    1997   *Places of Memory: Whiteman's School and Native American Communities*. Mahwah, N.J.: Lawrence Erlbaum Associates.

Pinar, William F.
    1993   "Notes on Understanding Curriculum as a Racial Text," pp. 60–70 in Cameron McCarthy and Warren Crichlow, eds., *Race, Identity, and Representation in Education*. New York: Routledge.

Pinto Molina, Angel Alberto, ed.
    1993   *Antología salud ocupacional*. San José: Consejo de Salud Ocupacional y Ministerio de Educación Pública.

Price, John
    1966   "A History of the Outcaste: Untouchability in Japan," pp. 6–30 in George De Vos and Hiroshi Wagatsuma, eds., *Japan's Invisible Race*. Berkeley: University of California Press.

Quesada, Juan Rafael, et al.
    1988   *Carlos Monge Alfaro*. San José: Editorial de la Universidad de Costa Rica.

Ramos, Alcida Rita
    1998   *Indigenism: Ethnic Politics in Brazil*. Madison: University of Wisconsin Press.
    2002   "Cutting Through State and Class: Sources and Strategies of Self-Representation in Latin America," pp. 251–279 in Kay B. Warren and Jean E. Jackson, eds., *Indigenous Movements, Self-Representation, and the State in Latin America*. Austin: University of Texas Press.

Relph, Edward
    1976   *Place and Placelessness*. London: Pion.

Renan, Ernest
    1990   "What Is a Nation?" pp. 8–22 in Homi K. Bhabha, ed., *Nation and Narration*. London: Routledge.

Rist, Ray C.
    1970   "Student Social Class and Teacher Expectations: The Self-Fulfilling Prophecy in Ghetto Education," *Harvard Educational Review* 40(3): 411–451.
    1978   *The Invisible Children: School Integration in American Society*. Cambridge: Harvard University Press.

Rival, Laura
  1996   "Formal Schooling and the Production of Modern Citizens in the Ecua-
          dorian Amazon," pp. 153–167 in Bradley A.U. Levinson, Douglas E. Foley,
          and Dorothy C. Holland, eds., *The Cultural Production of the Educated Person:
          Critical Ethnographies of Schooling and Local Practice.* Albany: State University of
          New York Press.

Rivas, Ramón D.
  1993   *Pueblos indígenas y Garífuna de Honduras.* Tegucigalpa, Honduras: Editorial
          Guaymaras.

Rizo Zeledón, Mario
  1992   "Etnicidad, legalidad y demandas de las comunidades indígenas del norte,
          centro, y del pacífico de Nicaragua," pp. 59–103 in Germán Romero, ed.,
          Persistencia indígena en Nicaragua. Managua: CIDCA-UCA.

Rizvi, Fazal
  1993   "Children and the Grammar of Popular Racism," pp. 126–139 in Cameron
          McCarthy and Warren Crichlow, eds., *Race, Identity, and Representation in Edu-
          cation.* New York: Routledge.

Rodríguez Vega, Eugenio
  1953   *Apuntes para una sociología costarricense.* San José: Editorial Universitaria de la
          Universidad de Costa Rica.

Romo, Harriett D., and Toni Falbo
  1996   *Latino High School Graduation: Defying the Odds.* Austin: University of Texas
          Press.

Roosens, Eugeen
  1989   *Creating Ethnicity: The Process of Ethnogenesis.* Newbury Park, Calif.: Sage.

Rosaldo, Renato
  1993   *Culture and Truth.* Boston: Beacon.

Salguero, Miguel
  1991   *Cantones de Costa Rica.* San José: Editorial Costa Rica.
  1999   *La familia mena mora* (nationally produced television show for Costa Rican
          Channel 6).

Sarris, Greg
  1993   "Keeping Slug Woman Alive: The Challenge of Reading in a Reservation
          Classroom," pp. 238–269 in Jonathan Boyarin, ed., *The Ethnography of Reading.*
          Berkeley: University of California Press.

Schaller, Susanna Francesca
  1998   "Identity Politics in Search of Community-Based Development: A Case Study
          of the Indigenous Movement in Costa Rica." Masters' thesis, Department of
          Community and Regional Planning and Department of Latin American
          Studies, University of New Mexico, Albuquerque.

Schermerhorn, Richard
  1996   "Ethnicity and Minority Groups," pp. 17–18 in John Hutchinson and An-
          thony D. Smith, eds., *Ethnicity.* Oxford: Oxford University Press.

Scott, James C.
  1990   *Domination and the Arts of Resistance: Hidden Transcripts.* New Haven: Yale Uni-
          versity Press.

Sharp, John
1996   "Ethnogenesis and Ethnic Mobilization: A Comparative Perspective on a South African Dilemma," pp. 85–103 in Edwin N. Wilmsen and Patrick McAllister, eds., *The Politics of Difference: Ethnic Premises in a World of Power.* Chicago: University of Chicago Press.

Shimahara, Nubuo
1971   *Burakumin: A Japanese Minority and Education.* The Hague: Martinus Nijhoff.

Shostak, Marjorie
1981   *Nisa: The Life and Words of a !Kung Woman.* New York: Vintage.

Sibley, David
1995   *Geographies of Exclusion.* London: Routledge.

Silverblatt, Irene
1987   *Moon, Sun, and Witches: Gender Ideologies and Class in Inca and Colonial Peru.* Princeton: Princeton University Press.

Sleeter, Christine
1993   "How White Teachers Construct Race," pp. 157–171 in Cameron McCarthy and Warren Crichlow, eds., *Race, Identity, and Representation in Education.* New York: Routledge.

Solórzano, Juan Carlos
1992   "Conquista, colonización, y resistencia indígena en Costa Rica," *Revista de Historia* 25: 191–205.

Sommer, Doris
1990   "Irresistible Romance: The Foundational Fictions of Latin America," pp. 71–98 in Homi K. Bhabha, ed., *Nation and Narration.* London: Routledge.

Spicer, Edward H.
1971   "Persistent Cultural Systems: A Comparative Study of Identity Systems That Can Adapt to Contrasting Environments," *Science* 174(4011): 795–800.

Spindler, George, ed.
1982   *Doing the Ethnography of Schooling: Educational Anthropology in Action.* Prospect Heights, Ill.: Waveland.

Spindler, George, and Louise Spindler
1982   "Roger Harker and Schönhausen: From Familiar to Strange and Back Again," pp. 21–46 in George Spindler, ed., *Doing the Ethnography of Schooling: Educational Anthropology in Action.* Prospect Heights, Ill.: Waveland.

Stephen, Lynn
1991   *Zapotec Women.* Austin: University of Texas Press.

Stocker, Karen
1995   *Historias matambugueñas.* Heredia, Costa Rica: EUNA (Editorial de la Universidad Nacional Autónoma).

1997   "Contradictions in History, Identity, and Memory: The Interpretations and Negotiation of Imposed Identity Among 'the Chorotega' of Costa Rica," Master's thesis, Department of Latin American Studies, University of New Mexico, Albuquerque.

2001   "The Effects of Schooling on Ethnic Identity: The Dynamics of Discrimination in a Rural Costa Rican High School," PhD dissertation, Department of Anthropology, University of New Mexico, Albuquerque.

   2002   " 'Ellos se comen las eses/heces': The Perceived Language Difference of
           Matambú," pp. 185–211 in Stanton Wortham and Betsy Rymes, eds., *Linguis-
           tic Anthropology of Education*. Westport, Conn.: Greenwood.
Stoler, Ann Laura
   1995   *Race and the Education of Desire*. Durham, N.C.: Duke University Press.
Talpade Mohanty, Chandra
   1994   "On Race and Voice: Challenges for Liberal Education in the 1990s," pp.
           145–166 in Henry A. Giroux and Peter McLaren, eds., *Between Borders: Peda-
           gogy and the Politics of Cultural Studies*. New York: Routledge.
Taussig, Michael
   1984   "Culture of Terror—Space of Death: Roger Casement's Putumayo Reports
           and the Explanation of Torture," *Comparative Studies in Society and History*
           26(3): 467–497.
Tedlock, Barbara
   1995   "Works and Wives: On the Sexual Division of Textual Labor," pp. 267–286 in
           Ruth Behar and Deborah Gordon, eds., *Women Writing Culture*. Berkeley:
           University of California Press.
Thomas, Robert K., and Albert L. Wahrhaftig
   1971   "Indians, Hillbillies, and the Educational Problem," pp. 230–251 in Murray
           Wax, Stanley Diamond, and Fred O. Gearing, eds., *Anthropological Perspectives
           on Education*. New York: Basic.
Tsing, Anna Lowenhaupt
   1993   *In the Realm of the Diamond Queen: Marginality in an Out-of-the-Way Place*.
           Princeton: Princeton University Press.
Tuan, Yi-Fu
   1977   *Space and Place: The Perspective of Experience*. Minneapolis: University of Min-
           nesota Press.
   1992   "Place and Culture: Analeptic for Individuality and the World's Indiffer-
           ence," pp. 27–49 in Wayne Franklin and Michael Steiner, eds., *Mapping American
           Culture*. Iowa City: University of Iowa Press.
van Willigan, John
   1981   "Applied Anthropology and Cultural Persistence," pp. 153–167 in George
           Piere Castile and Gilbert Kushner, eds., *Persistent Peoples: Cultural Enclavement
           in Perspective*. Tucson: University of Arizona Press.
Wade, Peter
   1997   *Race and Ethnicity in Latin America*. London: Pluto.
Warren, Kay B.
   1978   *The Symbolism of Subordination*. Austin: University of Texas Press.
Warren, Kay B., and Jean E. Jackson, eds.
   2002   "Introduction: Studying Indigenous Activism in Latin America," pp. 1–46 in
           Kay B. Warren and Jean E. Jackson, eds., *Indigenous Movements, Self-Representa-
           tion, and the State in Latin America*. Austin: University of Texas Press.
Waters, Roger
   1977   "Another Brick in the Wall—Part 2," *The Wall*. Recorded by Pink Floyd.
           Capitol Records.

Weber, Max
1996 "The Origins of Ethnic Groups," pp. 35–40 in John Hutchinson and Anthony D. Smith, eds., *Ethnicity.* Oxford: Oxford University Press.

Wexler, Philip
1989 "Curriculum in the Closed Society," pp. 92–104 in Henry A. Giroux, ed., *Critical Pedagogy, the State, and Cultural Struggle.* Albany: State University of New York Press.

Wilcox, Kathleen
1982 "Differential Socialization in the Classroom: Implications for Equal Opportunity," pp. 268–309 in George Spindler, ed., *Doing the Ethnography of Schooling: Educational Anthropology in Action.* Prospect Heights, Ill.: Waveland.

Williams, Brackette F.
1989 "A Class Act: Anthropology and the Race to Nation Across Ethnic Terrain," *Annual Review of Anthropology* 18: 401–444.

Willis, Paul E.
1977 *Learning to Labor: How Working Class Kids Get Working Class Jobs.* Westmead, England: Saxon House.

Wilmsen, Edwin N., and Patrick McAllister, eds.
1996 *The Politics of Difference: Ethnic Premises in a World of Power.* Chicago: University of Chicago Press.

Wolf, Diane L.
1996 *Feminist Dilemmas in Fieldwork.* Boulder: Westview.

Wolf, Margery
1996 "Afterword: Musings From an Old Gray Wolf," pp. 215–221 in Diane Wolf, ed., *Feminist Dilemmas in Fieldwork.* Boulder: Westview.

Yon, Daniel A.
2000 *Elusive Culture: Schooling, Race, and Identity in Global Times.* Albany: State University of New York Press.

Zavella, Patricia
1993 "Feminist Insider Dilemmas: Constructing Ethnic Identity With 'Chicana' Informants," *Frontiers* 13(3): 53–76.

Index